MW00436849

FREEMAN'S CHALLENGE

FREEMAN'S CHALLENGE

THE MURDER THAT SHOOK AMERICA'S ORIGINAL PRISON FOR PROFIT

Robin Bernstein

The University of Chicago Press   CHICAGO

The University of Chicago Press, Chicago 60637
© 2024 by Robin Bernstein
All rights reserved. No part of this book may be used or reproduced in any
manner whatsoever without written permission, except in the case of brief
quotations in critical articles and reviews. For more information, contact
the University of Chicago Press, 1427 E. 60th St., Chicago, IL 60637.
Published 2024
Printed in the United States of America

33 32 31 30 29 28 27 26 25 24   1 2 3 4 5

ISBN-13: 978-0-226-74423-0 (cloth)
ISBN-13: 978-0-226-74437-7 (e-book)
DOI: https://doi.org/10.7208/chicago/9780226744377.001.0001

Library of Congress Cataloging-in-Publication Data

Names: Bernstein, Robin, author.
Title: Freeman's challenge : the murder that shook America's original
    prison for profit / Robin Bernstein.
Description: Chicago : The University of Chicago Press, 2024. | Includes
    bibliographical references and index.
Identifiers: LCCN 2023037521 | ISBN 9780226744230 (cloth) |
    ISBN 9780226744377 (ebook)
Subjects: LCSH: Freeman, William, 1824–1847—Trials, litigation, etc. |
    Trials (Murder)—New York (State)—Auburn. | Auburn Correctional
    Facility. | Prisoners—Legal status, laws, etc.—New York (State)—
    Auburn—History. | Insanity (Law)—New York (State)—Auburn—
    History. | Prisoners—Legal status, laws, etc.—United States. |
    Prisons—Law and legislation—United States. | African Americans—
    Civil rights—United States—History. | Prisons and race relations—
    United States—History.
Classification: LCC KF223.F74 B47 2024 | DDC 364.152/3092 [B]—dc23/
    eng/20230926
LC record available at https://lccn.loc.gov/2023037521

♾ This paper meets the requirements of ANSI/NISO Z39.48-1992
(Permanence of Paper).

For Elizabeth Bernstein; her parents, Marty and Pat;
and her grandparents, Annette and Henry:
three generations of justice-seekers.

Contents

Illustrations

Plates (after p. 130)

Figures

"Slaves of the State"

American prisons are worksites. Of the 1.2 million Americans currently incarcerated in state and federal prisons, two-thirds have jobs. They cook, scrub floors, wash laundry, or maintain buildings. Beyond the prison, they fix roads or fight forest fires. Some raise crops or work in factories. Unlike their free counterparts, incarcerated workers do not have the right to refuse to work, and almost none earn more than one dollar per hour. In many states, prisoners earn nothing at all. Yet every year they produce more than $2 billion worth of commodities and $9 billion in services.[1]

How did prisoners become a lucrative labor force? Many people trace the origins of profit-driven prison labor to the Thirteenth Amendment to the United States Constitution. This amendment, passed in 1865, states that "neither slavery nor involuntary servitude" shall exist in the United States—"except as a punishment for crime." In the eyes of many, this amendment ended slavery while licensing a new form of unfree labor: the de facto reenslavement of African Americans through Southern chain gangs and convict leasing.[2]

But the post–Civil War South did not, in fact, invent profit-driven prison labor. Incarceration and capitalism entangled half a century earlier in the North, in the context of that region's rising industrialism and gradual abolition of slavery.[3] The key location was New York State, in a village called Auburn. There, a group of white businessmen built a new kind of prison: one that did not aim primarily to punish, confine, or redeem criminals, but instead to stimulate economic development.[4]

Auburn's state prison enclosed industrial factories where prisoners were leased to private companies, usually for thirty cents per day. The prison pocketed this money; prisoners received no cut. Yet they manufactured furniture and animal harnesses, carpets and combs, and more, which consumers bought throughout New York State. The system did more than enrich the prison and its contractors. It made Auburn prosperous, internationally admired, and proud. Meanwhile, it made prisoners, as one warden put it in 1826, "slaves of the state."[5]

A young Black and Native American man named William Freeman challenged this status. Freeman was convicted of horse theft and incarcerated in Auburn for five years, starting in 1840, when he was fifteen years old. When set to work in the prison factories, Freeman resisted. The freeborn son of a manumitted Black father and a free Black and Stockbridge-Narragansett mother, Freeman was incensed at being forced to work, as he put it, "for nothing."[6] He demanded wages. His claim was simple, but it threatened Auburn's defining idea: he insisted he was not a slave but a citizen with rights, a worker. The assertion triggered violence—first against him, then by him. Freeman committed a quadruple murder that terrified and bewildered white America.

William Freeman's challenge to the prison deserves to be heard. Nearly two centuries ago, when the prison industry was in its infancy, Freeman exposed profit-driven incarceration as a form of organized labor-theft, criminality disguised as justice. This book tells that story. To grasp the target of Freeman's challenge, Part I focuses on the Auburn State Prison: how it was uniquely significant, how it affected the people incarcerated there, and how it shaped the world beyond its walls. "Auburn" was the name of a prison, a system of incarceration, and a village that became a city. Over time, Auburn became even more: an economic engine, a microcosm for New York's politics, and a crucible in which state-funded capitalism boiled into a racialized criminal justice system. Part II narrates how Freeman fought this hydra—through words, then violence. Part III shows the aftermath: how white and Black people, differently devastated by Freeman, managed the terror he unleashed. This section reveals consequences that no one could have predicted—with aftereffects that reverberate into our lives.

Today, many activists decry private prisons and corporations that profit from incarcerated labor. But as Ruth Wilson Gilmore argues, a hyperfocus on privatization can distract from a more capacious understanding of what she calls "carceral geographies." Gilmore explains that private companies are best understood as "opportunists slurping at the public trough rather than the prime movers" in the construction of the modern prison.[7] Events in nineteenth-century Auburn confirm and expand on this insight. The Auburn State Prison was never a private prison. It was a state prison that partnered with private companies for the purpose of making money. The immediate beneficiaries were, of course, the prison and its contractors. But as this book shows, private companies were but one aspect of a much larger system involving state-funded capitalism, businesses outside the physical boundaries of the prison, reform societies, churches, intellectuals, political parties, and more. By the mid-nineteenth century, Auburn had become a kind of "company town," where the prison directly or indirectly affected every business, every person.

Prison, as Angela Y. Davis, Ruth Wilson Gilmore, and others have explained, is much more than a bounded place. It is a set of relationships, a collective process of spacemaking.[8] This book uncovers these economic, political, and personal relationships at their roots, as they germinated in the soil of central New York. By telling a story of penal capitalism on a human scale—through one young man, his family, and his city—this book exposes the contingency of prisons themselves. The making of the modern prison was not inevitable. Prison as we know it was constructed, challenged, defended, adjusted, and reentrenched by individuals working in concert. By understanding their actions, we can imagine alternatives. We can question the economic and cultural systems that insist prisons are necessary. We can know the world before mass incarceration—and create one after it.

PART I

THE PRISON

CHAPTER ONE

Sweet Auburn, Loveliest Prison

A Haudenosaunee creation story called rivers "the veins of Mother Earth," but to Lieutenant John L. Hardenbergh, rivers were power. Tall, white, and twenty-eight years old, Hardenbergh was on mission with Sullivan's Campaign, a military operation ordered in 1779 by General George Washington. The campaign's purpose: to crush the Haudenosaunee, also called Iroquois, who had allied with British forces and raided American settlements. The soldiers recorded their destruction of at least forty Native communities: "We found a very pretty town of 10 houses and a considerable quantity of corn, all which we burnt. We discovered another small town about a mile above this, we likewise destroyed." If any Haudenosaunee survived, the soldiers aimed to starve them by torching their crops. "This morning went to destroying corn, beans, and orchards. Destroyed about 1500 Peach Trees, besides apple trees and other fruit trees," one soldier wrote. John Hardenbergh pursued this mission, along with a second, personal one: he wanted to find an exceptionally swift river. There, he hoped to settle after the war and build a mill. He found what he sought in the Owasco Outlet in central New York State. "Good mill site," Hardenbergh noted on his hand-drawn map.[1]

After the war, Hardenbergh obtained the lot he wanted: Military Tract 47, on the banks of the Owasco. In spring 1793, he took possession. He brought along three people: his infant daughter Cornelia, whose mother had just died, and an enslaved man and woman named Harry and Kate. Harry was forty; Kate may have been younger.[2] We

FIGURE 1.1 Military Tract Map

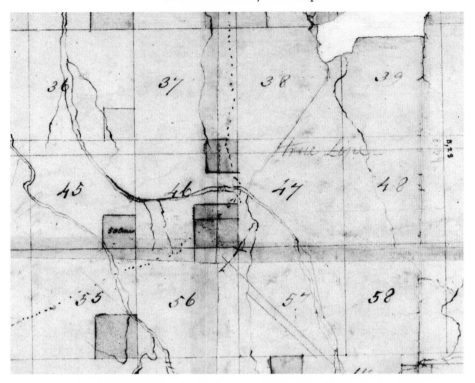

Lot 47 and surrounding area. Detail, "The Military Tract in 1792," *The Balloting Book, and Other Documents Relating to Military Bounty Lands, in the State of New-York* (Albany: printed by Packard & VanBenthuysen, 1825), n.p. Image prepared by Dennis McClendon.

cannot know what Harry and Kate thought about leaving their home. We know they had no choice in the matter. We can trust they lost people they loved. Whatever their relationship was before the move, now they had only each other.

The three adults built a log cabin, then a dam and a mill. The mill became the center of a village that was first called Hardenbergh's Corners, then Aurelius. By 1805 it took on an aspirational name based on "Sweet Auburn, loveliest village," the subject of a 1770 poem by Oliver Goldsmith. The town's founders envisioned a city to mirror the one described at the outset of Goldsmith's poem: entrepreneurial, modern, healthy, decent, simultaneously industrial and bucolic, and above all, prosperous. (They were undaunted by the fate of the poetic Auburn, which collapses due to its inhabitants' greed and is abandoned.) At first, the august name outshone the town's reality of a dozen or so log cabins, two mills, two tanneries, and a tavern. But Auburn grew. In 1802, the state widened the Great Genesee Trail, which the Haudenosaunee had built across New York and which bisected Tract 47.[3] By this path, more white families arrived—many of them, like Hardenbergh, conscripting enslaved people to work the land.

Within five years, Black and white labor caused Auburn's manufacturing to mushroom. The two mills grew to four, two tanneries became three. These businesses were soon joined by five sawmills, an ashery, a brick factory, a carding mill, three shoemakers, and two distilleries. In 1815, Auburn incorporated and became the official seat of Cayuga County.[4] By then, the government was seeking a site for a new state prison. In this fact, Auburn's businessmen saw an opportunity: a prison could constitute one more industry, yet another moneymaker alongside factories producing leather and bricks. To Auburn's leaders, it was an enticing, modern vision. Worthy of Goldsmith.

Becoming Freemans

While white entrepreneurs built Auburn's factories and prison, Harry and Kate grew a family. They had a daughter, Jane, in 1793 and a son, James, in 1795—both enslaved, like their parents, to Hardenbergh. Then New York launched a process known as "gradual emancipation." The state passed the "Act for the Gradual Abolition of Slavery," which freed no one. Instead, it declared that after July 4, 1799, all children born of enslaved New Yorkers would be technically free—but that they would be unpaid indentured servants, serving their mothers' enslavers until the age of twenty-eight for men and twenty-five for women. Shortly after this law passed, Harry and Kate had two more sons: Luke in 1803 and Sidney in 1805.[5] Because of their birth dates, Luke and Sidney were free but indentured to Hardenbergh.

Eventually, the Hardenbergh family released Kate and Harry. Kate was freed first, in December 1805, shortly before John Hardenbergh died. Harry was freed by Hardenbergh's heirs seven months later.

Whatever joy the couple felt must have been chilled by the knowledge that the Hardenbergh family still gripped their children. Then, in 1817, a new law set an end for slavery in New York: as of July 4, 1827, all enslaved people would become legally free. The law retained slavery-based indenture like Luke's and Sidney's but shortened its length to twenty-one years.[6]

By 1820, eighteen people remained enslaved in Auburn and the immediate area. Two of them were Jane and James, whom John Hardenbergh's descendants finally manumitted on April 25 of that year.[7] There is no record of Luke and Sidney shedding their indenture, but it would have occurred automatically when each turned twenty-one, in 1824 and 1826, respectively. Through the twists and ironies of gradual emancipation, then, the first nonenslaved members of Harry and Kate's family were the last to cast off bondage.

As Kate, Harry, and their children became emancipated, they chose for themselves a surname: Freeman. The name is an act of writing, an autobiography in one word. It articulated the family's values; it said who they were and who they wanted to be. The name, too, spoke hope: the future was free. By the 1820s, the first cohort of indentured-but-not-enslaved New Yorkers began raising their own children—the first fully free generation. Every day, more free Black children were born. One of them was Harry and Kate's grandson William.

William Freeman in New Guinea

William, the son of Harry and Kate's son James, grew up in New Guinea, a close-knit, lively Black neighborhood near Auburn's southern border.[8] When William was born in 1824, about 115 African Americans lived in and near Auburn, and New Guinea was the center of their social world. With his family and neighbors, he attended parties, dances, and church meetings and took recreational rides in carriages and sleighs. Several times, the community attempted to establish schools for Black children. One recently freed man named Albert Hagerman (or Hagaman) opened a Sunday school, which he ran from at least 1818 through 1820, but white attacks forced the school to close.[9] Wil-

FIGURE 1.2 New Guinea, "Negro Settlement"

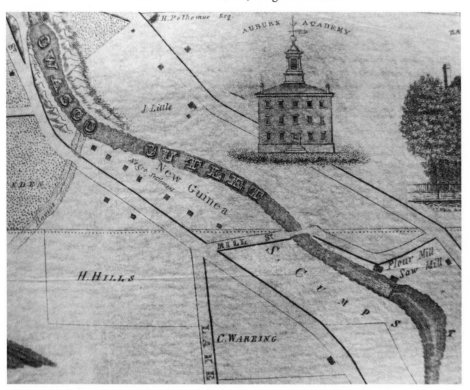

This map, originally published in 1834, shows nine homes comprising Auburn's Black neighborhood. The home of Henry Polhemus is marked to the north of New Guinea, across the Owasco Outlet. Detail, *Map of the Village of Auburn.* Engraved by M. M. Peabody for the publishers [Auburn, NY]. Published by Hagaman & Markham, 1837. Courtesy of the American Antiquarian Society.

liam's family must have attended to his education, however, because he learned to read and compute.

Above all, William Freeman was loved. To be a descendant of Harry and Kate, whom many revered as New Guinea's founders, was to be "born...a great favorite." William enjoyed that status. His mother, Sally Peters Freeman—a freeborn Afro-Native woman—described him as "very playful and good natured." Her view was biased, certainly. But other people, both in his family and beyond it, agreed. Physically energetic, he was "stout and springy," and in the eyes of some, his mother's Stockbridge-Narragansett heritage visibly shaped his face.[10]

William's father, James, died in 1829, most likely from a fall while intoxicated. His death left Sally Freeman a widow with a low income and three children, including a daughter who may have been mentally disabled.[11] And Sally, like her deceased husband, drank habitually. Unable to care for all her children, she decided to place William in the home of a white employer. She found it easy to line up reputable employers because William was smart and likable. As one employer said later, he could tell that William was "a bright boy, and took him for that reason."[12]

But the plan did not work as Sally Freeman had hoped. Six-year-old William chafed against his labors of scrubbing cutlery, driving horses, and running errands. He surely noticed that Auburn's white children generally lived with their parents and attended school while Black children like him labored, often in homes not their own. Nearly every day, he ran away from work, back to his mother. Each time, she carted him back to his employers. They whipped him, yet he ran away again. For nearly a decade, he cycled through white employers—he as unhappy with them as they became with him.[13]

He began getting in trouble. He broke into a peddler's cart, stole hens. When an officer tried to arrest him, he jumped clear of the officer's sulky and escaped. Another time, he hid from a constable under his brother-in-law's bed. When another constable confronted him for throwing stones at white boys, Freeman "boasted of his running," taunting the officer that he "could not catch him."[14]

William Freeman's life changed forever in 1840 when a horse was stolen near Auburn. The sheriff found Freeman with the horse in a nearby town. Freeman said that Jack Furman, the stepfather of his friend in New Guinea, had put him on the horse to send him on an errand.[15] The sheriff then arrested Furman—but he returned an accusation against Freeman. Freeman insisted he did not steal the horse, but the sheriff believed Furman. Freeman was arrested for grand larceny. While awaiting trial, he was held in the Cayuga County Jail, which was a few blocks south of the Auburn State Prison.

Freeman knew exactly what was at stake if he was convicted because eight years earlier, his uncle Sidney Freeman had served four years in that prison on a charge of petty larceny. The experience had shattered him. For years afterward, Sidney wandered the streets, ranting that Jesus Christ was trapped in his throat, choking him—surely a disturbing sight for his young nephew.[16]

Freeman refused to relinquish his freedom without a fight. One morning, when the prisoners were called from their cells, he played sick. After jailor Israel Wood led the other prisoners outside, Freeman used the handle of a shovel to break the lock on his cell door. He and another prisoner fled, with Freeman wearing only checkered pantaloons, a striped vest made of silk and worsted, and a black fur hat. The other fugitive was quickly apprehended, but Freeman raced west, barefoot, for eight miles. He reached the Cayuga Reservation on Cayuga Lake, where he took a boat north. Wood advertised a reward of twenty-five dollars for his arrest, and Freeman was captured in Lyons. He was then tried and convicted. The sentence: five years' hard labor.[17]

On September 25, 1840, William Freeman, a scion of Auburn's founding Black family, traveled in chains from the courthouse to the Auburn State Prison.

Throughout his life, Freeman had seen the prison grow. When he was born, it was a hollow square, five hundred feet on each side. As the prison's fame spread, its factories expanded and its walls advanced westward five hundred feet, doubling the prison's footprint to ten acres. Now, Freeman faced a titanic rectangle. The outer stone walls reached fifty-one feet high and four feet thick, all the color of a storm cloud. Iron fretted every aperture. Within the walls, the prison rose even higher, to five stories, or fifty-six feet.[18] It was Auburn's tallest, widest, and deepest structure. Its towers obtruded above houses and trees, making them visible from the downtown to the south and the Hardenbergh land to the east. Atop the central tower was "Copper John," an eleven-foot statue of a Revolutionary War soldier, which some thought was a likeness of John Hardenbergh.[19] To a night guard, the moonlit prison resembled "ancient ruins, or deserted palaces, & castles." The prison's champions called it "grand"; a critic called it a

FIGURE 1.3 *Ground View of the Auburn Prison*

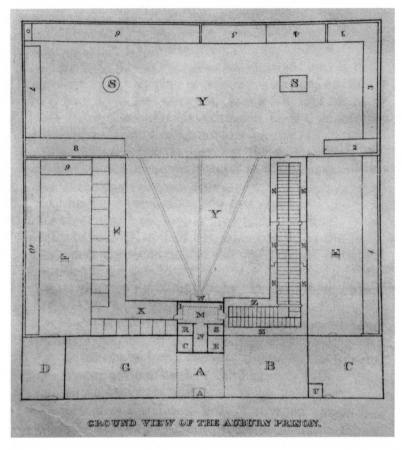

GROUND VIEW OF THE AUBURN PRISON.

When Freeman was a boy, the Auburn State Prison was square. By the time of his incarceration, the prison had doubled in size. In this view, the top is west and the bottom is east. Gershom Powers, *Report of Gershom Powers, Agent and Keeper of the State Prison, at Auburn* (Albany: Croswell and Van Benthuysen, 1828), 8.

"mansion of horror"; and those condemned to it struggled against its crushing gloom.[20] To all, the prison was impressive, dominating. Its heft was Auburn's gravitas, its smokestacks were Auburn's economic hope, its walls were Auburn's security. It was a monument to power. And now, it would become the site of William Freeman's captive labor, the crucible of his resentment and resistance.

FIGURE 1.4 Auburn State Prison

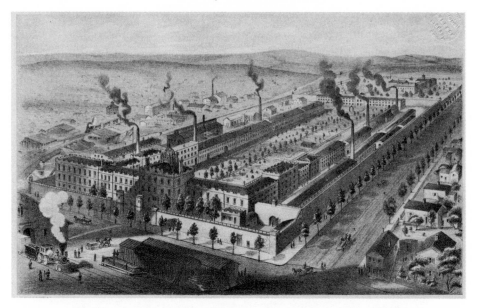

Auburn State Prison as seen from the northeast corner, facing southwest.
Smokestacks mark the locations of factories. The taller corridor along the north
side (lower right) without smokestacks is the cellblock. The railroad is visible,
bottom left, across the street from the prison's main entrance. Documents of the
Senate of the State of New York, 93rd sess., vol. 3, no. 71, 1870, between 92 and 93.

State Capitalism Transforms the Prison

How, in only a few decades, had torched Haudenosaunee land become
home to New York's flagship prison? Why did the prison rise in Auburn, not elsewhere?

The answer is that the prison grew in Auburn because of a combination of waterpower—the same reason that John Hardenbergh chose
the site for his mill—and changes in New York's political economy.

Among the early white settlers attracted to the Owasco Outlet's currents was one John H. Beach, who began buying up Auburn real estate
in 1811. Beach built businesses in lumber, flour, cotton fabric, oil, and
liquor. Most acutely, Beach yearned to establish a bank. Through these
entwined ventures, Beach aimed to grow Auburn into a commercial
center.[21]

Had he been in Massachusetts or another nearby state, Beach might have tried to reach this goal by building a large factory. But New York was undergoing changes that created a different possibility. For over two decades, New York's government had incubated the idea that the state had a responsibility to develop its economy. Toward this end, the state devoted massive funds to infrastructure projects, most notably the Erie Canal, for which surveying had just begun.[22] Meanwhile, the state's only prison—Newgate, in New York City—had become overcrowded and notoriously corrupt.[23] The state decided to fund a second prison to manage the overflow and was seeking a site. From the government's perspective, a canal and a prison were fundamentally different. The purpose of the first, in the words of Governor DeWitt Clinton, was to "augment the general opulence, to animate all the springs of industry and exertion."[24] In contrast, a prison existed to control, punish, or rehabilitate criminals. But between these apparently different ventures, John Beach saw a confluence—and in that confluence, an opportunity.

A canal and a prison each demanded massive state funding—and that funding itself, Beach realized, could transform local economies. The process of prison construction would draw skilled and unskilled workers from across the state. They, and then the prison itself, would constitute a market for lumber, flour, cotton fabric, oil, and liquor— the very goods Beach sold. And a prison in Auburn would not only support but also necessitate the establishment of the bank Beach wanted. The state's prison contract would result in $20,000 (about half a million in today's dollars) immediately flowing into the village of fewer than two thousand people, with more cash to come every year in perpetuity; a bank would be needed to manage the funds.[25] In short, a prison could enhance Auburn's economy as the Erie Canal could enhance that of New York.

Beach enacted this strategy in 1816, when he was elected to the state assembly. Immediately, he lobbied for Auburn to be awarded the state's contract to build a prison.[26] Although Beach had no prior documented interest in carceral systems or reform movements, his political maneuvers succeeded in landing the state contract. Two partners joined him in the venture: James Glover, a businessman about whom little is known, and Elijah Miller, a businessman, judge, and investor in real estate (plate 1).

Once they secured the contract, the three entrepreneurs confronted a question: where in Auburn should they build? Their answer revealed yet more about their business strategy. Beach and his partners, along with a neighbor named Samuel Dill, sold a six-acre plot on the north bank of the Owasco Outlet—a portion of Tract 46, next to Hardenbergh's Tract 47, on the second-swiftest portion of the river—to the state for one dollar. The deed granted the right to build a dam across the outlet. The reason was explicit: waterpower would "drive... machinery... for the use of the state prison." In other words, the land was transferred with the assumption that the prison would enclose factories. Furthermore, the deed stipulated that after state prison funds were used to build the dam, "only one half of the water of said Creek shall be appropriated for the use of said prison." The other half was retained by Beach and his partners.[27]

The strategy triumphed: by 1823, the prison directly and indirectly infused Auburn with the equivalent of two million of today's dollars. As Beach hoped, the inflow of state funds supported a mighty financial industry, led by the Auburn Bank, of which Beach was president from 1836 through 1839.[28]

In less than a decade, the white entrepreneurs and politicians of Auburn accomplished something unprecedented: they sited and planned a prison around factories, in relation to their power source, with the purpose of enriching a town, its businesses, and its businessmen. Unlike their counterparts who built prisons in Pennsylvania, Massachusetts, and other nearby states, Auburn's leaders had no discernible interest in reform. They viewed a prison as a vehicle by which to soak up state funds, build banking, stimulate commerce, manufacture goods, and develop land and waterways. In short, they reimagined the prison as an infrastructure for capitalism.

Developing the Auburn System

With the land secured, construction began. Beach hired his longtime business associate William Brittin as the general contractor; then Brittin hired stone contractor Isaac Lytle and architect John Cray. Together, these men oversaw a process that employed every available builder in Auburn and drew many more from across the state. Visiting workers and suppliers needed accommodations, so Lytle built a three-story tavern called the Prison Hotel.[29] It was the first private business in Auburn to be defined by, and dependent on, the prison.

Soon, the construction needed more builders than were freely available. The prison's leaders looked for another source of labor, and they found it in an unexpected place: local jails. Fifty-three prisoners, all likely white, were conscripted. Unlike the free workers, the prisoners received no pay—an appealing arrangement for Brittin, Beach, and the other partners.[30]

But the scheme backfired. As the free and jailed laborers worked together, the free workers developed sympathy for the prisoners' "punishment and privations."[31] Free laborers agitated on behalf of their incarcerated coworkers. Tensions peaked when a free overseer was ordered to whip three incarcerated workers. He refused, but a blacksmith named Jonathan Thompson volunteered to do the job. In retribution, free laborers seized Thompson, tarred and feathered him, and paraded him through the streets of Auburn.

To regain control, Brittin hired Captain Elam Lynds, a veteran of the War of 1812 with the square face and underbite of a bulldog. Lynds was charged with overseeing construction and commanding workers, both free and incarcerated, with militaristic precision.[32] He devised a way to break the alliance between free and incarcerated workers: he forbade all speech. If workers could not communicate, Lynds reasoned, they could not build solidarity.

Lynds's innovation coordinated with that of architect Cray, who began designing prison factories along with cells for solitary confinement. Solitary confinement was then an experimental practice; its debilitating effects were not yet fully acknowledged. In Pennsylvania, reformers forced each prisoner into near-total, permanent solitary confinement, which they believed would provoke self-reflection leading to penitence and spiritual redemption (instead, the practice induced widespread mental illness and suicide). In New York, however, Cray

FIGURE 1.5 *Elam Lynds*

Charles Henderson, *Correction and Prevention*, vol. 2 (New York: Charities Publication Committee, 1910), facing 32.

designed solitary cells for the same reason that Lynds forbid speech: to control and silence prisoners, thus increasing productivity. When the Auburn State Prison opened in 1817, Cray and Lynds's system became its hallmark: by day, prisoners worked silently in factories; by night, each prisoner endured solitary confinement.[33]

At first, Auburn prisoners manufactured goods exclusively for use in the prison: uniforms, shoes, buckets, and barrels, for example. In this way, Auburn resembled some other prisons. That changed, however, in 1821, when Brittin died and Lynds became the agent and keeper, a role similar to warden. Lynds then expanded manufacturing to include goods for outside sale.

This move reoriented the Auburn State Prison around surplus value: the difference between what workers cost (in wages or, in the case of slavery or the prison, in the minimal maintenance of life) and what they produce. Initially, Lynds collaborated with a hardware manufacturer and merchant named Samuel C. Dunham to make tools, leasing prisoners' labor for thirty cents per man per day. By 1824, Lynds expanded the contract system by building more in-prison factories and signing new contracts to produce clothing, shoes, and metalwork. Before long, nearly all able-bodied male prisoners were contracted to private companies, which paid the prison—through Lynds, with zero wages reaching prisoners—for their labor. Now the prison, and Lynds personally, not only *saved* money but *profited* off prisoners' forced labor.[34]

This development overturned some core concepts of incarceration—and attendant concepts of prison labor. Early systems, from ancient Rome to premodern Europe, had aimed mainly to confine, punish, or deter wrongdoers. If prisoners labored, they did so mainly as punishment, to settle debt, or to offset operating costs. Then, in the late eighteenth century, Quakers and other reformers developed a new model of incarceration. They believed that a prison's most important function was to lead sinners to spiritual redemption. They created the "Pennsylvania System" (also called the "solitary" or "separate" system), which posited repentance and reformation as a prison's goals. Solitary confinement was Pennsylvania's defining strategy. In the Pennsylvania System, prisoners were isolated in individual cells, where they manufactured shoes and other goods. This labor was believed to provide vocational instruction, protect from the sins of idleness, and most importantly, transform sinners into disciplined, spiritually redeemed Christians.[35] Before the founding of the Auburn State Prison, then, the prevailing belief was that incarcerated laborers had an inalienable *right* to benefit from their work. Even when labor was forced as punishment, it was considered beneficial because it could provoke penitence, balance moral scales, or discourage others from committing crimes.

Furthermore, prison officials assumed there was a *limit* to how much anyone else should benefit from the labor of an incarcerated person.

In contrast, Lynds rejected the goal of reforming prisoners—an endeavor he dismissed as "hopeless"—and he believed that no amount of punishment could diminish criminality.[36] Instead, Lynds aimed for profit. To him, a prisoner was like a slave, a machine, or a river: a resource to be exploited. Therefore, the extraction of prisoners' labor, like that of slaves, should be limited only by the capacity of their human bodies. He believed that incarcerated men had no inherent right to benefit from their labor—vocationally, morally, or otherwise. Lynds's ideal prisoner was "reduced to a silent and insulated human working machine."[37]

People are not machines, and it is difficult to compel them to work without compensation of any kind. Only violence—physical and otherwise—can do that. And Lynds embraced cruelty. His preferred weapon was the cat-o'-nine-tails whip, which he used so extensively that his administration was called a "cat-ocracy." Lynds developed a distinctive cat with a cow-hide handle, eighteen inches long and wound with leather, with six hemp or flax strands that were twelve to fifteen inches long. Each strand was saturated in shoemaker's wax, the weight of which increased the severity of the blows.[38] To break prisoners psychologically as well as physically, Lynds instituted the striped uniform, which would become iconic, and he prevented prisoners from communicating with their families.[39] For Lynds, these tortures were not punishments to provoke repentance, but instead methods of control by which to extract labor. His logic mirrored that of Southern enslavers, who were simultaneously calibrating torture to maximize the productivity of enslaved agricultural workers.[40]

By 1823, Lynds, Brittin, Cray, and their collaborators had improvised their way to create the distinctive Auburn System of incarceration: for-profit, silent group work by day combined with solitary confinement every night, all enforced by extreme violence, with the overwhelming goal of growing a city rather than enacting justice. The system spread fast, far, and hard. In 1825, New York hired Lynds to build and run its third state prison, to be called Sing Sing, under the Auburn System. By 1829, prisons employing the Auburn System were built in Connecti-

FIGURE 1.6 Whipping at the Auburn State Prison

FRONTISPIECE.

CHRISTIAN REFORMATION !!

The chin-heavy, wavy-haired man with the heavy eyebrows wielding the whip clearly resembles Elam Lynds (see figure 1.5). The prisoner wears Auburn's iconic striped uniform. The image's caption, "CHRISTIAN REFORMATION!!," refers sarcastically to Lynds's disinterest in redeeming prisoners. Frontispiece by unidentified artist, *A Peep into the State Prison at Auburn, N.Y., By One Who Knows* (published for the author, 1839; n.p.: copyrighted, 1838), 10–12. Main Collection, Y1839, New-York Historical Society.

cut, Massachusetts, Maryland, and Washington, DC. Over the next fifteen years, the Auburn System spread further across the North, to Vermont, New Hampshire, Maine, and Upper Canada. It spread, too, to the South and West: Virginia, Georgia, Tennessee, Illinois, Ohio, Louisiana, Mississippi, Alabama, Kentucky, Indiana, and Michigan all instituted Auburn-style prisons.[41] These states absorbed not only a system of incarceration but also a *relationship* between prisons and state-funded capitalism.

This proliferation was not unopposed. Advocates for the rival Pennsylvania System—in which prisoners labored in perpetual solitary confinement for the purpose of repentance and reformation—defended their own practices and ideology by waging a "pamphlet war."[42] At stake for Pennsylvania's advocates: prisoners' souls. For Auburn's promoters: money. For the town of Auburn, whose name had become synonymous with a system of incarceration, what was at stake was its very identity.

The feud between prison systems prompted state and European governments, reform societies, and prison administrations to send representatives to assess the Auburn System. The best known of these envoys were Alexis de Tocqueville and Gustave de Beaumont, who visited Auburn and its rivals in 1831–1832 at the request of France's minister of interior. Other luminaries included the Marquis de Lafayette, social thinker Harriet Martineau, reformer Dorothea Dix, and US president John Quincy Adams. Auburn welcomed these visits, which prison officials viewed as opportunities for self-promotion. When an ambassador came from other prison systems or from reform societies, he or she was assigned a special escort, often the agent himself, who answered all questions and put the Auburn System in the best light. For example, when the prominent Scottish phrenologist George Combe visited in June 1839, the governor himself accompanied him.[43]

Auburn sought to augment its status further by appealing to another audience: tourists. The prison eagerly opened its doors to travelers from across the United States and the world. They gawked at Auburn's famous spectacle of silent factory labor and then reported their impressions—which were overwhelmingly positive—in private letters and published accounts.[44] (Tourists never witnessed the physical violence that coerced this work. Before an officer whipped a prisoner, he always "ascertain[ed] if there be visitors in the prison, or at least in that part of it which he attends." If there was, he "postpone[d] the punishment for a few minutes until after the visitor shall have retired.") Women, men, and children of all races, often more than ten thousand a year, came "almost every hour of the day." They walked onto factory floors and filed past the prisoners, who were forbidden to look directly at them. In some areas, visitors were escorted through tunnels from which they could watch prisoners while remaining unobserved. The prison-as-spectacle established Auburn as a highlight along a railroad route that delivered tourists from Boston and New York City to Niagara Falls. An 1842 children's story titled *A Journey to Niagara Falls* articulated this status. The story's narrator told readers that if they travel to the Falls, "I hope you will request your father and mother to show you all the most important places on the route, such as the State Prison, at Auburn.... The prisoners are employed in making combs, and carpets, and clothes, and shoes, and a good many other useful articles.... It is a solemn sight."[45]

Tourism was important not only to the prison's reputation and management, but also to its bottom line. Each adult tourist paid $.25 admission; children were half price. In September 1840, William Freeman's first month of incarceration, the prison collected almost $459 in admission—the proceeds from at least 1,836 visitors, an average of 62 per day.[46] Submitting to tourists' gaze was the prisoners' unpaid job as much as their factory work. Tourists, in turn, injected money into Auburn's railroads, hotels, taverns, and more—which grew those businesses and employed locals.

The increasingly famous term *Auburn System* referred, in its narrowest sense, to a practice of incarceration. But it also described a set of economic relationships among the prison, the state, and endeavors with no obvious connection to incarceration. One such enterprise was the Owasco Canal Company, founded in 1835 by a group of Auburn's businessmen and local politicians, including a young lawyer named William Henry Seward. These men petitioned the state to fund a dam and a canal that would increase the waterpower available to the prison's factories—and link Auburn to the Erie Canal, which opened in

1825 but bypassed Auburn eight miles to the north. Thus, the Auburn System of factory labor became, itself, a justification for appropriating state funding for infrastructure beyond the prison.[47] A second prison-linked enterprise was the Auburn Theological Seminary. It was built in 1819 in part by Auburn prisoners under supervision by Brittin and Lytle; for decades, the prison employed seminary students as assistant chaplains and religious teachers.[48] Later, when some critics objected to the Auburn Prison's disinterest in reform, agents pointed to the presence of seminary students to claim that the prison did indeed minister to souls. Thus, prison labor built the seminary, which later deflected criticism from the prison. A third example was the Auburn Medical Institution—that is, medical school—which was established in 1825 in direct partnership with the Auburn State Prison. Various doctors associated with the prison, as well as William Henry Seward, helped to establish the medical school with the reasoning that it would benefit from yet one more product that the Auburn State Prison yielded: corpses. When a prisoner died, relatives were permitted only twenty-four hours to collect the body—an impossibility in many cases, especially for families from distant parts of the state. After one day, a body was designated "unclaimed" and appropriated for medical dissection. Thus, the Auburn Medical Institution drew on the prison and in turn enhanced Auburn's prestige—and brought yet more people, yet more business, to the town.[49] A canal, a seminary, a medical school: none obviously conjoined with the Auburn State Prison but all interdependent with it. Overtly or subtly, directly or indirectly, the prison affected all Auburn's industries and financially benefited almost every free individual—white or Black.

Black Freedom and Unfreedom Side by Side

From its early days, the Auburn State Prison disproportionately imprisoned African Americans. In 1840, the year William Freeman was incarcerated, it held 62 Black men, 629 white men, 2 Indian men, 1 Black woman, and 1 white woman—a total that was just over 9 percent Black. That same year, Black people comprised 2.1 percent of the population of New York State.[50] Black people were overrepresented in the prison, then, by more than fourfold. However, Auburn's free Black community did not describe the prison as a racial threat. If anything, Auburn's new form of unfreedom emerged alongside and in apparent harmony with expanding Black freedom. Why was this the case?

Black people did not organize in opposition to the Auburn State Prison in part because they were busy organizing around other issues that seemed more urgent. The year 1821, when Lynds assumed control, was also the year an amendment to New York's constitution stripped almost all Black men of the right to vote.[51] Accordingly, voting rights, along with Southern abolition, topped Black New Yorkers' political agenda. Around 1840, however, African American activists in New York shifted toward a broader agenda of racial equality, encompassing education, women's rights, segregation, and labor and its relationship to class status.[52]

This growing emphasis on racial equality created a potential bind for any Black people who might have wanted to criticize the prison. Enslaved people were generally denied jury trials and legal sentences. Access to jury trials—and therefore vulnerability to convictions and sentences—was a feature of citizenship. From a white perspective, these rights might even define personhood.[53] Ironically, then, legal imprisonment was a privilege of freedom, so in the years when slavery lingered in the North and dominated the South, it was risky to oppose a prison in racial terms. To protest Black imprisonment would have been, in a sense, to undermine Black freedom.

Furthermore, if free Black people had called attention to their over-representation in the Auburn State Prison, they would have risked augmenting proslavery rhetoric that associated Black freedom with crime. These arguments gained traction in 1837 when white abolitionists in Philadelphia conducted a census of the city's Black neighborhoods. The study found a higher incidence of crime than in the general population—but also showed that crime rates for Black communities paralleled those of white communities of a comparable class. The abolitionists argued that this equivalence demonstrated both the need and the promise of Black people in Philadelphia. The logic ran thus: most members of the older Black generation were freed people who had been denied formal education and all members of the community were burdened with discrimination—but despite these impediments, poor African Americans' achievements equaled those of white poor people. Therefore, abolitionists argued, Black communities both deserved and would benefit from reform efforts, including economic support. The abolitionists' data were soon hijacked, however. Proslavery forces appropriated the statistics to argue that free Blacks in the North were more likely than enslaved Blacks in the South to be imprisoned. This claim was technically true, but it ignored the fact that enslaved African Americans who committed crimes were punished mainly by enslavers and were denied access to the courts. Thus, white supremacists twisted the Philadelphia data to argue that freedom caused Black criminality. They then similarly manipulated city, state, and national censuses to give this white supremacist story an appearance of statistical fact, an aura of objective truth.[54] These travesties surely had a chilling effect on any New Yorkers who might have wanted to decry Black overrepresentation in the Auburn State Prison.[55]

Finally, Black people did not criticize the prison because the overall number of incarcerated African Americans was small. In 1840, the census counted 50,031 Black New Yorkers, of whom 63 were held at the Auburn State Prison.[56] Some Black Auburnites, including William Freeman, knew someone who had served time there. But many did not. Mass incarceration was unimaginable. For all these reasons, it is no wonder that the fledgling prison scarcely concerned Black New Yorkers.

If anything, many African Americans, like their non-Black neighbors, viewed the prison positively. In October 1840, just one month after William Freeman began serving his sentence, the Black newspaper the *Colored American* ran a "splendid view" of Auburn that praised the town's beauty, its ever-expanding businesses, and especially its prison, which it accurately claimed was "admired as a model, both in Europe and in this country."[57] Although the prison excluded Black people from its payrolls (employing only white guards, for example), it fed local industries that employed many of New Guinea's residents. As Auburn prospered, many Black Auburnites benefited from new jobs, especially in hotels and transportation.

William Freeman's uncle Luke, the first of Harry and Kate's children to be born indentured rather than enslaved, was among the African Americans who thrived in this prison-fed economy. Luke Freeman became a successful barber and owner of barbershops, including one in the American Hotel, which served tourists visiting the Auburn State Prison. (William Freeman, too, gained employment through prison tourism: shortly before his incarceration, he washed knives in the American Hotel's kitchen.) White customers recommended Luke Freeman to each other: "when a man is so fortunate as to fall into his hands," wrote one, he will "leave his shop a happier man." Because Luke Freeman served prison tourists, his reputation traveled far beyond Auburn—so much so that the makers of "Dr. Denton's Hair Invigorator" solicited his endorsement, which they then published in dozens of advertisements in newspapers across New York State. By the 1830s, Luke Freeman was likely Auburn's most prominent and highly esteemed African American, being praised as "worthy and trusty," "humane," "eloquent," and "clever, kind, generous, good." He bought multiple properties, including a home on Court Street, across the street from the Cayuga County Courthouse and jail.[58]

Luke Freeman leveraged his financial and social success to fight slavery. By 1834, he became a figure on the Underground Railroad, sheltering fugitives from the South. He organized with others, including his son Burget, another relative named Platt R. Freeman, and a business partner named Sebeo Hornbeck.[59] One of Luke Freeman's barbershops, at 113 Genesee Street, shared an address with an abolitionist newspaper, the *Northern Independent*. Although this newspaper listed a white man as publisher, Luke Freeman was likely involved.[60] In part because of such abolitionist organizing, New Guinea became a destination for fugitives from Southern slavery. This influx of self-freed people in turn expanded and strengthened New Guinea.

Abolition, economic growth, community development, voting: these were Black Auburn's goals. The prison seemed a mere backdrop, a monument that wielded force through its banality. An 1834 map shows how the prison figured in everyday Auburn. In a magnified illustration in the top right corner, the map depicts business dealings and social life playing out in front of the prison. We see white people in fine dresses and top hats promenading, a white man managing a horse, and a cart laden with barrels and sacks—either supplies entering the prison or consumer goods, ready for sale, exiting it.

FIGURE 1.7 Auburn State Prison

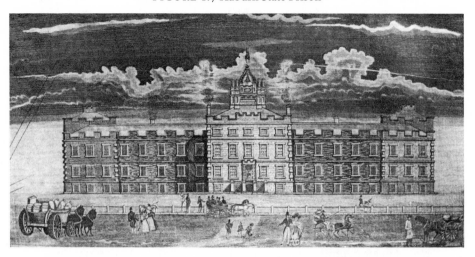

Detail of *Map of the Village of Auburn*. Engraved by M. M. Peabody for the publishers [Auburn, NY]. Published by Hagaman & Markham, 1837 (first published 1834). Courtesy of the American Antiquarian Society.

FIGURE 1.8 Three Figures in Front of the Auburn State Prison

Detail of *Map of the Village of Auburn*. Engraved by M. M. Peabody for the publishers [Auburn, NY]. Published by Hagaman & Markham, 1837 (first published 1834). Courtesy of the American Antiquarian Society.

At the image's center, however, is a different vignette. Two white figures face the prison: a top-hatted man carrying a horse whip and a boy with his hat in his hand. Behind them is a Black boy in profile. In contrast to all the stiffly upright white people, the Black boy bends backward—playing, perhaps, or dancing? When the map was made, about fifteen Black boys under the age of ten lived in Auburn.[61] One of them was William Freeman. The boy on the map could have been him: resisting labor, playfully leaning away from the prison that seemed little more than background scenery to a social drama.

But on September 25, 1840, the prison seized the foreground in William Freeman's life. Rather than prance past it, he trudged, weighted by shackles and manacles. Guards dragged open the prison's iron gates. Freeman breathed a last sip of street air. He stepped forward. The gates closed behind him.

CHAPTER TWO

Outer Stone, Inner Rot

Immediately after William Freeman entered the Auburn State Prison, an assistant keeper took him to the prison's machine shop, where his shackles could be knocked off.[1] There, an extraordinary sight commanded the attention of newcomers: a steam locomotive under construction.[2] The gleaming machine, nearly complete, dominated the workspace. Soon the locomotive would roll out of the prison yard and onto the tracks across the street, whistling the industrial might of the Auburn State Prison.

But this outer show of power contrasted with inner disintegration. The prison was barely two decades old but the machine shop's walls were decayed, its leaky roof, timbers, and floor rotted beyond repair. Trash was piled about. Dust and mold hung in the stagnant air, along with smells of smoldering metal, sawdust, oil, and sweat. The machine shop featured modern equipment: punches, grinders, blowers, cutters, and more, powered by the dam across the Owasco Outlet. But all was in hazardous disrepair, with the blades dull and dangerous.[3]

The sound was as striking as the sight. Machines clanked: metal ground metal, chewed wood, and punched through leather. But no human voices. No communication, no instruction, no banter among workers. Only machines and thirty-two men moving among them, like them.

Freeman surely knew that Auburn's prisoners were forbidden from speaking. He likely learned about this silence from his uncle Sidney

FIGURE 2.1 Auburn State Prison

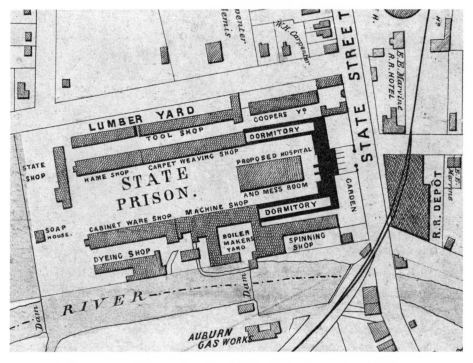

"Dormitory" is a euphemism for the cellblock. Freeman labored in the hame shop (upper left) and later the dyeing shop (lower left). The dam across the Owasco River powered the prison factories. Detail, *Map of Auburn, Cayuga Co., N.Y.* Surveyed and published by John Bevan, 7 Broad St., N. York, & 26 Barrow St., Jersey City, 1851. Map courtesy of Bill Hecht. Image prepared by Dennis McClendon.

and other former prisoners in Auburn's Black community. And when Freeman worked in the American Hotel, he must have overheard the chatter of tourists who traveled long distances to goggle at the silent laboring prisoners. But nothing could have prepared him for the reality of almost three dozen men working shoulder to shoulder in endless silence. "To be duly felt, it must be seen," one tourist wrote.[4] No one was permitted to look up from his work to regard the new boy in chains. The only sound from prisoners' mouths was deep coughing: lung disease, the reported cause of half the prison's deaths.[5] Most of the prison's men were white, but one in eleven was Black.[6] They were as old as sixty-eight and as young as twelve.[7] They looked worn and pale. On witnessing Auburn's factories, one visitor wrote, "so miserable, jaded, desponding a row of faces I never beheld—such sunken, lacklustre eyes I never encountered."[8]

As per the standard intake process, a guard would have searched Freeman's pockets and then led him to an anvil, instructing him to lay his foot on the metal slab. Another prisoner would have raised a sledge-hammer, then slammed it down, shattering the clasp of the shackle around Freeman's ankle. If Freeman cried out in fear or pain, the guard would have responded, "Stop your noise, if we break legs here we do not care, we can mend them again."[9] Three more blows were needed to crack the irons from Freeman's other joints.

Next, Freeman was taken to the kitchen to be shaved, shorn, and uniformed. The shave, always performed by an African American prisoner, could be an ordeal: one man described the barber "tear[ing] out the beard by the roots." Freeman's shave was likely less painful because he had little facial hair—just a shadow across the chin and upper lip. The barber removed what was there and then clipped Freeman's hair close to the scalp.[10] Not a word was permitted between them.

A guard ordered Freeman to strip, likely threatening to whip him if he dawdled. Freeman relinquished his hat, pantaloons, and vest. A Black prisoner would have dunked him in a barrel of water—a "severe ceremony," admitted one prison administrator. As a new prisoner dripped, nude, an officer threw clothes at him: one cotton shirt, two pairs of wool socks, leather shoes, a cap. Then the prison uniform: canvas trousers and jacket, all in broad, horizontal black and white stripes. Austin Reed, an African American who entered the Auburn Prison four months before Freeman, called the outfit "robes of disgrace"; reformer Samuel Gridley Howe called the stripes "poison" that dissolved self-respect. A lucky few received new uniforms, but Freeman likely received one that was patched, too big for his small frame, and mephitic.[11]

As he put it on, he wept.[12]

Freeman was then delivered to the office of Abraham Gridley, the prison clerk.[13] Gridley measured Freeman and recorded his height—five feet, four and a half inches—in the thick prison register. Then he questioned his prisoner.

"How old are you?"

Fifteen.

"Where was you born? What county did you come from?"

Here. Cayuga.

"And what's the crime you are charged with?"

They said 'twas for stealing a horse, but I didn't do it.

"Are your parents living, and are you a married man? How many children have you?"

Mother living, father dead. No wife, no children.

"And what kind of an education have you?"

Not much.

"How many times have you ever been in a county jail, or how many times have you ever been fined?"

Arrested for stealing fowl and for breaking into a peddler's cart. They say I stole a horse, but I didn't.[14]

After recording each answer, Gridley asked about past work for the purpose of assigning the new prisoner to a shop. Freeman had sawed wood, driven horses, run errands, scrubbed cutlery, and cared for younger children. He had no skills of value to a factory. Gridley assigned him to the hame shop, where animal harnesses were manufactured. There, Freeman would file metal for plating.[15]

Unshackled, shaved, shorn, uniformed, measured, questioned, and assigned, Freeman had one last step: to meet with the prison's top authority, Agent Henry Polhemus.

The Agent

Like many of Auburn's officers, Henry Polhemus got his job for his accomplishments in party politics, not prison administration. Since its establishment, the Auburn State Prison had been New York's political seesaw: each time a faction gained control of state government, it sank members of opposing parties and boosted its own loyalists to leadership. As a result, the prison's administrators were chronically inexperienced. From 1834 to 1851, the Auburn State Prison had twelve agents, or wardens, who served an average of 1.5 years apiece.[16]

Polhemus fit this pattern. He began his business life as a merchant, tavern keeper, and landlord, but in 1818 he became a politician. Running as a Clintonian, he was elected twice to the state assembly and served briefly as commissioner of a poorhouse. By the 1830s, Polhemus became a Federalist and then, with many members of that party, a Whig. In 1836 he was elected as one of the first trustees of the village of Auburn.[17]

Polhemus owed his accomplishments in government—including prison administration—in part to his alliance with local rising political star William Henry Seward. The two men worked together: first on a failed committee, chaired by Polhemus, to establish a Christian political party that would enforce sabbath observance in New York; next, on the Board of Directors, also chaired by Polhemus, of the Auburn and Owasco Canal Company. In 1838, each man won an election: Polhemus became president of the Whigs of the County of Cayuga and Seward, governor of New York. Whigs also took control of the state's Congress.[18] Soon after Seward was inaugurated in 1839, he appointed Polhemus to the Board of Inspectors of the Auburn State Prison—Polhemus's first prison gig.[19] One year later, and four months before William Freeman arrived in the prison, Seward's loyal associate became the agent.

But when Polhemus accepted the prison's top position, he inherited a firestorm of controversy kindled by his predecessor, Captain Elam Lynds. The brawl reshaped the prison and framed the experience of every person incarcerated there—including, now, William Freeman.

Party Battles

The fight began in 1838, when Lynds started a second, nonconsecutive term as agent and keeper of the Auburn State Prison (he had left Auburn for thirteen years, during which time he built Sing Sing Prison along Auburn's model).[20] When Lynds returned to Auburn, he discovered that other agents had loosened some of the prison's most draconian methods of control. One agent, Gershom Powers, had even

endeavored to reinvent the prison as a "means of [prisoners'] reformation; that, when restored to their liberty, they may prove honest,
industrious, and wholesome members of society." Lynds set out to re-
verse this direction. Within days of resuming his leadership, he closed
the dining hall and forced prisoners to eat meals in their cells. He dras-
tically reduced rations to the point of starvation. Meals were eaten out
of "kids," or food buckets, which went unwashed for days, attracting
vermin and sickening the men. These measures, Lynds insisted, were
necessary cost-savers. State law required the agent to record "every
complaint made by any convict of bad or insufficient food," but Lynds
refused. When Willet Lounsbury, a member of the Board of Prison Inspectors, said Lynds was legally bound to record prisoners' complaints,
Lynds scoffed, "I care not for the law."[21]

Lounsbury tried to rally inspectors to force Lynds to reinstate adequate meals.[22] When they rebuffed him, Lounsbury quit the Board of
Inspectors and published a blistering exposé in the Democrat-affiliated
newspaper the *Cayuga Patriot*, which he edited. Lounsbury predicted
that his insubordination would "incur the denunciation of a few political harpies, who consider their future political prospects based upon
sustaining Capt. Lynds, right or wrong."[23] But the expected denunci-
ations proved unexpectedly fearsome. The stakes were high because a
schism within the Democratic Party jeopardized state elections. The
split even bore national implications because New York controlled
one-seventh of the Electoral College—so united Democratic votes
were important to the reelection campaign of President Martin Van
Buren, a Democrat from New York.[24] To manage these threats, Lynds's
supporters noisily refuted Lounsbury's claims—and accused the former inspector of hypocrisy, knavery, slander, abuse, and unspecified
"nefarious purpose."[25]

As Democrats firebombed Democrats, Whigs sprayed accelerant.
The Whig-leaning *Auburn Journal and Advertiser* published Democrats' screeds for and against Lynds, including a full-page, Democrat-
authored denunciation of Lounsbury and an anonymous provocation
by a Democrat-appointed Auburn guard alleging that Lynds's prisoners, being denied forks and knives, "tore their meat from the bones

with their teeth" like "carniverous [*sic*] animals." The *Auburn Journal and Advertiser* aimed through Lynds at the Democratic Party itself: the fact that Democrats did not fire Lynds and his cronies, "notwithstanding the horrid cruelty perpetrated daily upon the wretched convicts by these worse than barbarians," proved that "their conduct meets the approbation of the leaders of the party, whose whole history has been one continued scene of fraud, speculation, and oppression."[26]

Summer turned to winter, and controversy snowballed. *Frostbite! Meal buckets crusted with mouse dung!* Each new disclosure and subsequent Democratic denial intensified public outrage. *Men so hungry they eat paste and filch turnip skins from swill pails! Mass diarrhea!*[27] Accusations, defenses, cross-accusations, petitions, anonymous pamphlets, libel lawsuits, perjury trials, and criminal charges were volleyed.[28] *Evidence destroyed! Whippings deliberately undercounted! Embezzlement!* One Whig paper covered every moment of the fracas while commenting disingenuously, "All is excitement at the present time... and the events of almost every day seem calculated to feed and keep alive such feeling, rather than allay it."[29]

The orchestrated controversy paid off for the Whigs in November 1838 when William Henry Seward was elected governor. He was the first member of his party to hold the office, breaking a decade-long run of Democrats. Many attributed Seward's win in part to the storm in Auburn.[30] The stakes of prison politics were now undeniable: Auburn was a bellwether, even a microcosm for the state.

In January 1839, just after Seward took office, a grand jury indicted Lynds on three counts: for "beating, bruising, wounding, and ill treating" prisoners; for ordering his officers to commit similar abuses; and for "causing to be withheld from the convicts a quantity of food necessary to their health" as well as insufficiently heating the factories and cells. Polhemus, now a Whig-appointed prison inspector, took Lynds on by fighting to reopen the dining hall.[31]

Just when it seemed the conflagration could not burn hotter, two prisoners perished. John Winterscale choked on a piece of pilfered meat—a death the press attributed to desperate hunger. Then a keeper lashed to death Louis von Eck, a twenty-two-year-old German forger. The death of a white, middle-class man convicted of a nonviolent crime set off yet another round of public indignation. Lynds refused the coroner entry to the prison to examine von Eck's body. A crowd gathered at the gates demanding they be opened. Lynds finally allowed the coroner's inquest provided his political allies were present and his enemies—Polhemus, Lounsbury, and nineteen others—were not. Auburnites pelted Lynds with rotten eggs and attempted to tar and feather him. Despite Lynds's interference, the inquest determined that von Eck had died as a result of disease, "hastened by flogging, labor and general harsh treatment" combined with "want of proper care on the part of the Physician."[32]

Lynds was defeated. The day after the coroners' verdict, he resigned, aggrieved that "my motives have been traduced and my character assailed" in a "vindictive war" of "fierce, personal and political conflict."[33] In return for his resignation, the state dropped criminal charges against him.

Over the next year, the prison transitioned acrimoniously from Democratic to Whig power. One month, a guard was fired on the mere suspicion that he voted Whig; a few months later, Whigs gained control and discharged Democrats and other non-Whigs. The purge of Democratic employees ended only when nineteen officers resigned and the Whig-dominated Board of Inspectors became "afraid to discharge [more] because of the inefficiency of new hands."[34]

The prison's power to swing elections now seemed confirmed, and all factions were left bruised and vindictive. Far from being silenced, Lynds's supporters founded a newspaper, the *Corrector*, to defend the former agent and attack the Whigs including "Billy O'Seward." The *Corrector* claimed the Board of Inspectors, on which Polhemus sat, had embezzled, framed Lynds, and staged a disingenuous investigation. "How long will the [W]higs make asses of themselves by getting up humbugs about investigating this and investigating that?" The *Corrector* mocked. Whig papers were "filled with recitals of 'shocking barbarities'" in the Auburn Prison. "Crocodile tears trickle down upon vapid jeremiads." "Let the galled jade wince!"[35]

Amid this rancor, Polhemus became agent in May 1840. Democrats immediately targeted him in the *Tocsin* newspaper, which published "grave charges and foul insinuations" that Polhemus had embezzled from the prison.[36]

The Whigs expected Polhemus to right Lynds's wrongs in meals, cold, and violence and thus deliver yet another win to the party. Polhemus, in contrast to Lynds, seems to have cared genuinely about the bodies and souls of prisoners like William Freeman. After the dining hall reopened, Polhemus addressed heating.[37] He was horrified by the "almost intolerable degree of suffering from cold," which he considered "palpably wrong in principle, as well as inhumane in effect." He decommissioned a leaky system of steam heat that his predecessors had installed and mounted four furnaces to heat the cells at night. He improved the bedding: each prisoner received a new mattress and comforter, each of which contained about five pounds of cotton batting.[38] The problem of violence against prisoners was thornier. Polhemus discontinued Lynds's practice of destroying punishment reports and managed to avoid the use of lethal whippings while he sought more measured approaches to prison discipline.

Hardest to resolve, however, were the financial knots tied by Polhemus's predecessors. Rumors of embezzlement and fraud had long dogged Lynds. One former prisoner claimed that Lynds's officers prevented prisoners from eating their full rations because Lynds sold leftovers "for swill, to enrich himself." Two anonymous sources accused officers of stealing funds and goods.[39] Polhemus discovered that his predecessors had muddied the books and omitted key facts from annual reports. For example, the agent was required to inventory the state's property inside the prison, but Polhemus's predecessors refused—and thus gave themselves the opportunity to carry off whatever they wished. They did not even account for consumables such as firewood, bedding, and clothing, which obscured lucrative transactions. Furthermore, previous agents omitted outstanding debts from the annual reports. If the amount of confirmed debt was subtracted from the claimed profit, the prison's annual profit shrank more than 40 percent, from Lynds's claimed $8,490.25 to Polhemus's calculated $5,000.11. Lynds's clerk had omitted the dates from the receipts, which made conducting an accurate audit impossible. If the true amount of debt were accounted for, the prison might show no profit at all.[40]

Four months into his job, Polhemus faced a sickening truth: the celebrated Auburn Prison was in financial peril. He led inexperienced staff while dodging cross fire among Democrats, Democrats, and Whigs. The prison was built for business, not penitence. But earnest, reform-minded Polhemus wanted what he saw as the best of all worlds: to show profits—legitimately—and to transform prisoners into law-abiding Christians. To please his Whig bosses by reducing criminality while benefiting state coffers. To neutralize criticism by curbing whipping without sacrificing productivity. Above all, to protect the vulnerable prison—and the Whigs—from external and internal threats. He did not yet have a plan. But he was determined to hatch one. With it, Agent Polhemus envisioned himself reforming *and* profiting off his prisoners—like this one, William Freeman, who now sat before him in his office.[41]

The Ritual

Polhemus considered prisoners "vicious and degraded men" who "sullied" all they touched—but unlike Lynds, he shrank from whipping them. Polhemus wanted William Freeman to obey the rules and thus spare officers the pain of punishing him. That outcome depended on the success of a ritual: Polhemus, like agents before him, met with the new prisoner to intimidate and cajole him into docility. As Lynds put it, prison officers took "great pains" to make each incoming prisoner "acquainted with the rules by which his conduct is to be governed" and to make clear the consequences for violations.[42]

Each agent began the initiation by explaining the warp of prison's reality. "You have come to a hard place," the agent recited. "For the term of your sentence you must consider yourself dead to the world." Prisoners, the agent explained, were "deprived of all their rights of freemen"— William's hard-earned family name thus undone—because "by their willful misconduct and depravity, they had forfeited all rights."[43]

A prisoner should blame no one but himself, the agent continued. "You exhibit a sad picture of human degradation. From 'bad example, idleness, or the indulgence of evil passions,' you have been led to the commission of crime, by which you have violated the laws of your country, forfeited your liberty, and offended your God."[44]

If Freeman protested his innocence or raged against his accusers, the agent would have quickly silenced him. "Cherish no malevolent feelings against society, or the government, for arresting you in your career of criminality, but rather be thankful for the mildness of our laws; that instead of forfeiting your life on ignominious gallows, as would have been the case under most other governments, you are only restrained for a time." According to the agent, Freeman's fate was in his own hands: "If you will but faithfully improve the opportunities with which you will be thus favored, your case is far from being hopeless; your suffering during confinement will be greatly mitigated."[45]

After the agent painted a sunny picture, he flipped the canvas. "This place is meant as a punishment of the mind, but if you do not conform to the rules laid down to you by myself or the keeper of your shop; we have the power of punishing very severely, even to the *taking of life*."[46]

The rules were rigid. Most important: silence. "Above all things you are prohibited from any intercourse with your fellow convicts, either by talking or making signs." Silence, as Freeman saw in the machine shop, served the prison's overarching directive: to "labor diligently.... No convict is willfully or negligently to injure his work, tools, wearing apparel or bedding; nor is he to make the articles carelessly or badly on which he is at work, when he has the ability to make them well. For the willful or repeated neglect or violation of these or other rules, chastisement is inflicted by the keepers." If communication became necessary, Freeman "must approach the officers of the institution with deference; and when addressing them must bestow on them their usual civic titles, and make use of none but the most respectful language."[47]

Submit, Freeman was commanded, in body as well as speech. "Every movement and whole demeanor are to be in strict accordance to the most perfect order." You "may not sing, dance, whistle, run, jump, or do any thing which will have the least tendency to disturb or alarm the prison." You "must not be seen a running through the yard when sent from one shop to another on some errand." When visitors — tourists, family members, or inspectors—entered the factories, you "must not look up off your work" or "speak a word." As Austin Reed recalled of his own initiation four months before Freeman's, the agent warned that the prisoners' posture would be constantly monitored: "When goin' through the yard on any particular business, you must keep your arms folded and your head bowed towards the ground."[48]

Prisoners were never to look at each other's faces—even during meals or religious services. This rule, as important as Auburn's silence, aimed to extend the social isolation of solitary confinement into communal situations. "When in church, you must keep your eyes directly on the chaplain and not be gazing around you." And "when sitting at the table, you must keep your arms folded, our head bowed, with your eyes directly down on your dishes before you, not allowed to touch a knife or a fork or to unfold your arms until the bell rings as a signal for you to eat. Must not pass a piece of bread or meat or a potato from one man to another."[49]

Even when alone in his cell, Freeman learned, his every movement would be regulated. The "convict must not swing his hammock and go to bed until the bell rings at eight o'clock," the agent said. "He must then strip off his clothes, swing his hammock, and go right to bed, and not be seen by the guard through the night until the bell rings for him to get up in the morning at half past five." On rising, "he must hang up his bed clothes... and not let them be seen on his bed." He "must then be up and dressed and be standing at his door in readiness so as when the Keeper comes along and raises the lever of his door, he may push it open and come out."[50]

Guards, the agent promised, will "enforce these regulations" with "unceasing vigilance and untiring zeal." Any transgression, and "off comes your shirt, and [in] less than a minute's time you are suffering under the pain of the cats." You cannot negotiate your punishment: "*A convict's word is never taken, even against another convict, and much less against an officer.*"[51]

On hearing these rules, some men resolved to "assimilate themselves to puppets"—that is, to acquiesce outwardly to avoid punishment. Prison officials understood this phenomenon. "I have always observed," Lynds told Alexis de Tocqueville and Gustave de Beaumont,

FIGURE 2.2 Architectural Diagram of the Auburn State Prison

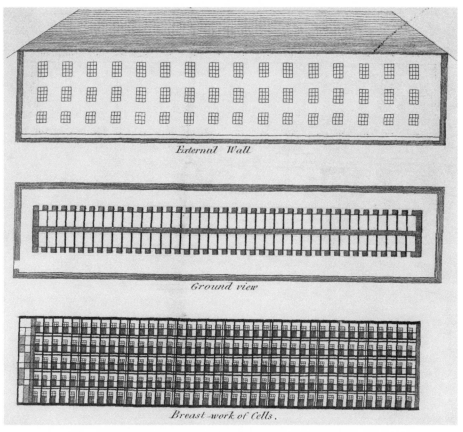

External Wall

Ground view

Breast-work of Cells.

The middle, bird's-eye view depicts the layout of each of the five floors of the north wing. Each cell looked out only into the hall, or "gallery." Each door was recessed, as seen in figure 2.3. "This engraving represents a building, designed to contain four hundred cells, on the plan of the north wing of the prison, at Auburn, in the state of New York." Printed by T. R. Marvin, Boston, 1826. Courtesy of the American Antiquarian Society.

"that the worst subjects made excellent prisoners." These men "generally have more skill and intelligence than the others," so "they perceive much more quickly" that the only way "to avoid painful and repeated punishments" is to "behave well"—but "without being the better for it." Thus, Lynds said, "hypocrites only are made."[52]

William Freeman was no hypocrite.

FIGURE 2.3 *Exterior of a Convict's Cell*

EXTERIOR OF A CONVICT'S CELL.

Agent and keeper Gershom Powers explained the cell's exterior design: "The recess, in front of each door, increases the difficulty of conversation between the prisoners; prevents them from making signs to each other, or from seeing far to the right or left on the galleries; and furnishes a convenient place for an officer of the prison to converse with the prisoner, without being seen or heard by those in the adjoining cells. The fastening of the door is by a strong latch, connected by a hook, with a bar of iron placed over it. The bar extends from a latch two feet horizontally to the outer edge of the wall; thence at a right angle eighteen inches horizontally to the lock." Powers, *Report of Gershom Powers, Agent and Keeper of the State Prison, At Auburn* (Albany: Croswell and Van Benthuysen, 1828), 113. The box to the right of the recess is not described in any prison documents; it seems to be the invention of the illustrator. *Harper's Weekly*, 18 December 1858, 809.

Into the Cell

After meeting with Polhemus, Freeman climbed a stone stairway to the north wing. For the first time, he saw the notorious cellblock from the inside: five tiers, each with a double row of back-to-back cells ringed by a narrow oak walkway—the "gallery"—with a guard rail. Five hundred and fifty cells.[53] He would sleep here for the next 1,826 nights.

The galleries opened around a central shaft that was heated by the furnaces Polhemus had installed. But they were scant help: the air penetrating Freeman's uniform was cold, damp, and still. The stones themselves seemed to be in a cold sweat: water trickled from the mortar and pooled on the plank floor. Wet, smelly clothes hung off the gallery rails.[54] Little light and no air permeated the windows of the central shaft. Outside it was fall, but in the cell block it felt like winter.

While awaiting trial, Freeman had spent three months in the Cayuga County Jail, where prisoners in separate cells could see and hear each other. In contrast, the shape of the prison's cells prevented communication. Each cell's door was recessed two feet; this cavity made it difficult for a prisoner in one cell to hear or to glimpse, even with a mirroring object, interaction between a prisoner and a guard at the next cell. An aperture on each door stretched eighteen by twenty inches. Across it lay iron rounds, each three-quarters of an inch thick, welded into a grill with two-inch gaps—too close to permit the passage of a man's hand. As one prison officer put it, these architectural features physically "embod[ied]" the "genius" of the Auburn System.[55]

The turnkey opened Freeman's cell. If it was typical, it stank of Camphine, a purified spirit of turpentine used to kill bugs. Strong enough to make a man faint. Inside, Freeman saw a pocket of space: three and a half feet wide, seven feet long, and seven feet high. A man could wedge his shoulder against one wall and flatten his palm against the opposite one. A lead pipe, two and a half inches in diameter, snaked from the cell's rear to the roof—that, with the aperture on the cell's door, was the only source of air. The cell contained a bucket for waste and a canvas hammock on which lay the bedding that Polhemus had procured. An abundance of fleas, bedbugs, and other insects defied the Camphine to crawl about the cell.[56]

The turnkey closed the door and locked it. Now there was almost total darkness, with but a glimmer from the door's aperture.[57] In four days, William Freeman would turn sixteen.[58] He was alone among five hundred forty-nine others in the belly of a ship sailing into the unknown.

CHAPTER THREE

Skirmishes and Stagnancy

Every morning at 5:30, a bell ordered William Freeman to leave his cell. Three, four, five dozen prisoners formed a single file on the gallery. Silently, Freeman placed his right hand on the shoulder of the man in front of him and felt the man behind him cup his. Each man's left hand held a night tub, or chamber pot. Every face turned toward the guard, heads bowed, eyes sweeping the floor, mouths immobile. They marched—closely, fluidly, appearing, one former prisoner wrote, like "a long reptile crawling out of a dead horse." This was the "lockstep," which Elam Lynds and John Cray instituted to prevent communication as prisoners moved to and from factories.[1]

But men found cracks of opportunity, and they bored into them. They whispered, passed notes, even taught each other ventriloquism. They learned each other's names and origins. Some prisoners, particularly African Americans, parodied the lockstep as they performed it, "stamping and gesticulating as if they were engaged in a game of romps."[2]

First they marched into the prison yard. They emptied their night tubs into an underground tank, rinsed them with pump water, and set them aside. Then they rejoined the lockstep and marched through factories that produced carpets, clothes, barrels, furniture, and more, with each chamber generating a different racket, a distinct shade of smoke as raw materials began to smolder or boil. As men peeled off to assume their workstations, the line dwindled. The last stop was Freeman's: the hame shop (figure 2.1). There, amid gusts of dust, seventy-two men made animal harnesses and hardware for carriages. In 1841, his first full year

FIGURE 3.1 *Prisoners at the State Prison at Auburn*

Prisoners at the State Prison at Auburn.

Prisoners at Auburn wore humiliating stripes and moved in "lockstep." All the prisoners depicted here appear white, but about 9 percent of the prisoners were African American. John W. Barber and Henry Howe, *Historical Collections of the State of New York* (New York: pub. for the authors by S. Tuttle, 1845), 78.

there, Freeman and others built 6,849 animal harnesses plus hundreds of saddles, stirrups, buckles, carriage lamps, and related items. Their work was sold wholesale to Cayuga County's merchants and saddlers at a total market value of almost thirty-two thousand dollars.[3] The contractor bought the year's labor from the prison for a fifth of that amount—just over seven thousand dollars, less than thirty-five cents per man per day.[4]

Freeman's job: to file rough iron imported from England, smoothing it in preparation for japanning, a lacquered finish. Alongside nine other filers, he burnished the surfaces of buckles, rings, and other hardware for saddles. It was "coarse work" that required muscle but also "judgment and comparison." Freeman filed every morning for two hours, then marched to the mess hall for a half-hour breakfast, marched back, filed more, marched, ate dinner, marched, filed. Every movement regimented, every day the same. Another prisoner described the life: "Each morning, when I seated myself in the shop and cast a look around me upon the things too familiar with my sight, my impression has been accompanied with a sigh, 'Ah! I am here yet.'"[5]

Sometimes Freeman relieved the tedium by clowning around. Laughter was prohibited, so men made a game of trying to make each other burst. When keepers looked away, Freeman made motions that were so silly the other men in the hame shop could not keep their faces straight—and they reciprocated. Austin Reed, who was incarcerated alongside Freeman, described another Black prisoner who "would come to my bench and pretend that he was showing me something about my work, when at the same time he would be talking about something else which would make me bust out and laugh."[6]

The games had serious underlying functions: not only to lighten the emotional burdens of imprisonment but also to reduce productivity and thereby profits. If the prison could steal their days' labor, the men could steal seconds back.[7]

But resistance incurred penalties. Nearly every day, jailors whipped the prisoners. They whipped them for working poorly or slowly, for "playing old soldier" by handing in the same work on multiple days, for whispering or laughing, for sharing food or pilfering. No disobedience was too small to warrant punishment. Jailors whipped prisoners in the factories, the mess hall, the yard, the cells—but always out of sight of tourists. Jailors whipped prisoners naked, and if they did not strip fast enough, they whipped them more. They whipped them as they stood; and those who could not stand were clamped into vices or tied by the wrists to rafters, their toes grazing the floor. The strands of the whip, Austin Reed wrote, "sting like the prick of a needle, and when sunken in very deep, the sufferer feels as though he had been bitten by the bite of a dog or been scratch[ed] by the paw of a cat."[8] Each day, keepers registered these punishments in the state-mandated ledger:

November 2, 1840: "J[ames E.] Tyler Reports the punishment of Allen, nine stripes with the cat for insolence."

November 5, 1840: "R[obert] D. Cook Reports the punishment of Lynch six stripes with the cat for Spoiling a piece of carpeting."

FIGURE 3.2 "T[homas] H. Toan reports the punishment of Freeman six strip[e]s with the cat for laughing & making motions to make others laugh"

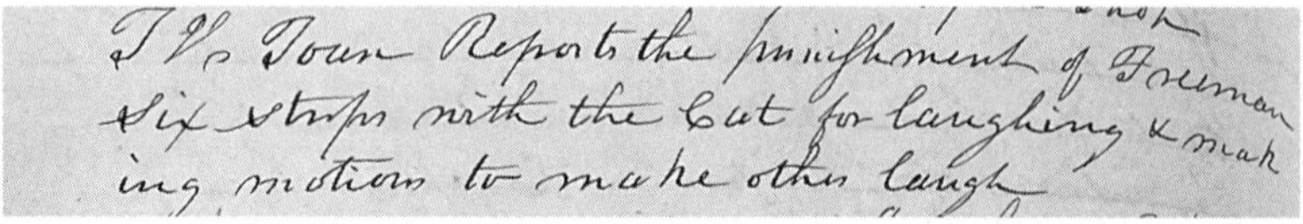
T H Toan Reports the punishment of Freeman
six strips with the Cat for laughing & mak
ing motions to make others laugh

Daily Punishment Reports of the Auburn State Prison, 1 November 1840. New York State Archives, New York State Education Department, Albany. Photograph courtesy of Joni Christel.

> November 6, 1840: "M. L. Owen Reports the Punishment of Washburn six stripes with the cat for giving in more cloth than he wove."

> November 9, 1840: "J. Underwood Reports the punishment of Durfey six stripes with the cat for writing & Robeson six stripes with the cat for stealing awls & carrying them to his cell."

> November 10, 1840: "H. Hawley Reports the Punishment of Lundy six stripes with the cat for not doing as much work as required of him."[9]

On November 1, 1840, barely five weeks into his sentence, Freeman suffered the whip for the first time: "T[homas] H. Toan Reports the punishment of Freeman six strip[e]s with the cat for laughing & making motions to make others laugh."[10] Humor could sustain a prisoner, but it could also cost him.

At day's end, the men extinguished the fires in the factories. They marched in lockstep to the prison yard, recovered the night tubs, and pumped some water into each one. They marched to their solitary cells. They slung their hammocks. They slept. The next morning, bells rang.[11] The routine began again.

Resistance and Retribution

Some prisoners may have reduced their labor simply to conserve effort, but Freeman did so within a broader pattern of protest. Repeatedly, he told his supervisors that he "did not want to work" because he "was deriving no benefit" from the labor. He deserved wages, he repeated. He "ought not to work" because had committed no crime, stolen no horse. He "didn't want to stay there and work for nothing." He was unyielding, certain in his repeated claims of injustice, quick to talk back to those with power over him. When his verbal arguments were ignored, Freeman resisted through other means: he worked slowly or submitted previously completed work as new.[12]

These protests attracted the attention of Samuel P. Hoskins and James E. Tyler, officers who oversaw the hame shop. Hoskins, "a man of unusual activity and vigor," once rubbed salt into the wounds of a whipped prisoner.[13] Tyler, who "consider[ed] blacks below whites in intellect" and declared Freeman "below the mediocrity of blacks," once bound a "crazy" prisoner naked to a post and "cut and lacerated" him "from his head to his heels."[14] Later, Tyler ordered another officer to wield a glowing-hot iron bar as a weapon against a prisoner, who later died. Prisoners who physically defied Tyler enraged him most. He once boasted, "I never allow a man to raise his arm at me and live." Together, Tyler and Hoskins made a routine of kicking Freeman. Tyler would "strike him and kick him generally when he passed him"; and Hoskins kicked Freeman whenever he "got the chance." The blows were so frequent that Freeman "thought he wouldn't stand it." He "made up his mind that he might just as well be dead as alive."[15]

One day, Freeman resisted physically. When Hoskins came at him yet again, Freeman "warded off the blows and weighed out Hoskins one." Freeman, by his own report, "struck Hoskins with his left hand and faced him around." Then Freeman "dropped his left hand over his face, and struck him with the right"—a move he called the "butcher's chop." Hoskins then ordered other prisoners to hold Freeman down, and the guards "pounded him." But the beating did not end Freeman's defiance. To the contrary, it made him resolve "to fight till he died."[16]

Freeman continued resisting. One day in early 1842, after he had worked in the hame shop about sixteen months, Tyler confronted him for withholding labor and demanded he increase production. Freeman refused. "He told me to go to work," Freeman said later, "and I wouldn't." Yet again contesting the prison's founding principle, Freeman told Tyler that he "was there wrongfully and ought not to work." Tyler then ordered Freeman to "take his clothes off" as preparation for whipping. Next, according to Freeman, Tyler "struck him [and] he struck back." Tyler told a different story: that Freeman grabbed a knife and lunged at him; "I then had to defend myself." Whatever the truth, Tyler was determined to force Freeman "to submit" to the whip. He kicked Freeman, knocked him down, and ordered other prisoners to "clinch" him. Then, instead of the intended whip, Tyler grabbed what was closest: a basswood board measuring four feet long, fourteen inches wide, and half an inch thick. He smashed the board against Freeman's left temple. The blow was so severe that the board split lengthwise along the grain, leaving in Tyler's hands a spike four inches wide. Tyler, who became "excited," used the remnant of the board to deliver "eight or ten" more blows—"pretty snug," without recovery time in between. "A black man's hide is thicker than a white man's," Tyler explained later, "and I meant to make him feel the punishment."[17]

When the board hit his temple, Freeman felt something fall. It was not only his body, knocked to the ground, nerves firing—but also something smaller, inside. He later described the sensation: "It felt as though stones dropp'd down my ears." Although Freeman did not know it specifically, the blow broke his ear drum, gave him a concussion, and damaged his left temporal bone—the thick bone at the side of the skull that protects the ear's nerves and other structures. After that—quiet. "The sound went down [my] throat," he said later. The hame shop became muffled, as if dampened by a heavy curtain. Most of his "hearing was gone, was all knocked off." It never returned.[18]

News of the deafening beating reached William Freeman's mother, Sally Freeman, who "heard that somebody had struck" her son "on his head, and that it was going to kill him." She asked her son-in-law, John De Puy, to check on him. It was no small request because African American visitors, while not barred from the prison, were few. One prison guard who regularly escorted outsiders counted hundreds in his diary, noting gender and race; only six in a year were Black. Defying any barriers, De Puy visited Freeman five times during his sentence. To his dismay, De Puy saw evidence that the blow to his brother-in-law's head had affected more than his hearing: his brain, too, seemed injured. He saw Freeman shuffling about the prison yard. "He would walk a little way and turn round" without apparent reason, De Puy said later. He went home and told his wife, Freeman's sister Caroline, "I don't think he was in his right mind."[19]

The Shower-Bath

In Henry Polhemus's view, whipping and other punishments were problems—not only because they maimed and killed prisoners, not only because injured or dead prisoners could not work, not only because blood fed public outrage that abetted whichever party was out of power, and not only because spontaneous, unauthorized beatings undermined his power as agent. Whipping was all that and more: a symbolic problem.

FIGURE 3.3 *The Cat O'Nine-Tails*

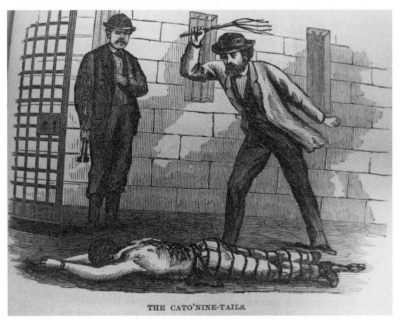

Despite the book's title, this image depicts a whipping at the Auburn State Prison. Charles Sutton, *The New York Tombs: Its Secrets and Its Mysteries, Being a History of Noted Criminals, with Narratives of their Crimes, as Gathered by Charles Sutton, Warden of the Prison*, ed. James B. Mix and Samuel A. MacKeever (New York: United States Publishing Company, 1874), 591.

Whips hearkened to the South, amplifying echoes between enslaved and prison labor. Previously, these racial implications had been tolerated, even touted. An early agent boasted that Auburn made slaves of its prisoners, most of whom were white. But as abolitionism swelled in the North during the 1830s, the mirror between whipped white prisoners and Black slaves became a liability for the prison.[20] Now, when the whipped prisoner was white, his slave-likeness constituted an epistemological emergency: whipping threatened to smudge the line between white and Black. As one white prisoner was widely quoted, "It is hard for one white man to take off his shirt to be flogged by another."[21]

Polhemus needed a modern, distinctly Northern punishment that could intimidate men into compliant productivity without damaging their white bodies or souls—or the prison's reputation. An idea came from Louis Dwight, president of the Boston-based Prison Discipline Society, who described experiments in dousing defiant prisoners with cold water. One of Auburn's physicians, Joseph Pitney, liked the idea but was unimpressed by Massachusetts's disorganized practice of throwing water at prisoners. The Auburn State Prison, idealized as a machine run by machinelike workers, warranted nothing less than a machine for punishment. In 1842, Pitney invented it: the shower-bath.[22]

The shower-bath was a stocks-like structure that constrained a seated man at the neck, wrists, and sometimes ankles. Above the man's head was a source of water, which trickled or gushed down. Some shower-baths encased the man's lower head in a hopper or trellis-box that pooled water. The box forced the man to twist his face up—into the stream—to avoid drowning. A shower usually ran fifteen to twenty minutes but could run as long as forty-five.[23]

In fantasy, the shower-bath reflected Auburn's self-image: it was modern, innovative, and rational; the "most *efficient, time-saving* and *humane* mode of punishment that could be devised," Pitney proclaimed.[24] Like the prison and its factories, it drew power from rushing water. Like the Auburn System, it promised results without damage—a rejoinder to Lynds's "cat-ocracy." One admirer described the invention as "somewhat like an easy chair" in which the "patient" is "securely confined." Water travels through a tube at a "proper distance above the head," de-

FIGURE 3.4 An Idealized View of the Shower-Bath

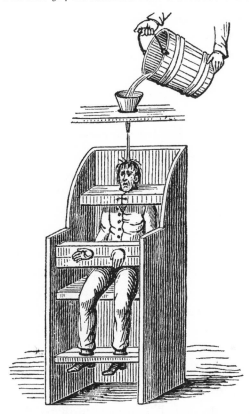

Frederick A. Packard, *Memorandum of a Late Visit to the Auburn Penitentiary; Prepared for the Philadelphia Society for the Alleviation of the Miseries of Public Prisons* (Philadelphia: J. Harding, 1842), 5. Courtesy of the American Antiquarian Society.

livering water "of an ordinary temperature" in a "steady stream." In one illustration, a clothed white man looks unhappy, even remorseful, as water sprinkles harmlessly over his scalp. The man's right hand is outstretched, receptive, while his left hand and feet are relaxed. The water's external source, a bucket, is held lightly by a pair of disembodied white hands. This punishment is impersonal, rationalized. Whipping "hardens the keeper and stimulates his anger," wrote another prison doctor, Blanchard Fosgate, but "the contemplation of his victim under the water excites his pity and better feelings. The shower-bath cools his passion, while the whip inflames it." Pitney called his invention "perfectly innocent," while a prison inspector declared that showering "has in most cases been beneficial to health," like the many water-cure spas that had recently opened in Auburn's environs.[25]

In reality, the shower-bath induced agony, terror, and debility. Austin Reed metaphorized the shower-bath as a "little water craft" called the "*Conqueror.*" He wrote, "I pity the passenger that ever steps on board of her.... She is a dangerous little craft to sail on, and the passenger who steps aboard of her is continually in danger of his life, or of getting his good reason lost." Fosgate called the machine "but a modification of the water punishments of the Spanish inquisition [*sic*]."[26]

Like many forms of water torture, showering made people feel as if they were drowning. "The first effect," Fosgate reported, "is strangulation of the most painful degree." High volume and low temperatures increased the torment: a shower used up to eleven barrels of water, and added ice or snow sometimes lowered the temperature to thirty-five degrees. "The muscles involuntarily shrink upon the application of cold. But here they must bear the shock, in all its severity." The result, Fosgate noted, is "aberration of mind, convulsions, congestion of the brain, liver, and bowels." Blood "reced[es] from the surface," to be "thrown suddenly and violently upon those organs." The machine sometimes caused deafness, blindness, or madness. "Have no doubt," wrote one inspector, "that the minds of convicts have been impaired, and in some cases ruined by the bath." Fosgate described one prisoner in "good health" who was showered and subsequently suffered "mental derangement."[27]

The machine not only maimed but killed. One Black man, Samuel Moore, died as a prison doctor watched: his "death struggles which were so fierce that, wrenching his hands free from their firm fastening, he slipped from his seat, and was actually hung by his neck in the stocks."[28]

The threat of the shower-bath did not, however, intimidate William Freeman into compliance. He continued to talk back and to resist factory labor. One day in spring 1842, only a few weeks after the installation of the shower-bath, he told Benjamin Van Keuren, the foreman in the hame shop, that he needed a new file. Freeman said, "You must be

FIGURE 3.5 *The Negro Convict, Mo[o]re, Showered to Death*

Harper's Weekly, 18 December 1858, 808.

a fool to s'pose a man can do as much with a dull file as with a sharp one." Van Keuren threatened to report him for insolence, and Freeman replied, "Report and be damn'd."[29]

Van Keuren did report Freeman—to none other than James Tyler. The officer forced Freeman to the shower-bath's corridor, which was "continually wet" from the device's frequent use. Freeman was stripped, locked into the machine, and showered. Austin Reed described what he and Freeman both endured: "my hands head and feet were made fast, and then the cruel work commenced and did not stop (only at intervals for me to get breath) till I had received eleven barrels of water." The mere thought of the shower-bath "makes me shiver and ache all over."[30]

As squeamish as Henry Polhemus seemed about whipping, he never championed showering. He installed the machine quietly, without mention in his governmental reports or communications with the press. And starting on Christmas Day 1840, the *Daily Punishment Reports*—the ledger in which Lynds scandalously underreported whippings—also went silent. From that day forward, in defiance of the law, Polhemus's staff ceased recording punishments of any kind.

Reformers were less reticent. Aware of the shower-bath's dangers, they called for the punishment to be adjusted or controlled—but not eliminated. Dorothea Dix, for example, was "convinced that, with due care, and under proper direction, the shower bath, (not the *douche*, or bolt bath,) is a very effectual means of procuring submission to proper rules and regulations. It is a mode of discipline which may be, and which has been abused, but so has and may be every other form of punishment." Dix favored the controlled use of mild showers for familiar reasons: "the lash hardens a hard nature, and degrades a degraded one."[31]

These limited debates perpetuated the system. As doctors like Fosgate and social reformers like Dix publicly weighed showering against whipping, one type of showering mechanism versus another, or abuse versus proper use of the machine, their squabbles short-circuited larger questions: If the Auburn System could not function without torture, might the system itself be immoral? Should the Auburn State Prison—or any profit-driven prison, or even any prison at all—continue to exist?

Tradesmen's Challenges to the Auburn System

While Freeman and other prisoners resisted the Auburn System from inside, another group did so from without—but for different reasons. That group was New York's white tradesmen, or "mechanics." As the North transitioned out of slavery and as capitalism arose, working-class white tradesmen needed to define their place in a changing economy. They did so largely by defining themselves as industrial "workers." They used this term to distinguish themselves from African Americans, whom they imagined as preindustrial "servants." Midcentury African Americans refused this label, claiming the term "worker" for themselves. The white and Black workers agreed on one point, however: both considered the two groups to be competitors.[32] When Freeman entered the prison, then, the idea of *worker* was itself a category of racial competition. New York's white mechanics understood prison labor in this context—and opposed it as unfair competition with their industries. They organized themselves as free white men in opposition to the unfree—who were mostly white but also, disproportionately, Black.

The mechanics' resistance launched almost as soon as factories arose along with the prison. In 1835, after almost a decade of protests, the mechanics pushed through a law stating that "no mechanical trade shall hereafter be taught to convicts in the State Prisons of this State, except the making of those articles of which the chief supply for the consumption of the country is imported from foreign countries." This law left Auburn's principles unchallenged, mitigating only competition with white free labor (which was the mechanics' sole objection). But Lynds and other agents ignored and evaded even this law. In 1840, mechanics reorganized to decry prison labor as "unjust and oppressive towards a single class"—namely, white mechanics. Each product made with cheap prison labor, they argued, forced them to reduce their own prices. Thus, state income rose *because* mechanics' earnings declined. The mechanics characterized this dynamic as "a tax upon labor and not upon property" because it "throws the whole burden of its support upon one class of community—a class the least able to sustain it." For this reason, they petitioned the state legislature to "abolish… all mechanical labor in the State Prisons" and instead support prisons with tax revenue unless prisoners could be employed in noncompeting industries.[33]

The mechanics' petition, which was signed by nearly four thousand people including the mayor of New York City, failed. The state legislature rejected it on the grounds that abolishing for-profit prison labor was "the equivalent to requesting the State to change its whole code of criminal jurisprudence and its entire system of prison discipline, at the expense of the entire change of the constitutions of the prisons" of New York.[34]

Despite the decision, the white mechanics still plagued Polhemus, who "felt extremely desirous" to develop a new form of labor that would "remov[e] all just cause of complaint." That new mode was suggested by Polhemus's collaborator William Henry Seward. The Whig governor's proposal: silk manufacturing.[35] If the state could stimulate the economy by building canals and prisons, surely it could do the same with a silk venture.

Silk

During the 1830s, silkmaking boomed and then busted in New York State. By the time Polhemus became agent, demand for silk was again skyrocketing, and patriotic Americans increasingly rejected the European manufacturers who dominated the US silk market (which one newspaper estimated at $1.5 million per year).[36] Because the silk industry had recently collapsed in New York State, regional artisans could not complain of unfair competition. Silkmaking, like showering, seemed refined, civilized, and therefore fit for a modern factory-prison. For all these reasons, Seward advocated in-prison silkmaking, also known as sericulture.

Silkmaking was attractive to Polhemus because it offered him a way to heal the ruptured relationships between the prison and the townspeople (who still simmered over the Lynds fiasco). Auburnites with little capital and no experience could raise silkworm cocoons and sell them to Polhemus. One acre of mulberry trees had the potential to yield one hundred bushels of cocoons, for which the prison would pay about $350. Because the labor of cultivating cocoons required little muscle, children could perform it and thus augment a family's income. One supporter of the venture described a family with a "small cocoonery" that housed 100,000 worms. "The worms are entirely fed and managed by two little girls from 12 to 14 years of age. A boy about the same age collects and brings the leaves. This is *all* the labor employed in the cocoonery."[37] The cocoon market, Polhemus strategized, would make even more Auburn families financially interdependent with the prison—and thus buy their continuing allegiance.

Although Polhemus had even less experience in sericulture than in prison administration, he predicted future profits with confidence—and, he often reminded the public, with the governor's support. Ignoring the previous decade's silk bust, Polhemus calculated optimistically. The prison would buy cocoons for three to four dollars per pound. Processing those cocoons—reeling, dyeing, and winding—would cost two dollars per pound. The resulting silk, which, Polhemus averred, would "no doubt" be of "superior quality," would sell for ten dollars per pound, yielding a profit margin of one hundred percent. Since the business eliminated middleman contractors (in contrast to the other commercial factories in the prison), the state would net all the profits.[38]

Polhemus aired his plan nationally through a newspaper call for families to cultivate cocoons and sell them to the Auburn State Prison. The advertisement, which newspapers—mainly Whig—ran for free, promised easy, quick cash plus a chance for patriots to counter foreign interests.[39] With this countrywide campaign, Polhemus staked the prison's reputation—plus his own, and potentially even Seward's—on the success of the silk venture.

Construction began. Polhemus had one throwing mill built, to which he assigned two incarcerated men. He rapidly scaled up to five mills with ten workers, then ten mills with forty-one men. By the end of 1841 Polhemus had invested $2,792.35 in the silk business. A few weeks later, he bragged in his annual report that he had restored the Auburn State Prison to profitability. Seward, in his annual Governor's Message in January 1842, praised Polhemus's silkmaking effort and announced that the prison had paid Auburnites and other New Yorkers a total of $964 for cocoons in the business's first seven months. Following that prominent endorsement, Auburnites went into a "spasmodic mania," devoting acres of land to the cultivation of mulberry trees (whose leaves fed the silkworms) and building cocooneries in "barns, wood-houses, garrets," and "even their parlors."[40]

The results were promising. In 1842, the first full year of operation, the prison silkworks cost $9,766.51 and earned $12,763.51—a profit of 30 percent. By 1843, the Auburn State Prison had become the nation's top buyer of unprocessed cocoons. Whig newspapers continued to run Polhemus's notices, which publicized his products and buffed the prison's damaged image. Auburn silk won two regional contests: the American Institute of New York called it "worthy of notice" and the Annual Fair of the New-York State Agricultural Society awarded Polhemus's product first prize in the category of "Manufactured Silk," calling it "equal [to] the best class of imported articles." The prize committee affirmed "the feasibility of rendering [sericulture] a successful branch of industry in our penitentiaries." With these awards as evidence, Polhemus declared his prison-made silk "superior to the imported article, in strength and softness of texture, in smoothness and in color"—the fulfillment of his promises.[41]

As the silk business grew, Polhemus reassigned prisoners from other factories to the silkworks. In June 1842, William Freeman became one of them. Now seventeen years old, hearing impaired, brain injured, and half-drowned by the shower-bath, Freeman seemed to fit among the other silkworkers, whom the prison clerk described as "cripples, boys, and negroes." Freeman worked in the dye house, where copper kettles, each one five feet tall, boiled color into silk. He worked the fires beneath the kettles. He hauled wood. He fetched water. He turned a kettle-crank to stir hundreds of pounds of soaked silk so the dye distributed evenly. The language of silk dyeing swirled around him: cochineal and copperas; peach leaves, fustic, lye. He must have strained to hear orders: boil, stir, rake, wring. Inspect the coppery scum. Mix the madder and pearl ash by bruising them together. Crystallize. Neutralize. Dissolve.[42]

Going Bust

After Freeman worked in the dye house for a year, America's silk balloon burst—again. In part because of overproduction—Seward had encouraged additional prisons, notably Sing Sing, to make silk—prices plunged by a third. Polhemus continued to promise that Auburn's silk business would "increase the force employed to an [sic] hundred men, with an increase of profits exceeding fifty per cent." Meanwhile,

FIGURE 3.6 Advertisement for Barber's Prison Carpets

Respectably dressed men (center) observe the prison factory while prisoners in striped uniforms (left and right) labor, eyes averted from the visitors. Detail, advertisement for Barber's Prison Carpets. *William H. Boyd's Auburn Directory, Containing the Names of the Citizens, a Business Directory of Cayuga County, and an Appendix Containing Much Useful Information. 1859–1860* (New York: William H. Boyd, Directory Publisher, Appletons' Building, 346 Broadway, 1859).

he obscured financial trouble by reporting the imputed value of silk produced rather than actual income from silk sold.[43] When silk prices plummeted nationally, however, Polhemus's cheery declarations rang false.

The Whigs, who had invested part of their reputation in the success of the Auburn State Prison, lost control of New York politics. In 1842, Seward did not run for reelection, and Democrat William C. Bouck became governor. Polhemus lost his job. John Beardsley, a Democrat who was President of the Cayuga County Bank, became Auburn's new agent.[44]

Aware that the silk business was losing money, Beardsley wanted to shut it down. To do so, however, would provoke Auburnites who "were feeling a deep interest" in it. "To have refused to purchase" cocoons, Beardsley realized, "would in most case have been a grievous disappointment," and therefore a political liability. So he continued buying cocoons and maintained the silk factory through the end of 1843.[45]

By 1844, however, silk became so unprofitable that even the threat of public opprobrium could not prevent Auburn's factory from closing. Beardsley dismantled the silkworks and sold off the machinery. The dye house and its workers, including William Freeman, were reallocated to the prison's carpet factory.

Democrats made a boon of silk's bust. With perceptible relish, Beardsley exposed the business failures of Polhemus—and thus of the Whigs. He reported that his predecessor had deposited six hundred pounds of silk with one New York City proprietor, then five hundred pounds with another, at a total value of $4,000—but only "a very trifling amount of the silk had been sold." The "silk," Beardsley gloated, was "badly twisted, badly assorted, and some of it defective in color, and consequently unsaleable." Beardsley felt "obliged to permit both houses to close the concern, and refund themselves, by a forced sale of the silk on hand," at a respective cost of $5.00 and $5.25 per pound, rather than the $7.25 that Polhemus had contracted. These defects and lost profits could be partially attributed to the resistance practices of Freeman and other allegedly "low grade" workers: they stole silk, "wasted" it, and worked at half the pace of their free counterparts.[46]

Freeman turned eighteen, then nineteen. The boy who liked to make others laugh still "made some music and fun about him." He danced. Punishment followed: three stripes with the cat. He disobeyed orders. Four stripes. Prison was "killing him by inches," he said.[47]

Anger rising, Freeman lashed out at a new target: other prisoners. He would "fly in a moment" at "anything that he thought was an insult." He argued with another prisoner, Andrew Aiken, "about the position of a pole of yarn in the dye house." Both were punished: Aiken, who was white, with four blows of the cat, Freeman, with six. The whip sliced a hole between Freeman's ribs big enough that "he could lay his fingers in." Once, another prisoner accidentally knocked over a pair of shoes Freeman had greased and set to dry near a dye house stove; in retaliation, Freeman struck him over the head with a board, sending him to the hospital for a week.[48] He hurt another prisoner as he had been hurt.

The Uses of Skirmishes

By fall 1845, the prison had accustomed itself to permanent flux. Every decade or so, white mechanics organized against competition and a weak law or two passed in their support—but was then ignored or circumvented. Critiques of the Auburn System occasionally arose, but they were scattered, disorganized, and ineffectual. Prisoners tactically reduced the value of their labor by stalling, stealing, or befouling their work, and officers retaliated. Tourists came, ogled, spent money, then hopped back on trains to Niagara Falls. One mode of punishment was declared inhumane so a new one supplanted it, and few asked whether a system that depended on torture might be fundamentally flawed. Prisoners died and reformers shrieked—until they stopped. A party won state control and denounced its predecessor, then another ascended and did the same, and then another. Factories made money, lost it, adjusted, and regrew. Corruption was discovered and investigated; reports were written; agents were fired and new ones hired. It seemed this cycle of disruption followed by accommodation and re-entrenchment would never change.

PART II

THE CHALLENGE

CHAPTER FOUR

Back Pay and Payback

Four coins. William Freeman eyed them. Too few even to make a heap on the desk of Jonathan Hubbard, the clerk who was processing his release from the Auburn State Prison. Four coins after five years' work. Freeman had no reason to see currency during that time, and he did not recognize these pieces. On one side of each coin, a seated white woman, her gown draped, wet-looking, clinging. On the tail side, an American bald eagle, arrows in its claws, muscles tense, ready to attack. Or to fly.[1]

Hubbard's eyes scanned the prison's register, where he entered the required information. Date: September 25, 1845. Where born: Cayuga County. Complexion: Negro. Height: 5′ 4.5.″ Occupation: laborer. Where convicted: Cayuga County Court of General Sessions. Crime: grand larceny. Hubbard dimly perceived the twenty-year-old man sitting before him; he incorrectly listed Freeman's age as eighteen. Had that been true, Freeman would have entered the Auburn State Prison at the age of thirteen.[2]

Five years. Four coins.

Freeman spoke. "I have been in Prison five years unjustly, and ain't going to settle so."

Freeman thought the money was payment for his labor in the prison factories. In fact, he received the four half-dollars because of a deal between the prison and the town. Auburnites were concerned that people who completed their prison sentences would remain in Auburn and commit crimes. Administrators therefore agreed to provide each released prisoner with a small sum to fund immediate needs and travel home. The sums ranged from two dollars for those like Freeman who resided nearby to five dollars for those bound for distant counties.[3]

William Freeman never doubted he had the right to be paid for his labor, and he never ceased asserting it. This scant handful of coins, in Freeman's view, constituted gross underpayment, and worse: evidence he was being cheated. He demanded more.

In response, the white men in the clerk's office—Hubbard, as well as prison chaplain Alonzo Wood and Russell Chappel, who became agent after Beardsley—chortled. To them, the prisoner's expectations were absurd. Freeman must have seethed as Hubbard instructed him to sign a receipt for the two dollars. Freeman said he couldn't write. If Freeman refused to "make his mark," the clerk threatened, he would forgo the money. Freeman acquiesced, marked the receipt, pocketed the coins, and left.[4]

John De Puy had been waiting in the prison's entrance hall. Freeman's mother had asked De Puy to pick up her son. But Freeman did not acknowledge his brother-in-law. "He passed me as if he didn't know me," De Puy said later. He then asked if Freeman recognized him. Receiving no reply, De Puy reached out to touch him. Freeman responded with something like a laugh.[5] But he said nothing.

The brothers-in-law walked out through the iron gates onto State Street. There, Freeman saw a new Auburn: one that had become as unfamiliar as his family, as unrecognizable as the coins in his pocket. The village he remembered was now a city. One change was immediately visible: across the street from the prison gates, at the corner of State Street and Chapel Street, stood the new railroad depot. When Freeman entered prison in 1840, Auburn had just welcomed its first steam locomotive and the depot was but a plan and a promise.[6] Now, Freeman saw a sturdy wooden building accommodating prison-made locomotives and lively with people traveling on double tracks from Syracuse in the east to Rochester in the west. The train station and the prison mirrored each other, together testifying to Auburn's modernity, prosperity, and vitality, each one helping the other flourish.

De Puy led Freeman south on State Street, across the Owasco Out-

FIGURE 4.1 Map of Auburn

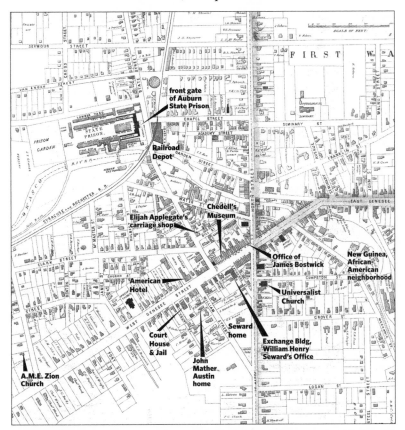

Detail, *Map of Auburn, Cayuga Co., N.Y.* Surveyed and published by John Bevan, 7 Broad St., N. York, & 26 Barrow St., Jersey City, 1851. Map courtesy of Bill Hecht. Image prepared by Dennis McClendon.

let, which powered the prison factories, then on toward Auburn's business district. Even the ground under Freeman's feet had changed. Only a few years earlier, State Street was a ribbon of mud, its sidewalks loose slabs that Auburnites sometimes stole to burn as fuel in the winter.[7] But during Freeman's incarceration, local government had undertaken an ambitious agenda of improvements, particularly to walkways. Streets that had been quagmires were now neatly paved with stones cut in prison factories. Multistory buildings of brick and limestone had risen. There were more people—6,171, up nearly 10 percent from 5,626 in 1840—and fewer trees. One of Auburn's hills had been flattened to accommodate increased traffic.[8]

De Puy led Freeman to Elijah Applegate's carriage shop at the corner of State and Dill Streets. There, De Puy was employed raising a building. As he returned to work, Freeman "sat on a pile of boards," De Puy recalled. "He sat there, and acted very stupid and dull, and said nothing." De Puy's coworkers asked "what dam'd fool that was, who was sitting there." The unkindness seemed to have stung him: "I remembered it," he said later.[9]

Perhaps at this moment De Puy realized the extent of his brother-in-law's impairment. He had cared for Freeman since about 1832, when De Puy married Freeman's sister Caroline. For two years starting in 1836, when Freeman was about twelve old, Freeman lived with him in Fleming, a hamlet immediately south of Auburn. There, De Puy worked for a prosperous farmer named Peter Wyckoff, and he and Freeman lived on the Wyckoffs' land. But after a financial dispute with Wyckoff, De Puy and Freeman moved to Auburn and lived together for an additional two years.[10] (Caroline Freeman De Puy lived with them only intermittently; at other times, she was likely employed as a live-in domestic.)

The boy De Puy helped raise was playful and talkative; he "read in the spelling book, pretty well," De Puy recalled, "smooth and decent." But the silent man who emerged from the prison could not comprehend the words "Half Dol" on the tails of his coins. This man staggered, his gait slightly off-rhythm. When he spoke, he gestured in a forced, staccato way, his voice "dull and monotone." He moved his eyes independently of his head, which others found "peculiar" and "sharp." His head hung low or listed.[11]

De Puy brought Freeman home and asked "how they had used him in prison." Freeman replied that "they gave him enough to eat, and sleep on." He asked De Puy about the whereabouts of Jack Furman, the man who had blamed Freeman for the 1840 horse theft. De Puy explained that Furman was in the Auburn State Prison—which surprised Freeman, who, forbidden from looking at the faces of other prisoners, "had not seen him" there. Then Freeman narrated the prison's violence. Once he started talking, words flowed. For an hour and a half, he described beatings, whippings, and Tyler's deafening blows.[12]

Freeman told De Puy he wanted compensation—not for his injuries, but for his labor. He "had been there five years for nothing," he told De Puy, and he "wanted his pay for it." Freeman articulated this idea many times and with different phrases, but throughout, he repeated the word "nothing." He loaded a double meaning into the word: both the absence of a just reason (for he maintained his innocence) and the absence of payment. Sometimes the dual meanings appeared in rapid succession, as when, five years earlier, he told the supervisor in the hame shop that he had "done nothing worthy of confinement" and added, a breath later, that he "didn't want to stay there and work for nothing."[13] *Nothing*: no crime and no wages. Two meanings dancing through one word, tagging intertwined injustices. Now home, William Freeman launched a quest to remediate both.

Seeking Justice

In November 1845, two months after release, Freeman decided to seek justice through formal legal means. It was courageous, even audacious for any nineteenth-century African American to voluntarily navigate a legal system that was designed to protect white interests. Furthermore, Freeman invested hope in the law despite his negative experiences with it. But his hope was not unfounded. Other African Americans had used the law to their advantage. In 1828, Isabella Baumfree, who later renamed herself Sojourner Truth, successfully sued to recover her freeborn son Peter, who had been illegally sold into slavery.[14] Half a century earlier, in Stockbridge, Massachusetts, an enslaved woman called Mum Bett sued for her freedom and won—after which she renamed herself Elizabeth Freeman. William Freeman could have known of these cases.[15] Freeman's mother, Sally Freeman, grew up in the Berkshires—the region of Western Massachusetts that includes Stockbridge—in the wake of Elizabeth Freeman's triumph. She was likely aware of this local heroine and could have told the story to her son. And Sojourner Truth and her family had been enslaved by Johannes Hardenbergh, uncle of John L. Hardenbergh, in Rosendale, where Harry and Kate lived until their enslaver forced them to come to Military Tract 47.[16] In 1845, Sojourner had recently begun to lecture publicly, spreading her story across the North.

William turned to his brother-in-law for advice. He told De Puy that he "wanted pay for his time" in the Auburn State Prison and "asked if there were any Esquires" in Auburn who might help him. He sought a warrant by which to force the state to pay him. De Puy directed Freeman not to a lawyer but instead to a magistrate, James H. Bostwick.[17]

This may have compounded William Freeman's hopes, because he had known James Bostwick all his life—indeed, the Bostwick and Freeman families had been neighbors for three generations.[18] Freeman must have known that Bostwick could dismiss him as the criminal son of a drunkard and a slave. Or he could acknowledge Freeman as a member of Auburn's founding Black family, and perhaps even respect the grandson of the first non-Cayuga to fell a tree on Auburn's land.

Apparently placing hope on positive possibilities, Freeman brought three complaints to the magistrate. First, Freeman told Bostwick that he'd been put in prison wrongfully and "wanted pay for his time." Second, Freeman wanted warrants for the arrests of three people he blamed for his conviction and imprisonment: Jack Furman, his accuser; David Simpson, the white constable who arrested Freeman; and Martha Godfrey, the white woman who owned the horse he was accused of stealing. Finally, Freeman sought a summons for a current white employer, a harness-maker named Conklin for whom Freeman had sawed wood. Freeman said Conklin had promised him three shillings but then paid him only two.[19]

James Bostwick did recognize his former neighbor and remember him, with some affection, as a "smart" and "active boy." He responded to Freeman with a mix of consideration and disregard. He dismissed Freeman's demands for pay for his prison labor, as well as Freeman's desire to relitigate his conviction, but he took seriously Freeman's accusation against Conklin. Bostwick interviewed Conklin and concluded that Freeman had not been cheated. He then "declined issuing the summons."[20] Bostwick's assessment was likely correct: John De Puy similarly investigated Freeman's accusations against Conklin and another employer and reached the same conclusion. As De Puy observed at the hatter's, Freeman sometimes misidentified currency and confused numbers.

Having failed to achieve the justice he wanted through a legal process, Freeman raged to his brother-in-law. Employers "cheated him all the time," he said, so there "wasn't any law for him." Freeman now considered violence. He asked De Puy "whether he should whip" Conklin. De Puy advised restraint. "I told him not to do it," he said later, because "they'd put him in jail if he did."[21] De Puy did not name the additional danger of mob retribution against any Black man who attacked a white one.

But Freeman persisted, lamenting that he "couldn't live so," he "couldn't make any gain." De Puy finally appeased his brother-in-law by giving him, from his own pocket, the money that Freeman believed his current employers owed him: "I gave him the balance, because he thought he was wronged."[22] Thus John De Puy protected Freeman from himself—for a time.

Seeking Home

"Is that Sally's son?" David Winner asked when he saw William Freeman in Luke Freeman's barbershop in early October 1845. Winner—forty-seven, formerly enslaved, and a friend of the Freeman family—had known William Freeman for sixteen years. But he struggled to recognize the boy he knew in the man in Luke's shop. This man was "sniveling, snickering and laughing, and having a kind of simple look," Winner said later. "I spoke to him, but he didn't speak to me." Luke Freeman explained that his newly deaf, strange-acting nephew had been released from prison a week earlier.[23]

Other members of the Black community tried to reconnect with Freeman. Deborah De Puy, who was married to John De Puy's brother Hiram, had been one of Freeman's closest friends before his incarceration. Three years older than Freeman, she was short, "sprightly," and smart. She remembered Freeman as a buoyant spirit who enjoyed New Guinea's social life. But now, the injured Freeman avoided gatherings, refusing to "go in company." Freeman and Deborah De Puy tried to reinstate their friendship. Freeman visited Deborah De Puy nearly every day, but he did not initiate any conversation. "I never knew him to speak of his own accord" after prison, she said. "Sometimes he would answer me, and sometimes he wouldn't.... I used to ask him what made him appear so dull. He said he didn't know." Freeman similarly visited his mother, Sally Freeman, about once a month. In each visit, he sat for about an hour, saying almost nothing. But his silence was not placid: Sally Freeman said later her son seemed "roiled."[24]

In November 1845, John De Puy moved to Skaneateles, seven miles east of Auburn, and Freeman then boarded with Adam Gray. Gray, an elder of the African American community and a friend of Freeman's parents, observed odd behavior at night: Freeman repeatedly rose, danced, and sang nonsense."[25] Other times, Freeman seemed not to understand that it was nighttime. He "said it was day-light," picked up his saw, and declared "he was going to work." He then disappeared for hours—to where, Gray did not know. One time, Freeman returned from his nighttime foray drunk. "He came in and out," Gray later said, "hallooed, stamped, and went on." Freeman stomped and shouted for about an hour before returning to bed. Gray responded, gently, by asking his young friend to accompany him to church. Freeman just laughed.[26]

During the winter of 1845–1846, Freeman drank more, and John De Puy watched as Freeman's "mind" became "very unsteady. Half of the time he didn't know what he had done." De Puy saw his brother-in-law run from one end of Auburn to the other and back again, without errand. He talked to himself, especially when he drank. Freeman sometimes stayed overnight with his brother-in-law in Skaneateles, and De Puy witnessed the same nighttime disturbances that Adam Gray had. Freeman "got up out of his bed at night many times, some times two or three times in the same night." Again, Freeman danced and sang, but he would "sing but part of a verse, and then be off on to another." And De Puy saw something more: in the night, Freeman fought invisible foes. He would "spar, as if some one [was] with him, and fix his fists and say, come on, d—n you, I'll fix you out; and then let his hands fall, and say, Oh Pshaw." De Puy intervened yet again to protect Freeman: he visited Noah Gale's grocery and asked them not to sell Freeman alcohol. The temperance movement had ignited Auburn during the winter of

1841–1842—yet another change during Freeman's incarceration—so the grocery may have been accustomed to accommodating such requests. Gale's subsequently refused to sell spirits to Freeman—which enraged him and did not prevent him from buying alcohol elsewhere.[27]

In January 1846, Freeman began boarding with Laura Willard in New Guinea. There, he shared a bed—a common practice—with David Winner, the family friend who had barely recognized William at Luke's barbershop. Like De Puy and Gray, Winner saw that Freeman "talked to himself" and "got up nights two or three times," singing nonsensically. Winner found it additionally disturbing that Freeman "kept his trowsers [sic] always, and slept in 'em." De Puy confirmed: "Sometimes he wouldn't dress himself."[28] No mystery for a youth who had been forced for a quarter of his life to strip whenever a guard ordered, and whose whipped back likely bore keloids.

Drinking, talking to himself, refusing to change his clothes, shouting threats at imagined combatants in the night: eventually, William Freeman frightened the people closest to him. After David Winner boarded with Freeman for three nights, he told Laura Willard he wouldn't sleep alongside Freeman anymore. Even John and Caroline De Puy began to fear Freeman. Later, when asked "Did you say that you was afraid to have him at your house, and drove him away?" De Puy hedged, "I might have said something like that." Asked whether he told a constable "that you were afraid [for] your life," De Puy admitted, "I may have told him my wife was afraid."[29]

Freeman struggled because he had become unrecognizable to others, but also because his community had become unrecognizable to him. He told Adam Gray that he "didn't know people" anymore; they "seemed strange" to him.[30] There was good reason for this: during Freeman's time in prison, Auburn's Black world had transformed as much as the city overall.

The changes galvanized in 1839, just before Freeman entered prison. That year, Black Auburnites opened an African Methodist Episcopal (AME) Zion Church—not in New Guinea, but a mile to the west. Adam Gray was a founding trustee, and many in Freeman's family, including Sally Freeman, Caroline Freeman De Puy, and Luke and his wife, were members.[31] The church, along with Luke Freeman's barbershop, anchored a rising abolitionist movement in Auburn. Starting in the 1840s, the church sheltered fugitives from Southern slavery. Some of these freedom-seekers passed through the city en route to Canada, but many settled permanently in Auburn. With the church's support, Auburn's Black population swelled nearly 60 percent, from 140 in 1840 to 223 in 1845.[32] Some of these newcomers found homes in New Guinea, but most lived elsewhere.[33]

Meanwhile, African Americans who had lived in New Guinea for decades began moving north and west, closer to the church and to new jobs in Auburn's expanding downtown. Deborah De Puy exemplified this exodus: in 1840 she and her husband, Hiram, lived in New Guinea, but by 1845 De Puy became the caretaker for the AME Zion Church and moved into a small house behind it—which was where William Freeman visited her every day.[34] Meanwhile, a white abolitionist named Abijah Fitch began selling parcels of Auburn's land at fair market prices to African Americans. One of the Black Auburnites who benefited was Freeman's uncle Luke, who bought two lots: one for his home and another for his barbershop. Another was Mary Ann Newark, a fifty-two-year-old laundress.[35] Auburn's economic boom created new opportunities for African Americans: some, like Luke Freeman and Newark, became business owners. As Auburn's hotels flourished, they hired some Black men as waiters—a skilled position that signaled entrance to the Black middle class.[36]

These changes were richly positive for Black Auburn overall, but they splintered the community of New Guinea. When Freeman was released from prison, only a few African Americans, including Laura Willard and Mary Ann Newark, remained in the neighborhood. Harry Freeman, William's grandfather and an anchor of New Guinea, died on December 20, 1845—less than three months after William Freeman rejoined the community. White landlords sold parcels of New Guinea to other whites, some of whom then displaced African American tenants.[37] Throughout the 1840s, Irish Americans moved onto the blocks that had once defined Black Auburn. Meanwhile, Auburn's Black newcomers developed a fresh set of social connections that did not include William Freeman. They had not grown up venerating Harry and Kate Freeman and they had not known William as a child. They had little reason to care about the deaf, angry, hard-drinking man who spoke in a low monotone, gestured off-rhythm, and frightened even his family. The world that William Freeman remembered had been lost to him, occluded by a new one: alive with strangers, seemingly flush with money in everyone's hands but his, and, to his ears, muffled.

A Door Slams

Freeman knew "people talk[ed] about him," and he disliked it; he told a neighbor that sometimes he "wished they would let him alone." Still, he kept trying to secure work, a home, and most of all, justice. In the first week of March 1846, he approached Mary Ann Newark, who had known Freeman since his boyhood. Freeman proposed to barter: in exchange for a bed in Newark's New Guinea home, he would run errands for her laundry business. She accepted, and Freeman moved in. The arrangement raised some eyebrows. Aaron Demun, Freeman's uncle by marriage, asked Freeman if he had sex with Newark. Freeman replied, "No, she's a Christian, and don't do no such thing." Freeman hauled Newark's laundry, sawed her wood, and provided his own food which either he or Newark cooked. But he knew that this existence on the margin of the margin could not sustain him. So he grasped onto a new ambition: "to hire out by the month with some farmer." Demun affirmed the idea: "I told him that was the best way for him to do." And he followed that with a piece of advice: "I told him [even] if he didn't get more than seven or eight dollars a month, to take it."[38]

On March 2, 1846, Freeman acted on his plan. Wearing his cap and a brown coat against the late winter snow, he walked on Lake Road to Fleming, three miles south of New Guinea, back to the farmland where he and John De Puy had lived while De Puy worked for Peter Wyckoff.[39] Wyckoff had died shortly after Freeman and De Puy moved away, and Wyckoff's widow, Phebe Wyckoff, now lived there with her daughter Sarah; Sarah's husband, John Van Nest; the Van Nests' three children; a hired man; and Helen Holmes, a grandniece of Peter and Phebe Wyckoff.

Observing racial norms and perhaps retracing steps he had taken as a child, Freeman approached the house through the barnyard at the back. The rear door to the kitchen was unlocked, and Freeman entered. From the kitchen, he knocked on the door to the sitting room. Helen Holmes let him in. Freeman, appearing cold and tired, "stepped towards the stove," Holmes later remembered. "I handed him a chair and he sat down."[40]

John Van Nest joined Freeman and Holmes in the sitting room. Van Nest was forty-one years old, a justice of the peace, and supervisor of Fleming. Freeman asked him, "Do you want to hire a man?" Van Nest said no, he already "had a man engaged." Freeman had to lean forward to hear the answer. Hanging his head down and explaining that he was deaf, he asked Van Nest to speak louder. Van Nest asked Freeman "if he lived in Auburn." Freeman answered that "he was staying around there"—that is, New Guinea—"and had no work." Perhaps Freeman "could get work further up the lake," Van Nest suggested. Freeman fell silent. "Nothing more was said," Helen Holmes recalled later. Five minutes after he arrived at the Van Nest home, William Freeman left.[41]

Freeman's frustration grew. "I'm so deaf I can't get work; people won't employ me. I've been trying, and can't get work," he said. He then conceived his boldest plan: he would solicit former governor William Henry Seward. Seward, now working as an attorney in Auburn, was in the spotlight because he was defending Henry Wyatt, a white man incarcerated in the Auburn State Prison who had killed another white prisoner. Because Seward was using a novel defense—that Wyatt was not guilty by reason of insanity—the trial aroused public fascination. Hundreds of Auburnites (including, by some reports, Freeman) crowded into the courtroom to watch the drama.[42] Now, Freeman wanted Seward to help him obtain the justice that James Bostwick had refused him.

Perhaps in preparation for meeting the former governor, Freeman sought a shave. He avoided his uncle Luke's shop and the awkward interactions he had experienced there. Instead, he approached one of Luke's competitors: a Black barber named Joseph W. Quincy.

Quincy had been incarcerated at Auburn alongside Freeman for two years, but neither man seems to have recognized the other. The barber described himself colorfully as an "amputator of the superfluous hairs of the Physiognomy" who "deprecates the practice of puffing one's self, but at the same time modestly intimates that he is not to be excelled by any one in skillfully relieving a gentleman of a superabundance of bristles, or giving a delicate twist to a moustach [*sic*]." An advertisement invited "all to come and see for themselves" the glory of Quincy's shop.[43] But "all" did not mean all. When William Freeman asked for grooming services on Wednesday March 4, Quincy flatly declared that he "did not shave colored men" and threw Freeman out.[44]

Denied and insulted, Freeman went to Seward's office in the Exchange Building at the corner of Genesee and South Streets. Seward was unavailable, but his clerk, Charles A. Parsons, received him. Freeman told Parsons that he wanted Seward to help him obtain "damages" for his false imprisonment and forced labor. As De Puy had done months earlier, Parsons redirected Freeman to magistrates: Bostwick and another magistrate named Lyman Paine.[45]

Having failed previously with Bostwick, Freeman tried Paine. On Saturday March 7, Freeman entered Paine's office. Silently, he took one step. A second step. One step after another, until he was five feet inside. Then he stopped. Five seconds passed. Ten. For half a minute, William Freeman stood wordlessly as Lyman Paine watched.[46]

Finally, Freeman spoke: he wanted a warrant. For what?, Paine asked. Freeman couldn't hear him. Freeman came closer, and Paine repeated himself. Freeman then replied that he wanted a warrant for those who had falsely accused him of stealing a horse and subsequently forced him to labor for nothing in the Auburn State Prison. He specified Martha Godfrey, the woman who owned that horse. "In order to get a warrant," Paine said, Freeman "must get at the facts." Freeman then went into a rage. "I want a warrant," he said. He took out two shillings—the correct fee—and threw them down. "I demand a warrant," he repeated. Paine responded hotly that Freeman "better take his money and put it in his pocket." Paine said he would neither take the money nor issue the warrant "without further information." Then, Paine threatened to charge Freeman with vagrancy and idleness, both widespread excuses to jail African Americans: "Go away and find a place and go to work," Paine said, or else you will "go into prison again."[47]

The words must have hit Freeman heavily. As he left Paine's office, he slammed the door behind him. He slammed it, the magistrate later recalled, "very hard."[48]

Prisons and Pay

All Freeman's associates, both white and Black, disregarded his demand for payment for his labor in prison. Some laughed, as did the prison officials who discharged him. Others, like Bostwick and De Puy, dismissed Freeman, treating his demand for back pay as an irrational fantasy.

They were wrong. Freeman's claim was not ridiculous or irrational, nor was it isolated: practices for paying incarcerated people were well established in the United States. Since 1699, American Houses of Correction and later carceral systems had developed ways for prisoners to earn money to spend in captivity, send home to their families, or save in preparation for their release.[49] In 1846, the most widespread mechanism was called *overstint* (or *overstent*, or sometimes *over-work*). In this system, an incarcerated person was required to labor a set amount of time or until a predetermined amount of work was accomplished—and any work beyond that "stint" earned money for the prisoner. In 1846, overstints were available to incarcerated people in Connecticut, Vermont, Maryland, Massachusetts, and other states. Pennsylvania had previously offered overstints but had discontinued the system, after much public debate, in 1844.[50]

Auburn refused to provide overstints or any other form of payment because wages, no matter how small, would have contradicted the Auburn System's founding principle that prisoners, like slaves or machines, had no right to benefit from their labor. To pay William Freeman or any other prisoner would not only have reduced the Auburn State Prison's profits; it would have refuted the system's ideology. It should be no surprise, then, that Auburn had long refused to institute overstints.[51]

This refusal attracted opposition from prominent white reformers including Dorothea Dix and Samuel Gridley Howe. In 1845 and 1846—concurrent with William Freeman's quest for back pay for his labor in the prison—Dix and Howe penned critical appraisals of the Auburn System. Dix, who visited the Auburn State Prison during Freeman's incarceration, published *Remarks on Prisons and Prison Discipline in the United States,* in which she "strongly recommend[ed]" an overstint system by which incarcerated people may "earn ... a sum for themselves by 'over-work.'" Also in 1845, the powerful Boston Prison Discipline Society, which had vigorously supported the Auburn System, factionalized. A minority group within the society, led by Howe, coauthored a report that criticized the Auburn State Prison from many angles, including its refusal of overstints. The report praised prisons that encouraged an incarcerated man to earn overstints that would "be at his disposal" after incarceration. "Knowing that the government makes nothing out of him," the report argued, this prisoner "will not suspect it of cupidity or cruelty."[52]

Cupidity and cruelty were precisely the accusations William Freeman made against the Auburn State Prison, which had forced him to work "for nothing." And he was not alone: other men incarcerated in Auburn reached the same conclusion. In the mid-1840s, officers heard prisoners argue that they were "entitled to pay" for their labor in Auburn's factories. Freeman never showed an awareness of others' parallel claims, however.[53] With his family history, his life experiences, and his own beliefs, Freeman seems to have generated his argument independently.

When Auburnites dismissed Freeman, other incarcerated men, and white reformers like Dix or Howe, they not only defended the prison. They also protected every industry in Auburn, from mills and tanneries to law offices and newspapers and hat shops, that entangled, whether tightly or loosely, with the prison and its famous factories. Local distilleries bought whiskey casks from the prison's coopers' shops and then filled them with spirits that were sold to Auburn's hotels, taverns, and individual citizens. Hotels coordinated with the railroads to entice tourists to come to Auburn, stay overnight, and tour the prison. Students at the local medical school dissected prisoners' corpses.[54] Few individuals got rich off the prison, but many Auburnites made a modest, reliable income, either directly or indirectly, from incarcerated labor, and almost every family included someone whose livelihood depended on it. For this reason, most of Auburn's families had a vested interest in declaring Freeman's claims irrational.

The Bostwicks were one such family. Magistrate James H. Bostwick continually collected small fees from the Auburn State Prison for taking affidavits and performing other services. In November 1841, for example, Bostwick took twenty-three affidavits from the prison, for which he collected $2.88; in February 1842, the prison paid him $2.75; in August 1842, $2.15; and so on—not a life-changing amount of money in any one month, but steady income that added up. James Bostwick and his older brother, William, sold the prison three bushels of silkworm cocoons totaling $11.75 in 1841—cocoons that Freeman likely processed. And in 1838, A. and J. Bostwick—likely James's brother Augustus and possibly James himself—contracted with the prison to receive services worth $250.91. They received those services—presumably prisoners' labor—but as of January 1840 they had not paid for them. The prison admitted in its annual report that it did not expect ever to recover that money in full; A. and J. Bostwick had extracted value from the prison without cost or penalty.[55] When James H. Bostwick shrugged off William Freeman's challenge to the Auburn System, then, he protected his family's interests—and his own.

"They Have Got to Pay"

From the moment of his release from prison, William Freeman restated one idea: "I have worked five years for nothing, and they have got to pay." From the start, he wrung a double meaning from the word *nothing*: no wages and no crime. But *pay* initially had only a single meaning: wages. December 1845, for example, he told local physician Levi Hermance, "They have sent me to prison, and I wasn't guilty, and they won't pay me." After he had pursued justice for six months without success, however, Freeman began packing a double meaning into *pay* as well. He "was five years in State Prison wrongfully," he said, and "somebody must pay for it."[56] *Pay*: back pay, but also, now, payback.

William Freeman began gathering knives.

Freeman's leap from soliciting magistrates to planning violence was not as surprising as it may seem. During the 1840s, many Black abolitionists shifted tactics from moral suasion toward "more combative and violent strategies." The shift reflected escalating white aggression against African Americans. During the 1810s and 1820s, 28 physical attacks on abolitionists were recorded. During the 1830s, however, white people attacked free African Americans and abolitionists in at least 115 separate events. As white violence increased, so did Black activists' calls for violent rebellion. In 1829, David Walker famously appealed to Black people to fight their white oppressors. In Buffalo, New York, in 1843, Henry Highland Garnet, who had read Walker's writing, addressed the National Negro Convention with a call to "use every means" including "physical resistance" against white supremacy. Invoking Nat Turner, Denmark Vesey, Toussaint Louverture, Joseph Cinqué, and Madison Washington, Garnet urged convention-goers to "appeal" to white people's "sense of justice"—and if that failed, to "cease to toil for the heartless tyrants, who give you no other reward but stripes and abuse." If white people should respond to the work-stoppage with violence, then "they, not you, will be responsible for the consequences.... Let your motto be RESISTANCE! RESISTANCE! RESISTANCE!" Garnet intoned, "Let it no longer be a debateable [*sic*] question, whether it is better to choose LIBERTY or DEATH."[57] Freeman wanted a key right of citizenship: to be paid for his labor. He had tried refusing to work. He had tried legal appeals. Now, along with a growing number of African Americans, Freeman was ready to fight for what was his—and, if necessary, to die for it.

Freeman likely started acquiring weapons on March 5, 1846. That day, he approached Joseph Morris, a white blacksmith who had a shop on Seminary Avenue, near the Auburn Theological Seminary. Freeman must have passed Morris's shop often as he hauled seminary students' laundry for Mary Ann Newark, and he was familiar with blacksmithing because he had worked the forge of the prison hame shop. Freeman told Morris that he wanted a double-edged blade. "I enquired what he wanted it for," Morris later said. Freeman answered Morris's question with one of his own: what would Morris charge? The price, Morris replied, depended on the material. Freeman said he wanted "good cast steel." Morris quoted a price of four shillings. Freeman countered that Morris "could do it for two shillings." Later, Morris claimed to have intuited that Freeman intended violence: "I asked him what he was going to do with that. He made no reply. I said, you are going to murder or kill somebody with it." If Morris did have those suspicions in the moment, he did not bother to act on them. Freeman's reply—that it "was none of my business, so long as I got my pay for making it"—satisfied the blacksmith. Morris said Freeman "asked again if I could make it for two shillings. I told him I should not make it short of four shillings." Freeman left without a knife.[58]

He walked three blocks southwest to another white blacksmith, George W. Hyatt, on Exchange Street. Hyatt and his assistant showed him four blades, from which Freeman chose one. Hyatt asked for two shillings, six pence. Freeman again bargained: he wanted the blade for one shilling, six pence. Hyatt first said no, but then agreed. Freeman asked Hyatt to put a handle on the knife, which Hyatt did, and then he helped Freeman sharpen one edge of the blade. Freeman left Hyatt's shop but returned two hours later with an old jackknife. The blade had loosened from the handle, and Freeman asked Hyatt to install a rivet to steady the blade. The blacksmith did so.[59]

Several days later, on about March 10, Freeman took the knife Hyatt made to Robert Simpson, a turner and chairmaker. In Hyatt's shop, Freeman had sharpened one edge of the blade, but now he asked Simpson to grind the flat edge as well so as to reshape the knife into a dagger. Simpson said he did not have time to grind the knife, but he invited Freeman to do the work himself on the shop's grindstone. Freeman did so with care, taking three-quarters of an hour to perfect the double edge. Freeman was assisted by John Gabriel, an African American who, like many Black people in Auburn by 1846, knew nothing of William Freeman. Freeman paid Simpson three cents for the use of the grindstone and left.[60]

The next morning, likely March 11, Freeman returned to Simpson's shop. He brought a hickory club that was three and half feet long. Simpson again allowed Freeman to use his equipment—this time, to bore a hole at one end of the club. Freeman fitted a blade into the hole to form a kind of bayonet, making a rough double of the bayonets carried by Auburn's prison guards.[61] Freeman now owned three weapons:

two made to his original designs, a third fortified according to his instructions.

For six months, Freeman had articulated a rational argument about the exchange value of his labor, but to no effect. In March, he articulated the same economic thinking—not in words, but through actions. Over six days, with none of the numerical confusion that plagued him on his release from prison, he negotiated equitable exchanges with five artisans—four white, one Black. These exchanges reflected Freeman's clear sense of the value of his money and of the artisans' labor, materials, and equipment. He paid prices he considered fair and refused those he considered otherwise. He asserted that the consumer's intention was none of the seller's concern; payment alienated a commodity from its producer. Thus Freeman voiced the normally unarticulated principle by which Auburnites tolerated forced labor in their midst.

On March 12, the day after William Freeman built his bayonet, he traveled to the home of Martha Godfrey, the elderly white widow whose horse Freeman had been convicted of stealing. Later, he described his goal as monetary: "I went to Mrs. Godfrey to get pay."[62] But his accumulation of knives prepared for another possibility.

At 2:00 p.m., Freeman walked into Godfrey's home in Sennett, five miles northeast of Auburn. Afraid of the intruder, Godfrey offered Freeman a chair. Freeman asked "if this was the place where a woman had a horse stolen five years ago." Godfrey acknowledged it was. He told Godfrey he had been falsely convicted of the horse theft and had labored for five years in prison. He wanted, he said, to "settle it." His words echoed against the ones he had uttered six months earlier, when he saw four half-dollars piled on the prison clerk's desk: "I have been in Prison five years unjustly, and ain't going to settle so."[63] Then, "settle" meant settle *for*: to accept underpayment. In Martha Godfrey's parlor, however, "settle" acquired a new meaning: to settle *up*. To balance, to make fair, to pay what was due.

Godfrey deflected responsibility: during the trial, she said, she had testified that her horse had been stolen but she had not accused Freeman. "I told him I knew nothing about that, whether it was he, or not," Godfrey said.[64]

Then, Godfrey's neighbor, Joseph Johnson, happened by. He asked Freeman what he wanted. Freeman had come desiring back pay and prepared for payback, but he answered that he did not know. Often, it seemed, Freeman gave this response when he could not hear a question—or sometimes, perhaps, when he wanted to avoid answering. The three people sat silently in Godfrey's parlor, the two white ones staring at Freeman, who stared at the floor. Minutes ticked by. Johnson again asked Freeman what he wanted. Had he come to demand the horse as compensation?

It was the first time anyone had offered Freeman recompense. Perhaps Freeman was surprised. Perhaps he was moved. Perhaps he simply did not hear Johnson. Whatever the reason, Freeman sat silently and did not respond. More minutes passed, with all three frozen in their chairs.

Godfrey then tried a new tactic: she asked Freeman if he was hungry. He said he did not know. She offered him cakes, which he ate. Johnson again asked Freeman if he had come for the horse. This time, Freeman heard the question. He remained silent for several minutes, thinking. He looked up. He smiled. Then he said, "I don't want the horse now."[65]

If he brought his knives that afternoon, he never showed them.

After an hour in Martha Godfrey's parlor, William Freeman left. It was the last time he would attempt to secure monetary compensation for his work. He was done chasing back pay.

Freeman returned to New Guinea. He greased his boots. He filled a washtub with snow for Mary Ann Newark's laundry. He went upstairs to his bed chamber and tucked his dagger under his shirt, laying it flat against his left breast. He put on his cap and coat. There was no way to conceal the bayonet inside his clothes, so he threw it out the window. As church bells called people to evening meeting, Freeman retrieved his club from the snow. He left New Guinea and walked south, stodging through snowdrifts. His destination: Fleming, the farm of the Wyckoffs and Van Nests. He said later, "The world rolled me there."[66]

CHAPTER FIVE

Work

THURSDAY, MARCH 12, 6:06 P.M. The moon rose full and lus-
trous. Freeman regarded the sky: "Just at dark," he called it, "edge of
evening." Past nights, at Adam Gray's, Freeman had gathered his tools:
a saw, an axe. This night, the same but different: knife, jackknife, bayonet. "I had my work to do," he explained later. "The time had come."[1]

With the tools tucked into the pockets and folds of his clothes, Freeman set out south toward Lake Road. The road was narrow, muddy,
with foot-high snowbanks on each side. He walked two and a half miles
uphill, ascending 125 feet. Recent rain slicked the path and slowed his
steps. He likely made a wrong turn at the southern border of Auburn,
but then he corrected course toward Fleming.[2] As he walked south, the
houses gradually grew further apart, snow-covered grainfields stretch-
ing between them. Five hundred feet to his left, the Owasco Lake
pulsed against the shore. Freeman's feet crunched ice and squished
mud, but he would not have heard these sounds. If owls hooted or
wolves howled, he would not have heard them, either. But deafness
did not stop him. The full moon lit his path.

EIGHT O'CLOCK. Freeman reached the Sand Beach Church—a
wooden frame building with a patch of a graveyard. A white man in a
small sleigh came up behind him, also traveling south. Freeman stepped
off the road to allow the sleigh to pass. The maneuver forced the man
to ease his horse to a slow clop. As he passed Freeman, the white man
looked suspiciously at the Black one. His eyes traced the contours of

FIGURE 5.1 Map of Fleming, New York

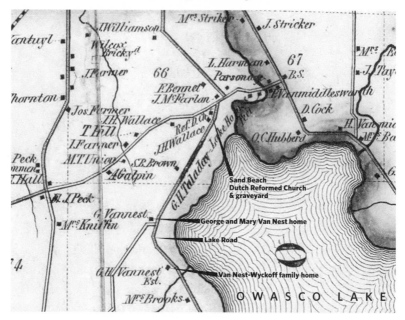

Detail, *Map of Cayuga County, New York: from actual surveys* (Philadelphia: published by Samuel Geil [& S. K. Godsalk], 1853. Map courtesy of Bill Hecht. Graphic design by Denis McClendon.

Freeman's coat, lingering on the lumps of covered weapons. Freeman returned the white man's gaze, pondering: the horse was slow enough that he could leap into the sleigh and kill the man. But he decided the time wasn't right. He let the man pass.[3]

After walking another half mile south, Freeman saw a house with a candle illuminating the second-floor window. Should he begin work here? he wondered. Freeman did not know the inhabitants, but they were George and Mary Van Nest, the elderly parents of John Van Nest, the man Freeman had asked for work a week earlier. Freeman entered their yard and walked halfway to the house. He could see Mary Van Nest watching him from her second-floor bedroom window. Later, she said that she could not see him clearly—not even the color of his skin—but she sensed there was something amiss. She blew out her candle so the stranger could not see her.[4]

Freeman paced by a gate and a woodpile. Then he paused and grasped the fence. He stood in the yard, thinking. The house had been light, but now it was dark. He looked north, back toward the Sand Beach Church. He looked south.[5] Then he returned to Lake Road and continued walking, keeping the Owasco on his left.

Freeman pressed south another quarter mile to the home of Mary and George's son John Van Nest—the house he had visited the previous week. It was bright with candlelight; Freeman could see half a dozen white people—old and young, women and men—shifting past the windows. He could not decide if this was the place to begin his work. He walked past the house, continuing a quarter mile more until he found another home—but that one was dark. "I didn't like to go into the house in the dark," he explained later.[6] He returned to the house with the light.

NINE TWENTY-FIVE. The bright home belonged to the Van Nest–Wyckoff family. Phebe Wyckoff, seventy years old, had raised six children there with her husband, Peter Wyckoff. For a few years in the late 1830s, the family had employed John De Puy, and he and Freeman had lived in a small log cabin not far from the house. After Freeman and De Puy left around 1838—two years before Freeman's incarceration at the Auburn State Prison—the family changed considerably. The Wyckoff children married and moved away, and Phebe's grandniece, Helen Holmes, joined the household. In 1840, Peter died and Phebe's youngest daughter, Sarah Wyckoff Van Nest, moved back home with her husband John and toddling daughter Julia. Like so many in the area, the family prospered: John Van Nest became a justice of the peace, and in 1844 he successfully ran for supervisor of Fleming as a Barnburner Democrat (the party faction opposed to extending slavery). Sarah Van Nest and Phebe Wyckoff became members of the Sand Beach Church. The young couple birthed two sons, George and Peter—the first named for his paternal grandfather, the second for his maternal one. The farm, too, flourished. One week earlier, just before William Freeman came knocking on the door, John Van Nest hired Cornelius Van Arsdale, a distant relative, as a farmhand.[7]

As Freeman approached the house, he could see three men sitting by the window in the front parlor. He had met one of them, John

Van Nest, the previous week. The two unfamiliar faces were Cornelius Van Arsdale and Peter Williamson, a visiting neighbor. Unseen by Freeman, a fourth person was also in the room: George, almost two years old, was asleep on a bed in the parlor's corner. Soon Van Arsdale went upstairs to his bedroom. Williamson left and began walking home, leaving two people in the sitting room: John Van Nest and his sleeping son.[8]

Freeman watched Williamson leave and head north. Freeman knew that the family would now likely retire—and blow out their candles. He had to begin work, fast. As he explained later, "I meant to kill 'em all; all I could see."[9]

NINE-THIRTY. Defying the racial convention he had obeyed the previous week, Freeman knocked on the front door, not the rear one. "What do you want?" John Van Nest asked. "Warm me," Freeman replied.[10] Did Van Nest bristle at the Black man at the front door? Did he recognize the person who had recently asked him for work? Regardless, he admitted Freeman, who stepped into the parlor and toward the stove.

Then Freeman heard John Van Nest say, "If you eat my liver, I'll eat yours." What could that mean? Later, people would try but fail to decipher these words. Most likely, Freeman misheard. But he did not puzzle over it, perhaps because the words Freeman perceived echoed his own purpose. A call to retribution, to balancing scales. He stabbed the man once, on the left side of the breastbone, penetrating the heart. Death overcame John Van Nest so quickly that he fell forward with his hand still in his pocket, bloodying his nose as his face smashed against the floor.[11]

Then Freeman saw a pregnant woman in the kitchen. It was Sarah Van Nest, who had just seen her husband die. She ran out the back door into the yard, and Freeman chased her while a dog barked. He stabbed her stomach, dragging the knife from left to right.[12]

Freeman then returned to the house, leaving Sarah Van Nest in the backyard. In his absence, she screamed to her family, "I was stabbed, and John was stabbed, and we're all going to be killed." Helen Holmes opened a first-floor window as a portal to safety, but Sarah, belly-heavy, could not pitch herself through it. Sarah ran to the east side of the house and Holmes raced to let her in the front door. Sarah Van Nest staggered into the front bedroom, where her mother and year-old son Peter slept. "They have killed me," Sarah told her mother, "and they will kill you." Holmes ushered Sarah to the rear bedroom, which she shared with nine-year-old Julia. As Julia and Holmes watched, Sarah collapsed on their bed and died.[13]

Freeman saw none of this. By now, he was in the front parlor, where he noticed a bed by the stove. Under the blankets, a person stirred. Freeman stabbed. The blade passed through the body, exiting the back and ripping the mattress beneath. Blood gushed, and guts too. But as Freeman said later, something was wrong—the person was too small, too soft. Why? He forced the question aside and continued his work.[14]

Now, someone was in the entryway near the front door. It was Phebe Wyckoff, whom Freeman must have known from the years when he and De Puy lived on the Wyckoff land. But Freeman did not recognize her. He stabbed, and Wyckoff fled, alive but wounded. Then he noticed stairs leading upstairs. "Is a man up there?" he called, but heard no answer.[15] The second floor was dark, so Freeman grabbed a candlestick before heading up. Suddenly, he saw Van Arsdale at the top of the stairs. Van Arsdale rushed Freeman, wresting the candlestick away. Freeman stabbed him in the chest. He tried to keep stabbing, but Van Arsdale blocked his blows with the candlestick, breaking his knife. Part of the blade flew off, landing on the first floor. Van Arsdale beat him with the candlestick, forcing him down the stairs. At the bottom of the stairs, Van Arsdale grabbed a broom and hit Freeman with it.

Freeman ran out the front door, toward the gate. Van Arsdale fell back, but Wyckoff chased Freeman, stamping red footprints into the snow. She grabbed his arm, and he saw something flash against the moonlight. A butcher knife: hers, not his. She slashed at him, cutting his right wrist. Blood from her wound, blood from his, spilled across the snow bed.[16] They struggled for half a minute; then she released him and fled south.

William Freeman was cut and bruised, his double-edged blade truncated. He had to hold it in his left hand now because he could no longer bend his right thumb. He had done his work on five people. As he said later, he had "meant to kill every body" in the house, but he "couldn't kill any more." Still, he did not give up. Echoing his vow from years earlier in the prison hame shop, he wanted "to fight and kill till some one killed him." He returned to the house and tried the front door—now locked. He peered through the southeast window, into the sitting room, but all the candles had been snuffed. He kicked the front door, and it broke open. But Freeman did not enter the dark home. He looked into another window—also dark.[17]

Now, the pain from Freeman's wound overtook him. His right hand was useless. He needed to go somewhere until his "wrist got well, and then come back and do some more work." As he explained later, an idea "came into my mind—take the horse—go." That way, he "could do more work" later, or perhaps soon, maybe even the same night.[18]

Freeman entered the barn and seized the first horse he saw: black with a white stripe down its nose. Overlooking three fine horses in the same stable and not even pausing to saddle up, Freeman took a halter and mounted the horse's bare back.[19] He rode north, back toward New Guinea. It was 9:35. He had been at the Van Nests' home for five minutes.

DARKNESS, THEN DAWN. Within moments, Freeman realized he had chosen a poor horse: old and slow, "he wasn't good for nothing." Like many African Americans in Auburn, Freeman had long worked with horses and handled them skillfully. Still, as he pressed downhill in snow and mud, the horse stumbled and slid into the sluiceway, the drainage trench by the road's side. The horse fell on top of Freeman, pinning his leg. The animal struggled to right himself and Freeman struggled to free himself—but neither succeeded. Freeman still had his broken blade, and that gave him an option. Knowing that horses respond to pain by moving away from it, he stabbed the horse behind the shoulder. If he had wanted to kill the animal, he could have. The jab must have been workmanlike, a strategy of horse management. It sufficed: the horse wriggled off his leg. Freeman stood up and continued on foot, leaving the horse flailing in the mud.[20]

Freeman crossed the Owasco Outlet via a dam and then walked about a mile and a half east. He found a barn with a fine gray mare that was well equipped with a leather halter, a lined plaid blanket, and a surcingle to secure the blanket. He took the horse, which proved "very fleet." He rode to the home of Martha Godfrey. His purpose was clear: "I meant to kill her." But when he reached Godfrey's, it was after 10 p.m., and all the lights had been extinguished. Freeman rode the mare off the road and onto Godfrey's yard, trampling the clean snow. He did not enter the house because it was too dark for him to work and "because my hand was cut, and I couldn't think to go in and handle my hand."[21]

So he rode further east toward Syracuse, reaching that city "about daylight" on the dawn of Friday, March 13. He paused once to dress his wounded wrist with tobacco; another time to discard his weapons where no one would find them; and two or three times, necessarily, to water the horse.

He passed through Syracuse and continued northeast to Schroeppel, where some of John De Puy's brothers lived. He needed a place to rest, to heal his hand. But when he arrived at the home of the De Puy brothers, they refused to shelter him. They questioned how their day-laboring brother-in-law could have acquired so valuable a horse. "Suspecting he had stolen" it, they "drove him off."[22]

FRIDAY MORNING, MARCH 13. Freeman had ridden an unfamiliar horse without a saddle fifty miles overnight in the snow—using only his left hand. He and the horse needed rest, food. He knew a place: Gregg's Tavern, near the town of Phoenix. "My hand was cut," he reasoned, "and I thought I'd go down back there till I'd cured it up."[23] He headed over to Gregg's.

A tavern was a promising shelter because strangers, including Black ones, could slip in without attracting much attention. For that reason, fugitives from slavery sometimes mixed into taverns to pass as free-people. A decade earlier, for example, J. W. Loguen sheltered in taverns several times during his flight to freedom in Canada and later Syracuse. Taverns were often dirty and dark, even at dawn. They offered a predictable mix of meat, pies, beer, fruit wines, and spirits. The inhabitants, too, were predictable: men and some women, many white and some not, many working class and some not, travelers and locals, smoking, fighting, and playing cards; doing business legal and shady. A meeting ground for work and leisure, ordered yet potentially explosive.[24]

As hungry and tired as Freeman must have been, another need took precedence: he had to ditch the mare before someone recognized her. As he approached Gregg's Tavern, he saw an opportunity: a white man, James Amos. Freeman knew Amos because the previous November he had hired Freeman, John De Puy, and three of De Puy's brothers to husk corn. Freeman thought Amos would recognize him as a former employee. He must have thought, also, that this work relationship would provide a basis for trust, which could in turn support a business transaction. As Amos watered his own horse, Freeman approached. Omitting any preliminaries, Freeman asked, "Do you want to trade horses?"[25]

Amos did not remember hiring Freeman and he declined the trade. Freeman then asked, "Do you want to buy one?" Amos repeated, "No." Freeman then pursued the same business with three other white men. He offered the mare to one man, Edwin Corning, for eighty dollars. Corning had seen Freeman talking with Amos, and Corning assumed the white man knew and could vouch for the Black one. Most likely, Corning thought Freeman worked for a white man on whose behalf he was selling the horse. This assumption would have been well founded because throughout both the North and the South, Black men managed white people's horses. In many regions, the most skillful and knowledgeable equine workers were African American; for this reason, white people eagerly hired and trusted Black coachmen, stablemen, grooms, ostlers, trainers, and jockeys.[26] Black equine workers bred excellence into white America's horses.

Corning inspected the mare and asked Freeman if he would accept a lower price. Freeman negotiated, eventually compromising: "I'll take fifty." Before finalizing the business deal, Corning asked Amos to confirm that he knew Freeman. But Amos told Corning that "I could'nt [sic] call him by name, but I thought I had seen him before."[27]

This statement suddenly raised the possibility that Freeman was independent. A Black man who managed a white man's horse was a supervised worker, a servant, and therefore a nonthreat. But a Black man who owned his own horse—especially one of quality, not a waste-hauling or a hack horse—disrupted racial expectations. Corning immediately stopped treating the negotiation as a neutral business transaction. Now, he voiced suspicion. "Where did you get the horse?" he demanded.[28]

Freeman replied, "I had a horse given to me, and I traded round and got this one."[29] This confirmed that he was not selling the horse on behalf of any white person.

Perhaps Corning found this explanation implausible. Perhaps he believed no Black man could—or should—own so fine a mare. "I guess you stole the horse," he said. Other taverngoers were watching, and one chimed in: "I guess he did, too."[30]

"No, I didn't," Freeman said. He looked to Amos for help: "It's my horse, and you know me." Freeman reminded Amos, "I husked corn with you in your barn last fall." Freeman positioned himself as a worker, Amos's worker, even if he was no white person's horseman. The strategy succeeded only partially: now, Amos recalled hiring Freeman, but that onetime gig did not recategorize Freeman as a trusted servant. The white men's suspicions swelled. Corning grabbed the horse's halter. Freeman "told him to let it go," but Corning refused. "It is my horse; I haven't stole him," Freeman insisted. Two other white men added their hands, trying to wrest the horse from Freeman. Using only his left hand, Freeman jerked the halter—and with it the horse's face—as the three white men tugged in the opposite direction. The horse must have backed up and tossed her head to shake them off. Freeman kicked two of the white men. Amos then stepped in, telling the three white men to drop the halter. They did so, and Freeman stopped kicking. Freeman again insisted that he "came honestly by the horse"—and this time promised to prove it. "I can satisfy you," he said, by having the De Puy brothers vouch for him.[31]

Why would Freeman dare Amos to summon family members who themselves believed he had stolen the mare? Perhaps Freeman thought that by invoking the De Puys, who had worked for Amos and many other white men in the area, he had one final opportunity to categorize himself as a servant by proxy and thus induce the men to release him. Maybe, as the accusations intensified, he panicked and blurted out whatever words came to mind. Perhaps he was buying time, angling to escape before the De Puys could arrive. Or maybe he believed that in the face of four hostile white men, the brothers would protect him, despite their own suspicions.

Amos accepted Freeman's proposal. He sent a messenger to the De Puys' home, and he and Freeman stood by the horse, waiting. After a while, Freeman again attempted to leave, but Amos held fast to the horse. Freeman kicked him, and they tussled. Until now, Freeman had held the halter only with his left hand, keeping his right hand in his breeches pocket. But when Freeman kicked Amos, he took his hand out of his pocket, and Amos saw that he "made no use of his right hand."[32]

"I see you've got your hand hurt," Amos said. "How was it done? I guess it was in a n—— fight."[33]

Freeman refused to explain, and Amos took his silence as further proof of guilt, warranting intensified retraints. He pried Freeman's left hand from the halter and grabbed his collar. While Corning took the horse and locked it in Gregg's barn, Amos pushed Freeman toward the tavern. Freeman fought hard. He kicked Amos and tripped him, making him fall to one knee. But the white men forced him into the tavern, roped him, tied him, and sent for a warrant for his arrest for horse theft.[34]

FRIDAY AFTERNOON. Gregg's Tavern—a site for business and leisure, necessities and excess—now became, also, a temporary jail. This transformation was commonplace. Taverns, where distinctions between the legal and illicit blurred, often metamorphosed into unofficial jails—especially to detain Black people. In 1841, for example, Madison Henderson, an African American accused of murder, was held captive and interrogated in a tavern prior to his formal arrest.[35] In both the South and the North, slave-catchers congregated and swapped information in taverns, which then became holding cells or even auction blocks for fugitives from slavery.[36] Taverns were easily converted into improvisational carceral spaces because they were plentiful, sturdily constructed (usually of logs or bricks), and often controlled and populated by white men. As private spaces open to the public, taverns provided an arena where people could watch each other while being shielded from the gaze, and potential approbrium, of outsiders. In contrast to the Auburn State Prison, taverns were neither monuments to power nor objects of governmental oversight. Along with other makeshift holding sites such as boardinghouses and even pits, taverns functioned as a capillary system that dispersed carcerality. North or South, free or enslaved, Black people were never far from sites of potential bondage. This presence suffused the lives of the Freemans, the De Puys, and all African Americans.[37]

The spectacle of a white man holding a Black one captive in a tavern was therefore not unique, but it surely attracted the curiosity of other customers—and Freeman, in turn, must have watched them watching him. The afternoon wore on as Amos and Freeman waited for the warrant and the De Puy brothers to arrive. Eventually, Amos asked Freeman if he was hungry. Freeman said he was. Amos loosened the bonds and provided a meal. Freeman could not use his right hand; Amos cut his meat for him.[38]

Near dusk, when the workday ended, John De Puy's brother Abram arrived at Gregg's Tavern. But he did not defend Freeman. Instead, Abram De Puy said "he didn't know that he [Freeman] owned such a horse—that he guessed he couldn't own such a one."[39] Amos, who had by now been formally deputized for the purpose of arresting Freeman for horse theft, made the arrest.

Neither Amos nor Freeman knew that hours earlier, back in Auburn, the publishers of the *Cayuga Tocsin* had fired up their presses in the middle of the night. They published an extra edition of their newspaper, alerting readers that a Black man had murdered a white family, sustained an injury to his right wrist, and stolen a horse. Based on the statements of surviving witnesses, the *Tocsin* identified William Freeman as the suspect. The news spurred a manhunt, and by dawn more than fifty men set aside their own labors and fanned out in every direction to find him.[40]

One of those men was Alonzo Taylor, a constable from Cato. Taylor was aware of a Black family named Freeman living in Syracuse, so he had headed there. The family said they knew William Freeman but were unrelated to him. So Taylor continued searching, and by afternoon encountered tavernkeeper Gregg. Gregg told Taylor "that the negro was at his house," and Taylor immediately headed there.[41]

Taylor found Freeman at the table, still eating the meat Amos had cut for him. "Ain't your name Freeman?" he demanded. Freeman did not respond. He did not even look up from his plate. Calmly, he "continued to put victuals into his mouth and to eat."[42]

"You're a damned murderer," Taylor said. "If I had a gun I would blow your brains out."[43]

The normally clattering tavern must have gone silent as all eyes turned to Freeman. The accused horse thief was a murderer? Freeman "seemed startled," but he calmly "raised his fork and continued eating."[44] He said nothing. Like anyone who had labored in the Auburn State Prison, he knew the power of silence.

"You're a black, infernal scoundrel," said Taylor. As he accused him of killing the Van Nests, Freeman kept his head down, toward his plate. He continued eating, turning only his eyes toward his accusor. Finally, he said quietly, "I don't know any thing about it."[45]

"You black rascal, you do!" Taylor shouted. He raised his cane to strike Freeman, but other white men in the tavern stopped him. Taylor and Amos forced Freeman into Gregg's kitchen. They stripped off his boots and cap, then searched his pockets, his body. They found one penny. "Nothing else but his clothes," Amos reported later. Freeman's knives were long gone, his tobacco used up to dress his wounded hand. Taylor and Amos returned Freeman's penny to him. Then they arrested him for murder.[46]

More law enforcers — official and self-appointed — arrived and commenced their work. Two white men, Walter D. Herrick and George B. Parker, took Freeman to another room in the tavern, where they interrogated him. Freeman resisted questioning. When Parker "asked whether he knew Van Nest," Freeman "said he didn't know any thing about him." Parker "pushed very hard for the reasons he had against Van Nest. He said, 'I don't know who you are talking about; don't know any thing about him.' He also said, 'I suppose you know I've been in State Prison five years. I was put there innocently. I've been whipped, and knocked, and abused, and made deaf. There won't any body pay me for it.' And there he stopped," Parker said. "I couldn't get him to admit he'd killed any body."[47]

Freeman's silence enraged his accusers. The men boxed Freeman's ears and grabbed him by the head and beard, jerking his head. Freeman cried out for Taylor, the constable: "I want to be protected. I don't want to be kicked and cuffed around in this way." Taylor said, "I guess they have not hurt you." Freeman retorted, "Yes they have."[48]

Freeman's interrogation dead-ended. "I got him to confess nothing," Parker conceded. "I thought he'd played a very strong game, and seemed to rely upon silence for his fortification." Freeman refused to admit knowledge of the murders, only saying, "there wouldn't any body pay me." Then Freeman declared, "I shan't answer any more; if they can prove any thing against me let them prove it."[49] His interrogators took him to a nearby jail—the permanent, official kind. There, for the first time in two days, Freeman slept.

SATURDAY, MARCH 14. In the morning, Freeman saw a white man, Abram Vanderheyden, a constable whom he had known since childhood. Vanderheyden had arrested Freeman in 1840 for horse theft and before that had arrested him for stealing hens.[50] Now, he came to remand Freeman to Auburn.

Freeman was chained into Vanderheyden's wagon, and the horses began their clop. Vanderheyden asked, "Bill, how came your hand cut?" Freeman refused to answer—or perhaps he did not hear the question. The constable asked again. Freeman replied, "by stabbing"— that is, by Phebe Wyckoff stabbing him. But Vanderheyden thought Freeman was referring to his own acts. "How did you come to commit such a deed, in murdering that family?" he asked. Freeman "turned his head and said, I don't want to say anything about it." Quietly, Vanderheyden said, "[You] might as well tell me about the matter." Freeman likely could not hear him but must have intuited his intent. He replied, "you know there is no law for me." Vanderheyden asked what he meant. Freeman answered, "They ought to pay me.'"[51] Then William Freeman fell silent. His work was done.

PART III

THE EFFECTS

CHAPTER SIX

Howling Why

THURSDAY, MARCH 12, 9:30 P.M. Neighbors heard shrieks. A dog barked. Then Phebe Wyckoff, bleeding and dressed only in socks and a nightgown, burst into a nearby house, screaming, "This way, quick, for God's sake."

From north and south along the Owasco Lake, neighbors lit lanterns, pulled on boots, and rushed along muddy Lake Road to the Van Nests' home. George and Mary Van Nest were among the first to arrive, and what they saw severed their lives into before and after: their only son on the floor, left pectoral gashed, face smashed, breath stopped. John's father heard something jingle: a neighbor had accidentally kicked the broken knife blade at the door's threshold. The elder Van Nest picked it up and found it wet with blood. At the north side of the house, they saw their daughter-in-law, Sarah Van Nest, "half doubled in a bed," her "eyes open and glaring." They watched their grandson George draw his final breaths as foot after foot of intestines cascaded from his abdomen. He would have turned two the next morning. They surely clutched George's siblings, Julia and Peter, now orphans. Cornelius Van Arsdale lay on a bed, "alive, but with the breast laid open," and "every thing about him clotted with his blood." Helen Holmes fanned him to keep his breath moving. Within minutes, additional neighbors converged. One neighbor could describe the sight only in gasping fragments: "Upon the floors—upon the snow—upon the steps—the doors—every where—blood, blood."[1]

Who had done this? And why? The first question was resolved

quickly: Holmes recognized the killer as the same man who had asked for work a week earlier. She did not know his name, but she described a deaf, Black laborer in his early twenties who lived in New Guinea.[2] Longtime Auburnites easily matched the description to the grandson of Harry and Kate and nephew of the barber Luke.

But why had William Freeman killed the Van Nests? For money? Holmes told her neighbors that Freeman had not tried to rob the family, and a wallet with almost twenty dollars in paper and silver was discovered on John Van Nest's body. All Freeman stole was a getaway horse—and the one he snatched was so old it was "worth little except for his shoes and hide."[3]

If not robbery, then surely revenge—an equally rote explanation. By the dawn of March 13, neighbors told each other that John Van Nest had testified at the 1840 trial for horse theft and Freeman had retaliated by killing him and his family. This recognizable story of a personal vendetta impelled neighbors toward an equally formulaic next chapter: blood for blood.

Revenge

That Saturday, three miles north, a white woman and her six-year-old son watched a mob chase the sheriff's wagon down Auburn's South Street. The woman was Frances Miller Seward, wife of the former governor and daughter of Elijah Miller, the cofounder of the Auburn State Prison (plate 2). The boy, William Henry Seward Jr., scaled a stone gatepost for the best view. The Sewards saw the sheriff's wagon careening south toward their house; then, at the edge of the property, the horses veered left onto Grover Street. The pursuing mob shouted, "Kill him! Kill him!" The mother and son realized that Freeman must be in the sheriff's covered wagon. Like many, the Seward family knew the Freemans through Luke; they called William, familiarly, "Bill." People in the mob, too, were well-known about town; the boy recognized a trustee of the Second Presbyterian Church swinging a noose above his head, roaring, "Hang him!" The fury shook Frances Seward, who wrote to her husband, "I trust in the mercy of God that I shall never again be

FIGURE 6.1 *Perspective of Van Nest's House*

Perspective of Van Nest's House.

Cayuga Tocsin, 9 April 1846, 1.

a witness to such an outburst of the spirit of vengeance as I saw while they were carrying the murderer past our door."[4]

The wagon and mob sped through Auburn, past New Guinea, and on to Lake Road—the same road Freeman had taken two nights earlier. At the Van Nest house, a crowd encircled Helen Holmes and Cornelius Van Arsdale, who waited to identify the killer (Phebe Wyckoff was too injured to participate). Three corpses—parents and child—lay unburied.[5]

Officers hustled Freeman out of the wagon and into the house; seconds later, Freeman's pursuers arrived and pooled into the crowd.[6] Inside, Freeman faced magistrate James H. Bostwick, who choreographed the process of identification. Bostwick posed Freeman, still chained, before Holmes and Van Arsdale. Freeman was noticeably "agitated" but stood motionless and silent, hanging his head down and looking up only with his eyes. Holmes and Van Arsdale studied him. Yes, said Holmes, Freeman was "the person who was in pursuit of a situation a week or so ago." He wore the same clothes that day, the night of the murders, and now. Van Arsdale agreed: "The colored man now shown me is the same individual who stabbed me on Thursday night," adding that he was sure because "he now has on the same cap and coat that he then wore."[7]

While Bostwick recorded this testimony, the white mob raged outside, yelling, "Hang the Negro!" They then strung a noose from an apple tree. But Bostwick came out of the house and commanded their attention. What if, Bostwick asked, Freeman had been "incited to the homicide by white men?" Perhaps "there were others who had instigated the negro to commit the horrid deed." If the mob lynched Freeman, Bostwick argued, "all means of detecting the guilty instigators would be lost."[8]

Bostwick's conjecture that Freeman was some white man's puppet bought the sheriff a breath's time. While the mob listened to Bostwick at the front door, officers slipped Freeman out the rear and shoved him into a carriage, which sped north.[9] Seconds later, the mob spurred horses in pursuit.

What happened next was a "race—a simple trial of speed," as one witness wrote later. The sheriff's destination was obvious: the Cayuga County Jail, which was in the basement of the courthouse. Auburnites filled the streets to watch the galloping horses. As many as six hundred people swarmed the snowy yard on the north side of the courthouse. "Kill him! kill him!," they chanted as they waited for the sheriff's wagon to deliver Freeman.[10]

But not everyone in the crowd was bent on lynching. A minister named John Mather Austin witnessed the scene aghast—not at Freeman, but at the white pursuers. Austin was horrified to watch a church deacon, the superintendent of an Evangelical Sabbath School, and a Methodist clergyman clawing for revenge. "'Quarter him'—'hang him'—'no, hanging is too good—tear him limb from limb'—'roast him alive,'" Austin heard them shout. Bloodlust, in the clergyman's view, disturbingly blurred distinctions between white people and barbarians. "'Where are we,'" Austin wondered, "'in the midst of the savage tribes who roam in the wilds of the Rocky Mountains, and who are about to sacrifice some captured enemy to their brutal ferocity, or in christianized [*sic*] and civilized Auburn?' The complexion, the dress, the names of the actors, would lead me to adopt the latter conclusion, while their spirit, their vengeful threats, and their deeds urged me to acquiesce in the former!"[11]

At about two in the afternoon, the sheriff's wagon approached the jail. A crowd, preparing to wrest Freeman from the law, swung a noose from a tree by the jail's main entrance on Genesee Street (figure 4.1). But the sheriff thwarted expectations by driving down an alley to the jail's less-used west-side door. When the crowd discovered the trick, "excitement rose to white heat," Austin observed. They "rushed across the intervening space, trampling fences and all other obstacles beneath their feet." But they did not run fast enough. "The jail entrance opened—the prisoner was thrust in—the door shut with an ominous bang!—the bolt within flew into its socket."[12]

Freeman was back in jail—the same one that had held him before the trial for horse theft. His cell was a familiar near-cube, seven by eight feet along the floor and eight feet high with a whitened rear wall, the only furnishings a tub and a tin cup. He had broken free from this jail five and a half years earlier, but now, flight would only deliver him to the mob. Even so, his jailers took no chances: they shackled Freeman's right ankle and chained it to an iron eye embedded in the floor.[13]

At the same time Freeman arrived at jail, 2 p.m. on March 14, Phebe Wyckoff died of her injuries.[14] Now, forever, William Freeman was a quadruple murderer.

Why?

Inside the cell, interrogations began. Auburnites wanted Freeman's confession: how he killed, in what sequence, who inside and who outside the house, with every detail cataloged. Even more, they wanted explanations. Why did he kill? Why the Van Nests? Why March 12, not earlier or later? Why did he stab a child?

James Bostwick was among the first questioners. Freeman confirmed he had killed the family but denied he was motivated by personal revenge. "Nobody ever told me that Mr. Van Nest got me to State Prison," he told Bostwick, deflating the rumor. "I know who did get me there; Simpson the constable, Jack Furman, and another, ... and a woman; her name is Godfrey; she swore to the loss of the horse."[15] Bostwick knew these names; they were the people for whom Freeman had demanded arrest warrants. Why, then, had Freeman killed the Van Nests rather than Simpson, Furman, or Godfrey?

Freeman's answer to Bostwick and many other interrogators was as clear as it was repetitious: he "said the state owed him for five years work, and they had to pay him, or someone had got to pay him." He "was five years in State Prison wrongfully, and ... made up his mind that somebody must pay for it." He believed "if he killed around the country, they would pay." "The only reason he assigns for the bloody deed, is that he had been five years in prison, and somebody must pay for it." "He said he had been sent to State prison innocently—the people refused to pay him, and he made up his mind he would kill some." He "was imprisoned wrongfully, and he ought to have pay for his time." He "had been five years in prison, and somebody must pay for it."[16]

Who was "somebody"? Anyone, everyone—or, as some inferred with the greatest alarm, any white person. As one white boy shouted, Freeman was "the negro who wants to kill us all." Freeman raised the ghost of Nat Turner, who fifteen years earlier had led an antislavery rebellion that slaughtered over fifty white Virginians. Turner's dead included men, women, and children who were not enslavers—a political strategy of attacking apparent "innocents" and thus terrorizing the broadest possible white population. Newspaper coverage made Auburnites well aware of Turner's Rebellion and other acts of violent Black resistance in the south. Only eight days before Freeman murdered the Van Nests, the *Auburn Journal and Advertiser* reported a nearly successful Black revolt in New Orleans "which for a time looked very much like giving the slaves the mastery." White Auburnites were primed to fear Black insurrection. The murders "produced a feeling of insecurity which I never experienced before," Frances Seward wrote, echoing a widespread emotion.[17]

But the city's older white citizens *had* felt something like this before: in the town's early years, four decades earlier, Cayugas regularly broke into white settlers' homes.[18] These events seldom ended in violence, but they terrified white people and precluded any illusion of invulnerability. As the decades passed, white settlers forced the Cayuga nation west and the intrusions ceased, which established a sense of white sovereignty and safety throughout the region. Now, however, Freeman's crimes stirred previous racialized terrors. "A murder so barbarous has never been committed in the United States except by Indians," Frances Seward wrote to her older son at West Point, adding that Freeman "has some indian [*sic*] blood by the mothers [*sic*] side." White feelings of security, only a few decades strong, shattered. The "fearful murder has made me feel very much alone with the little ones," she wrote to her husband.[19]

With old fears aroused and Freeman's words too disturbing to grasp, white Auburnites dismissed his statement of motive as nonsense and demanded to hear something else: the "real" reason why he killed the Van Nests. "[M]ultitudes of every class and sex" jammed the jail, agitating for access to the killer. Some were locals, but other people traveled in by train. They hurled racial epithets, swiped at Freeman through the cell bars, and spat on him. Barely beyond their reach in his tiny cell, Freeman sat on an overturned tub, motionless.[20] The crowd wanted to vent their outrage, but equally, they wanted answers — a new story that would bring closure and comfort. Over and over, self-appointed interrogators asked the same questions, repetitious and urgent: *Why did you kill? Why the Van Nests? Why March twelfth? Why murder a child?* And the unspoken but most important questions, the ones terrorism provokes by design: *Why kill that family and not mine? Why them, not me? How can I feel safe again?*

John Austin was one of the many people who posed these questions but refused to hear Freeman's answers. Forty-one years old, with a heavy brow above blue eyes and a jutting hypotenuse of a nose, Austin was an ambitious Universalist minister and respected author. In line with his denomination, he opposed slavery and capital punishment and embraced the doctrine of universal salvation — that is, that all human sin would ultimately be reconciled through God. Austin had moved to Auburn only two years earlier, and like many newcomers, he did not know the Freeman family. He had little regard for Freeman, whom he dismissed as a "colored man" whose crime "seemed more the act of a wild beast, than an intelligent being." Still, the minister called on Freeman in jail shortly after the murders and "had a long conversation with him—putting him many questions," as he noted in his diary. "I questioned him as to his motive in committing his horrid butchery—but could get nothing from him of an intelligent description—and nothing that could amount to a motive in a person possessing common sense." The minister asked Freeman "if the persons he killed, had any thing to do with putting him in prison. He answered No." Why kill the Van Nest family, then, and not another? Freeman gave Austin the same answer he had given before, and like other Auburnites, Austin interpreted it as nonresponsive: "I got no direct answer; except something about being put into prison wrongfully." Austin asked if Freeman "thought it was right to kill people who had no hand in putting him into prison. To this, his answer was in effect, 'Shall do something to get my pay.'"[21]

Freeman's explanations for why he killed were consistent and clear, but when asked why he chose March 12 or the Van Nest family, he tormented his interrogators with indeterminacy or pivoted back to the issue of his stolen labor.

Why kill on the twelfth, and not another night? Austin asked.

"The time had come."[22]

Why the Van Nests? asked a white former employer.

"I had my work to do."

Freeman's impaired hearing obliged interrogators to shout their questions. Still, Freeman sometimes seemed not to hear them. The president of the Village of Auburn, Ethan A. Worden, asked, why the Van Nests and not another family? Freeman responded, "Because I must go." A deliberately consternating non sequitur or a miscommunication? Following up, Worden "asked him why he must go." Now Freeman seemed to hear him. "I must begin my work," he said. "Why?" Worden asked again.

Freeman replied, "They brought me up so."

"Who brought you up to kill?" Worden pressed.

"The State," Freeman said. It was a stunning acknowledgment. Freeman saw what anyone could see if they cared to look: the state and the prison were operating through each other, both politically and economically. The resulting violence could not be confined to the prison, no matter how thick the walls.

The village president objected, "They did not ever tell you to kill, did they?"

"They won't pay me."

Worden then "asked him if the Van Nest folks had anything to do with it. He said no.... Asked him if he expected to get any money [from Van Nests]. He said no." Why, then, the Van Nests? Freeman shot back, "Why did they put me in the State Prison for nothing?"[23]

Only one question seemed to fluster Freeman: "Why did you kill a child?" Freeman gamely acknowledged that he had stabbed four adults and a horse, but the death of George Van Nest seemed to arouse in him a different set of emotions. Sometimes he denied this sole part of the crime: "I never killed a child"; "They tell me I killed the child, but ... I certainly did not." At other times, he claimed ignorance: "[I] didn't know it was a child; saw a person lying on the bed and stabbed it." When asked if he was sorry for killing the adults, his answers were blithe: "[I] don't think any thing about that," or flatly, "No." But was he sorry for killing a child? "I don't know but it was hard—it was little— I rather it was bigger."[24]

While white self-appointed interrogators clogged the jail, Auburn's Black community largely stayed away. African Americans had reasons to distance themselves: grief, shame, or anger, perhaps, that a member of Auburn's founding Black family shed so much blood. But fear, too, must have been a factor. For Black people to visit Freeman was to risk becoming, themselves, targets of a still-frothing white mob. Some white people snickered at that danger: a jailor told the *Auburn Journal and Advertiser* that he was tempted to "hire some negro to stand chained outside the jail, to personate Freeman, for the people to come and look at. 'But,' said he, 'I am afraid they would Lynch the n——!'"[25] The possibility of white fury against Freeman boiling over into violence against other African Americans may have amused some white people, but it surely haunted the Black community.

Despite the risks, three family members—John De Puy, Sally Peters Freeman, and Luke Freeman—visited William. They, too, asked questions. But whereas the white crowd's repetitious *whys* overlaid an unspoken self-concern—Why kill the Van Nests and not me?—the questions of Freeman's family showed concern for Freeman himself.

If white people's unspoken question was "Am I safe?," the family's was, "Are you safe?" But Freeman's answers would frustrate his family as much as his white interrogators.

John De Puy was the first to visit. He skipped the questions that obsessed the white crowd and instead "hallooed through the grates a few words" of greeting. Then he asked Freeman how "they used him, and he said pretty well." De Puy asked "if he had enough to eat," but "couldn't understand" Freeman's answer.[26] Perhaps Freeman did not hear De Puy. Perhaps De Puy did not hear Freeman. But one fact was clear: John De Puy cared more about Freeman's health than his explanation for the murders.

When Sally Freeman visited her son, she, like De Puy, immediately "asked him how he was." She said later that William "laughed when I went in, and said he was well." Then the questions became more intimate. "I asked him if he was glad to see me. To this he made no answer." Like others, she asked why he had killed, but she phrased the question in a unique way: "I asked how he came to do it"—a question of motivation but also of process, of the events that propelled her son. To this, too, "he made no answer." Sally Freeman "asked him if he knew what he'd been doing. He stood and laughed." Freeman looked at his mother with an expression—Was it blame, despair, indifference?—that devastated her. Silenced her. "I felt so bad, he looked at me so, I didn't know what he did say." Sally Freeman could not bear it. "I stayed a short time—a few minutes.... When I went away he didn't bid me good bye, nor ask me to come again."[27]

When Sally Freeman braved the mob to visit her son, she protected herself by entering the jail alongside a white man, attorney Christopher Morgan. Luke Freeman, too, visited with a white man: Leander Bigelow, a physician at the Auburn State Prison who had treated Freeman for ear pain after his deafening injury.[28] In this joint visit, the family's concerns clashed with the white interlopers' demands.

Bigelow, yet another self-appointed interrogator with no substantive connection to the case, called on Freeman "to ascertain the state of his mind"—that is, to determine yet again why Freeman killed. Bigelow asked factual questions to gauge Freeman's rationality.

"How old are you?"

"Twenty-one the 29th of September."

"What September?"

"Last September."

"How long have you been in jail?"

"About three months; don't know exactly." Freeman had been in jail less than two months, but it must have felt longer.

At this point, Luke Freeman interrupted the doctor's pursuit of *why* and inquired instead into Freeman's welfare. "Observing a scar on his wrist," Luke asked, "Bill, that cut you got in Weedsport?" Luke was referring to an injury that Freeman had incurred months earlier while chopping wood.

"No," William Freeman replied, "I have got another cut that I got there." He pulled his sleeve up to show the older scar from the work accident.

Luke Freeman wanted to know more about the wounds. "When did you get the other cut?"

"I got that up to the lake, where I was." That is, when Phebe Wyckoff defended herself.

At this moment, Leander Bigelow cut off Luke Freeman's attention to his nephew's body and relaunched the investigation of mental capacity. The doctor grilled Freeman on the days of the week and the number of hours in a day and a night, months in a year, shillings to a dollar, and cents to a shilling. Freeman answered the questions correctly, showing again that in the six months since his release from prison he had straightened out his confusion about currency.

"When did you come out of State Prison?" Bigelow asked.

"Last September."

"How long was you in prison?"

"Five years."

"Would it be right for me to kill Luke now?" At this sudden turn, Luke Freeman surely looked up in alarm.

But William Freeman was unruffled. "I don't know how you could kill him." A canny, frustrating answer that exposed Bigelow's question as impotent rhetoric.

Bigelow pressed the question as a neutral hypothetical to assess Freeman's capacity for moral reasoning. "Would it be right if I should?"

"I don't know."

"Would you like to see me do it?"

Freeman refused the bait. "I should not think any thing about it."[29] Another mocking answer, even a dare. Freeman knew Bigelow could not act on his threat.

If Luke Freeman said anything more to his nephew, his words went unrecorded. The barber and the doctor left the jail as they had entered. Freeman remained, sitting on an overturned tub, chained to the stone floor.

How?

As Freeman's explanations of *why* provoked frustration and emotional chaos, Auburnites scrambled to secure themselves in knowledge of the *how*. Newspapers answered this need—to their own profit. They printed moment-by-moment narrations of the murders, all in sensationalistic language, bespangled with gore, inflated with outrage. With details of the victims' wounds cribbed from the coroner's report, newspapers published blueprints of the Van Nest house so readers could track Freeman's footsteps, marking where each body fell. These stories spread from Auburn to Albany, Brooklyn to Buffalo. Telegraphs carried the news south from New York through every state in the mid-Atlantic and on to Virginia, Kentucky, and Georgia; west to Ohio, Indiana, and Wisconsin; and northeast to every state in New England.[30] Throughout, repetitious descriptions of the "devil incarnate" and his "revolting butchery" fit Freeman's crime into the familiar terms of melodrama— which delivered a sense of plotted control, a *sensation* of meaning even as interrogators failed to extract a *why* that they could comprehend.

White perspectives defined this narrative. Newspapers printed statements from any white person remotely connected to the case: not only survivors, law enforcement, and witnesses to Freeman's arrest, but also neighbors who congregated at the crime scene after the murders and tourists who swarmed the county jail. The slimmest connection warranted newspaper attention: one white man, William De Groff, was quoted merely because his sister, Maria De Groff, found the broken blade of the murder weapon.[31] Meanwhile, African Americans other than Freeman were almost absent from newspaper coverage. Even Luke Freeman and Leander Bigelow's joint visit to Freeman reached newspapers only through Bigelow's narration. Either the press did not interview Freeman's friends and family members or—reasonably, given the proximity of white rage—they declined to comment.

Even as white people skipped over Black perspectives and dismissed Freeman's own words as nonsense, they probed Freeman's racialized body, trying to make it explain the crime. Newspapers tapped Freeman's family tree, finding significance, as Frances Seward had, in his Native and African American heritage. There "must be some bad blood running in the veins of the Freeman tribe," declared the *Syracuse Journal*, because "Wm. Freeman is one-quarter Indian, his mother having been one-half Indian," and his father Black. A parade of doctors—not only Leander Bigelow but also Blanchard Fosgate, David Dimon, Joseph Pitney (inventor of the prison's shower-bath), and many more—examined Freeman's wounds, took his pulse, and inflicted pain to which they measured his response. Phrenologists palpated his head, then decreed his capacity for "destructiveness" large and for "benevolence and veneration, very small." Newspapers measured every bit of Freeman's body, describing him as "thick set," "short legged," and "compactly built"; five foot three or four, no more than 110 pounds; and "remarkably deaf" with "a downcast bearing of his head and eyes."[32] From blood to bone to nerves, white people bore into Freeman's flesh, seeking answers.

Seven days after the murders, the *Cayuga Tocsin* published a portrait based on a woodcut by Auburn artist George Clough. This three-quarters view showed Freeman with straight eyebrows above open eyes. His most prominent feature was his nose, large and slightly hooked, above full, pursed lips. His hair was angular and neat, his expression placidly neutral. The public objected that the portrait did not match their perception of the murderer. Clough conceded that the portrait "is not a correct transcript," and the *Tocsin* therefore promised to commission a revised engraving.[33]

Clough created a new portrait. Here, Freeman's torso was largely the

FIGURE 6.2 *Likeness of William Freeman, the Murderer of the Van Nest Family and Diagram of the House of the Late John G. Van Nest*

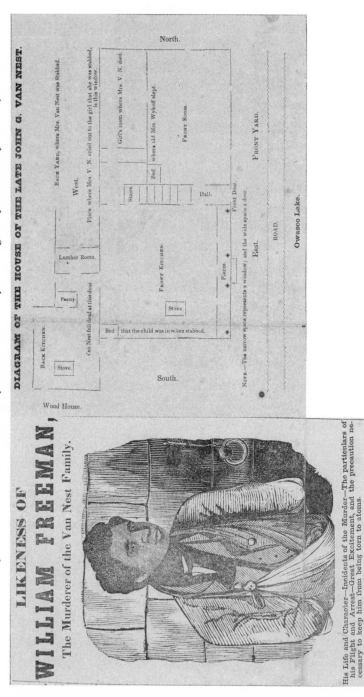

Daily Cayuga Tocsin—Extra, 19 March 1846, n.p. William L. Clements Library, University of Michigan, Ann Arbor.

FIGURE 6.3 *Correct Likeness of Wm. Freeman, the Murderer*

CORRECT LIKENESS OF WM. FREEMAN, THE MURDERER.
As sketched in his cell, by our young Artist, George L. Clough.

Illustration by George L. Clough, *Auburn Journal and Advertiser,* 25 March 1846, 1.

same, but his hair was disheveled, his eyebrows bushy. His eyes were unfocused and his nose sloped sharply downward. This full-body portrait included the overturned tub on which he sat, and, importantly, the shackle and chain that bound him to the floor. The newspaper declared Clough's second image "a *correct* likeness of FREEMAN in his cell." And indeed, the image seemed to satisfy readers—so much so that an Auburn bookstore offered it for sale as a lithograph, suitable for hanging

FIGURE 6.4 *Freeman, the Murderer of the Van Ness [sic] Family*

FREEMAN, THE MURDERER OF THE VAN NESS FAMILY.

National Police Gazette, 11 April 1846, 265. Courtesy of the American Antiquarian Society.

in a home.[34] An adaptation of Clough's portrait then ran on the front page of the lurid *National Police Gazette*. There, Freeman sneered, his nose almost grazing his upper lip. His eyes were half-closed and slightly crossed, producing a vacant yet vaguely malevolent look. Freeman's unfocused eyes suggested an unfocused man with no agenda, no *why* to explain his actions—only empty silence and menace.

For weeks, newspapers across the nation disgorged fact after fact, clarification after clarification, plotting each second of the murder and every contour of Freeman's flesh. But this glut of information of one kind—the *how*—could not fully muffle the *why* that white Auburnites could not accept. They kept asking, Why? Why?

CHAPTER SEVEN

Three Stories

William Freeman clearly stated his reason for killing four people: he wanted back pay or, failing that, payback. The murders challenged the Auburn System that extracted labor without compensation—the system on which Auburn's economy, pride, and identity depended. This was exactly what Auburnites refused to hear. But by dismissing Freeman's claim as incomprehensible, they created a narrative void, an absence of meaning, that was, itself, intolerable. Auburnites needed an explanation that satisfied and soothed them—and that protected their prison city. If Freeman would not provide one, they were determined to invent it.

Gallows Debates

Immediately after the murders, some Auburnites fit the crime into existing debates about capital punishment.[1] These debates were familiar because they had simmered for decades. Incarceration was itself an antigallows invention: it was created in Europe in the previous century to replace death and torture as the default units of punishment.[2] By refashioning Freeman's crime into a case study in the merits and drawbacks of capital punishment, Auburnites imbued the *case* with meaning, even as the *crimes* seemed depleted of it.

One of the first people to frame Freeman's crime as a referendum on capital punishment was the Reverend Aaron Burr Winfield. The Sunday after the murders, Winfield presided over the funerals of Phebe

Wyckoff and Sarah, John, and George Van Nest at the Dutch Reformed Sand Beach Church (figure 5.1). As many as three thousand people crowded to pay their respects and seek meaning and comfort.[3] Winfield responded with a bitter call for William Freeman's execution.

The absence of a fathomable motive, Winfield argued, was itself a dagger in the heart of Auburn, a crime on top of a crime. "How keen the smart, how deep the wound, how inscrutable the providence!" Winfield intoned, conflating the physical injuries of the Van Nest family with the emotional injuries of the community gathered in the church. Freeman, Winfield preached, was "fiendish"; a "monster" who "must answer for his horrid crimes"—including those against the terrorized general populace. Winfield thundered to a conclusion: Freeman's crimes exposed the folly of antigallows activists. "If ever there was just rebuke upon the falsely so-called sympathy of the day, here it is." Unless a man "loves the murderer more than his murdered victims," he must acknowledge as "reasonable" God's law that "he that sheddeth man's blood, by man shall his blood be shed."[4]

Winfield connected Freeman's crime to another that had been occupying Auburn's headlines for months: Henry Wyatt, a white prisoner at the Auburn State Prison, had killed James Gordon, another white prisoner. Wyatt murdered Gordon in the prison's tailor shop on March 16, 1845, and the trial began on February 11, 1846—a month and a day before Freeman murdered the Van Nests. William Henry Seward defended Wyatt, arguing that he was not guilty by reason of "moral insanity"—a school of thought maintaining that insanity could disorder the emotions while leaving intellectual capacity largely or even wholly intact. It was one of the first such defenses in US courts.[5] To the outrage of many, the jury could not reach a verdict, and Judge Bowen Whiting declared a mistrial. At the funeral of Wyckoff and the Van Nests, Winfield argued that Freeman had been emboldened by Wyatt's escape from the gallows. Thus he offered his congregants a new person to blame: Seward, by whose *"adroit counsel"* the law was "perverted, and jurors bewildered." "None of us are safe under such a false sympathy as this; for the murderer is almost certain of being acquitted!" Winfield charged. "If I shoot a man, to prevent him breaking in my house and killing my family, these gentlemen will say I did right. But if he succeeds, and murders my whole family, then it would be barbarous to put him to death! Oh, shame, shame!"[6]

Seward's son Frederick commented later on Winfield's oration and its effects: "Every word of this appeal, made under such solemn and mournful circumstances, fell upon the ears of the excited gathering like words of inspiration. It was fervently responded to, talked over, and praised." Swiftly, an Auburn publisher printed Winfield's sermon under the title, "Sermon at the Interment of the Bodies of John G. Van Nest, Mrs. Sarah Van Nest, G. W. Van Nest, Their Son, and Mrs. Phebe Wykoff [sic], Who were Murdered March Twelfth Inst., By a Colored Man Named William Freeman." This title, unlike the sermon itself, defined Freeman—and thereby his crimes—by race. "Thousands of copies" of this pamphlet were "scattered gratuitously far and wide." Following this publication, other progallows arguments also linked Freeman's crime to his race: the "false humanity of the anti-capital punishment advocates," wrote one newspaper, means that Freeman, "however *black* in heart and in skin, is as likely to escape, as to suffer the just punishment of his dreadful deeds of blood."[7] Thus progallows activists used Freeman to agitate white racial fears—and to mobilize those fears to support capital punishment.

Antigallows activists, too, refashioned the Freeman case into racialized evidence by which to bolster their preexisting arguments. Ten days after the murders, Reverend Austin preached against efforts to hang Freeman, arguing in lines echoed in the *Liberator* that white "Humanity and Common Sense" were threatened by "barbarous" impulses toward lynching. The *Prisoner's Friend* decried the anti-Black racism beneath calls for Freeman to hang, sarcastically arguing, "He is a colored man; and a negro is a large grade below a white man. If a white man kill a colored man, let him live; if a colored man kill a white man, hang him.... He killed,—let us kill."[8]

Most of the antigallows writers, in appropriating Freeman's case to their cause, not only ignored but *reversed* his challenge to the Auburn System: they supported incarceration as the just alternative to execution. To this rule, however, Walt Whitman flashed a rare exception. Writing in the *Brooklyn Eagle* eleven days after the murders, Whitman foregrounded Freeman's resistance to "labor[i]ous imprisonment," which took "possession of all his thoughts" and made "revenge," for Freeman, a form of "justice." The Auburn Prison, Whitman argued, was not necessarily "a milder penalty than death" because each man incarcerated there was "condemned to painful servile labor, dressed in the badges of degradation, his mouth deprived of its loved office of speech … and when night comes, to be shut in *alone* with darkness and silence."[9] Thus Whitman identified and criticized three hallmarks of the Auburn System: unpaid factory labor, silence, and isolation (he gestured, too, toward Auburn's iconic and humiliating prison stripes). Even when amplified by Whitman, however, Freeman's claims found few listeners. And Whitman never pursued Freeman's critique, but instead resumed arguments against capital punishment in general.

The connection between Freeman's case and existing debates on capital punishment imbued the murders with national significance — which in turn expanded national coverage. Cast in this context, the event was not just a lurid crime; it was an *important case*. And Whitman notwithstanding, this refashioning offered yet one more way to muffle, or even upend, Freeman's critique of the Auburn System. Antigallows activists considered prisons the solution, not the problem.

Lunatic or Fraud?

For progallows thinkers like the Reverend Winfield, Seward's "moral insanity" defense of Wyatt not only constituted a specious apology for murder, but also, alarmingly, provided grease by which Freeman might slip out of the noose. Freeman's crimes seemed an outgrowth and escalation of Henry Wyatt's. Wyatt killed one man; Freeman killed a man, a pregnant woman, a grandmother, and a toddler. Wyatt killed a convicted criminal; Freeman killed people who were not known to have committed any crime or even any offense against him. Wyatt's case entailed white-on-white violence; Freeman's, Black-on-white — and as such, the two rang different alarms for white people.

These alarms were shriller not only because of white people's ongoing fears of Black rebellions such as Nat Turner's, but also because in 1846, the concept of insanity was itself racialized. The census of 1840 had produced data that some interpreted as evidence that African Americans were disproportionately prone to insanity, especially in the free North.[10] This supposed correlation between insanity and Blackness shaped white perspectives: as one white Auburnite who had known Freeman since childhood said, "If Freeman is deranged, I should think a majority of the negroes were."[11] This association bore weighty implications for the moral insanity defense: if insanity excused murder and if Black people were more likely to be insane, then this defense licensed Black people to kill—especially, perhaps, to murder white people like the Van Nests. For these reasons, Freeman, unlike Wyatt, brought forward the racial stakes of the insanity defense.

Furthermore, the insanity defense had implications for the Auburn State Prison because many prisoners, including Freeman's uncle Sydney Freeman, went mad there. If madness excused murder and if prison caused madness, then the prison both caused and excused murder. This logic threatened to raise a question: if prison caused rather than controlled crime, why should it exist? For all these reasons, the idea that Freeman was insane undercut white people's sense of security, the prison, and everyone who benefited economically from the Auburn System.

An alternative explanation seemed to neutralize these implications: Freeman was sane but was feigning insanity. In this narrative, Freeman, emboldened by Seward, cynically copied Wyatt with the expectation that he, like his white antecedent, would dodge the hangman. On the surface, this view was worrisome because it confronted the possibility that Freeman would escape justice. But the idea of faked insanity reassured white Auburnites for several reasons. Immediately, this narrative diverted scrutiny from the Auburn State Prison and its damaging effects on prisoners. The narrative also short-circuited debates over Seward's moral insanity defense: if Freeman was faking insanity, it did not matter whether moral insanity was a valid defense because it simply did not apply. Most of all, however, the possibility that Freeman was faking insanity was heartening because it redefined the core question, not "Why did Freeman kill the Van Nests and not me?" but instead, "Is Freeman a fake or not?" This is what Leander Bigelow tested when he proposed to kill Luke Freeman "to ascertain the state" of William Freeman's "mind."[12]

The task of assessing Freeman's sanity transformed the city's emotional dynamics because it animated the practices of spectatorship that had been developed and popularized by the showman Phineas Taylor ("P. T.") Barnum. For over a decade, Barnum had famously displayed "humbugs" such as Joice Heth (the purported 161-year-old Black nursemaid of George Washington) and the Feejee Mermaid (the mythic exotic supposedly captured and preserved as taxidermy), challenging audiences to judge their authenticity. Barnum invited people to regard each exhibit with the understanding that it might be bogus or it might be real—and spectators' enjoyment lay partly in figuring out which was the case. Barnum positioned ordinary people as experts who were qualified to discern truth—and that flattery was part of what they bought with their admission fees.[13]

Auburnites were familiar with these habits of spectatorship because some of Barnum's most famous acts had performed recently in their city. Chang and Eng Bunker, the famous "Siamese Twins" managed by Barnum, performed in Auburn in 1832 and again in 1839. Barnum later visited Auburn with one of his stars, Charles Stratton, who was better known as General Tom Thumb. Furthermore, many people in Auburn knew Barnum personally. His half brother, Philo Barnum, lived in Auburn. Philo Barnum worked in the Auburn State Prison as a keeper in the weave shop; shortly before Freeman's incarceration, he testified against Elam Lynds and was widely believed to have contributed to Lynds's dismissal. The Reverend John Austin was another example of an Auburnite who knew Barnum. Four years earlier, Austin had called on Barnum at the American Museum in New York City; later, the showman and the minister traveled together to Utica, where they toured that city's famous insane asylum and dined together often.[14] Although Barnum never lived in Auburn, then, he was connected to the city, its people, its politics, and its prison—and vice versa.

When Auburnites regarded Freeman through a lens ground for Barnum's sideshow performers, they reinvented him as a freak—a "curious specimen" in the words of one newspaper article—and his cell as a stage.[15] A freak was, by definition, exceptional, an aberration that confirmed broader norms. Freaks made spectators normal; they gave people something to wonder at, something to fear in a controlled, pleasurable way. Most important, by staring at Freeman as they would stare at Barnum's freaks, Auburnites fashioned for themselves a new question: neither *why* nor *how*, but *what*. What was Freeman? Lunatic or humbug?

The *what* question gave Auburnites something new to *do*: they could interrogate Freeman to determine for themselves whether he was sane, insane, or sane but feigning insanity. Questions of *why* and *how* configured Freeman as a source of information—which he had the power to give or withhold. In contrast, when people like Leander Bigelow asked ever-more-clever questions to determine whether he was a humbug, they relocated the power to determine truth in *themselves*, not in Freeman and his "nonsensical" answers. *Why* and *how* generated emotional chaos, which white people managed by not hearing Freeman's answers; but *what* reinstated a sense of control, power, and racial superiority. It reinvented white spectators as cool-minded investigators rather than cowering victims, blood-lusting savages, or failed lynchers. If Freeman was a puzzle, he could be solved. Thus icy terror melted into intrigue.

The process of investigating Freeman as a possible humbug led some Auburnites, of course, to conclude that he was not one. And if Freeman was genuinely mad, then the insanity defense might save him from the gallows. Winfield and many others decried this possibility, but Frances Seward championed it. For her, the idea that Freeman was legitimately insane and therefore not criminally responsible was useful because it revisited the question of *why*—and seemed, finally, to resolve it.

Frances Seward moved toward this conclusion in stages. Immediately after the murder, she was anguished not only by Freeman's crime but also by his statement of motive, which she, like many white people, considered "incoherent and improbable." The "crime and the motive are so inadequate," so incommensurate to each other, she wrote to her older son, Augustus, "that I cannot avoid thinking with many others that something remains untold." In a letter to her husband, she further explained her certainty that the truth awaited discovery. Freeman, she noted, "did not know by sight the members of the family he has murdered," and his "imprisonment is all the reason he assigns for the commission of the horrible deed." To Frances Seward, his explanation was "incomprehensible." She wrote, "I cannot conceive it possible for a human being to commit a crime so awful without strong motive, either real or imaginary, for the act."[16]

Frances Seward proposed an explanation that satisfied her and promised to resolve her painful bewilderment: Freeman was indeed insane—and crucially, his lack of an "adequate motive" was *itself* the proof. She wrote again to her son: "Bill...must be insane as he does not profess to have any reason for selecting [his] objects of vengeance."[17] By this logic, white people's inability to comprehend Freeman's statement of motive became, itself, evidence of *Freeman's* mental deficiency. Frances Seward did not simply supply meaning that seemed missing; instead, she transformed a perceived absence of meaning into meaning itself.

Frances Seward had, she thought, resolved the *why* question: Freeman killed the Van Nests because he was insane. Simple. John Austin independently reached the same conclusion, but for him, this answer raised yet another *why* question: *Why* was Freeman insane? What had caused his mental infirmity? The minister looked to his faith for answers.

From Villain to Victim

Universalism distinguished itself from other forms of Christianity by rejecting the belief in Hell. Universal salvation, not punishment, awaited all souls. No human sin overrode God's benevolence. Compassion and reconciliation, God's ideals, should reverberate on earth. This optimistic orientation led Austin and many of his coreligionists to embrace liberal reform movements, especially temperance, abolition, opposition to capital punishment, and care for people with mental illness.[18]

Universalism had long informed Austin's stance on the relationship between mental incapacity and criminal culpability. When a person commits a crime, Austin argued in 1844, the "amount of guilt depends upon the *intentions* of the actor, and the degree of moral light under which the crime is committed." Rehearsing the logic by which Seward would later argue that Wyatt was not guilty by reason of moral insanity, Austin wrote that the intentions of an "insane person, or an idiot" are "beyond his control"; therefore he must "not be held responsible for his actions." Who, then, was responsible for the crimes of a mentally compromised person? Society, Austin answered. A society must teach moral reasoning to all its members, and each crime marked a lapsed lesson. "In the same degree that a man is deprived of moral light, whereby he can distinguish right from wrong," Austin explained, "to the same extent is the guilt of his crimes decreased."[19] In other words, society's shortcomings caused moral deficiencies, which in turn caused criminal behavior but mitigated criminal guilt—and all these human twists would ultimately be straightened, reconciled, by God.

Four days after Freeman killed the Van Nests, Austin recast this argument in newly racial terms: the society responsible for teaching morality was white, the lunatics and idiots whose crimes indexed society's failures were Black. Writing under the pseudonym "Justice," Austin characterized Auburn's Black community as "almost wholly without the benefits of moral, religious, or intellectual culture." Discounting the AME Zion Church half a mile from his home, Austin asserted that Black Auburnites "grow up almost literally heathen" because they were "thrust from our churches, with none to instruct them intelligently in their religious and moral duties." He similarly dismissed Black secular self-education: "Shut out from both public and private schools among the whites," Austin wrote, Black Auburnites were "unable to sustain schools themselves"—an unintentionally ironic statement given that a few years earlier, white "ridicule and secret opposition" had halted plans to open a Black school. Deprived of white moral leadership, Austin argued, Black people "imbibe[d] all the vices"—that is, from each other—"without being able to become imbued with the virtues, of those around them"—that is, white people. White neglect combined with Black inadequacy, Austin argued, made Black children "fall into crime." Speaking of Freeman's crimes, Austin asked, "[Is not] society in some degree, accountable for this sad catastrophe? Is it not to be traced as one of the legitimate effects of the utter indifference and neglect manifested toward the colored population of this place?"[20]

By this logic, Austin answered anew the question of *why*. Like Frances Seward, he asserted that Freeman killed because he was insane, but Austin elaborated that Freeman's mental infirmity and resulting crimes were themselves due to a "most heartless, cruel prejudice" against those with "complexions a few shades darker than some of the rest of our citizens." In short, white racial prejudice caused Black moral and mental debility, which in turn caused crime. Certainly, Austin was correct in asserting that racism suffused Auburn. But Freeman never claimed racism as either a motive for or target of his crimes. By repeatedly describing Freeman as a *"demented African"* and blaming his actions on shortcomings in white stewardship, Austin positioned Freeman as a piteous victim of prejudiced society in general.[21]

This move was emotionally useful not only because it forged yet one more way to suppress and distract from Freeman's challenge to the Auburn System, but also because Austin's story reversed the roles of victim and victor. Many white Auburnites, from Reverend Winfield to Frances Seward, felt themselves to be victims of Freeman's terrifying campaign. But Austin's argument promised to resolve that feeling: the general white population had victimized Freeman, not vice versa. In this flipped story, Freeman was weak and white Auburn was strong.

Austin's ideas traveled swiftly. The abolitionist *Liberator* soon called the "Justice" essays "excellent and reasonable"; the *Universalist Watchman, Repository and Chronicle* quoted them appreciatively. The *Prisoner's Friend*, a newspaper that advocated prison reform and opposed capital punishment, reprinted Austin's argument that African Americans constituted a "degraded caste" due to white neglect, arguing that "if we choose to let a portion of the people grow up in our very midst in a state of destitution and ignorance, we must expect vice and crime will be consequent." Another minister, Henry F. Harrington in Albany, amplified Austin's condescension, describing Freeman as a member of an "abject caste" whose life was determined by the experience of racism. "Let us follow the wretch from his cradle to his cell," Harrington intoned. "He was the son of a negro. Do you apprehend the force of that? He was the son of a negro!" Harrington painted Freeman as a helpless victim of Northern segregation, "born of outcasts, inevitably to become an outcast" because "it was the will of a free, noble, intelligent, civilized, Christian people to have it so." Ignoring all Freeman's statements, Harrington blamed "accursed prejudices" for the murder of the Van Nests, faulting the prison only for failing to impart Christian morality. Unsurprisingly, Austin's "Justice" essays also provoked rebuttals from Auburnites who wrote under pseudonyms including "Vindex," "The Public," "Law and Order," and "Fleming"—the first of whom was later revealed to be William Marcy, New York's governor immediately before Seward, and the last of whom may have been James E. Tyler, the guard who beat Freeman to the point of deafness.[22] Each of these columns induced Austin to write yet more "Justice" pieces, and the dueling essays further disseminated Austin's claims.

If the problem was that white neglect caused Black moral insanity, what was the solution? White Christian "duty," Austin wrote in his journal.[23] Freeman needed a champion, a protector, a steward. Austin knew where to find that person.

The Defense

John Austin lived less than a block from William Henry and Frances Seward, but he barely knew them. He first encountered the ex-governor in 1844 when Seward delivered a "most excellent address" on Christian charity before the Ladies' Martha Washington Benevolent Society. Austin felt a spiritual kinship with Seward. "Although he attends the Episcopal Church usually," Austin noted in his journal, he "has declared in so many words that he is a Universalist." Austin's enthusiasm grew in February 1846 when he witnessed Seward's defense of Wyatt. He effused in his journal, "My estimation of the noble and benevolent disposition, and the *splendid talent* of Gov. Seward" has "increased during this trial. I both *respect* and *love* him." In Austin's view, Seward's "*estimable* and *valuable* qualities," along with his defense of Wyatt, made the ex-governor an ideal advocate for Freeman.[24]

On March 26, Austin called on Freeman in his cell. The encounter seemed to confirm "Justice's" assumptions. Austin wrote in his journal that he found Freeman "very ignorant indeed—having but little more sense than the brutes." If Austin's diagnosis of social ill seemed correct, so too must be the prescribed remedy. "I asked [Freeman] if he would like to have Gov. Seward defend him," Austin related later. "He was agitated and hesitating. At length he answered Yes."[25]

Having procured Freeman's assent, Austin left the jail and walked two blocks to Seward's law office. He boldly introduced himself to the ex-governor, who "received me very cordially," Austin recorded in his journal. "I had a very interesting conversation with him descriptive of my interview with Freeman." As Austin left, Seward offered a "polite invitation to call again." Austin must have been pleased: in the space of a few hours, he had introduced himself to a murderer and a politician, and had prompted each to contemplate a relationship with the other. Over the coming weeks, Austin would accept Seward's invitation to return—several times—and gradually earn the ex-governor's trust.[26]

Meanwhile, Frances Seward independently concluded that her husband should defend Freeman, and she, too, pressed for that outcome. Frances Seward's and Austin's parallel campaigns tracked with parallel motives: both opposed the death penalty, both were horrified by their white neighbors' bloodlust, and both pitied Freeman as a helpless, impoverished, miserable, defenseless, demented, downtrodden, neglected, insane, idiotic, friendless Black wretch.[27]

Beneath these articulated motives, however, lay another, which was both unspoken and unacknowledged: Austin and the Seward family were both financially entangled with the Auburn System that Freeman challenged. Although they may not have consciously considered it, Austin and the Sewards stood to benefit from defining Freeman as insane—and his critique, therefore, as nonsense.

Austin was economically dependent on the Auburn State Prison because many in his congregation earned their income from it, and the church depended on their generosity. For example, Josiah Barber, who owned the carpet shop for which Freeman had dyed fiber, was one of the Auburn Prison's most profitable contractors and correspondingly one of the Universalist church's top donors. By March 1846, he had pledged the immense sum of $2,500 to Austin. In the same weeks when Austin penned his "Justice" articles, he and the carpet contractor traveled together to raise funds for a new church building.[28] Austin knew that the unpaid labor of prisoners like Freeman enriched Barber and other local businessmen, whose donations sustained Austin's church—and Austin himself.

Frances Miller Seward's finances and social standing, too, were tied to the prison. Frances grew up wealthy in part because her father, the judge Elijah Miller, was one of the prison's three cofounders (plate 1). Working with John Beach, another cofounder, Miller built a successful cotton factory equipped with prison-built machinery.[29] Miller invested, too, in real estate that increased in value as the prison-fed village grew. Everyone in Auburn was economically tied to the prison, but Frances Seward owed her exceptional wealth to it.

Seward listened to his wife and his pious, persuasive new friend, but he was initially unconvinced. Despite his motives to defend Freeman, he had many reasons not to do so. The first was closest: Seward's father-in-law, in whose home Seward and his family lived, inveighed against it. As Frances Seward wrote to her sister, Elijah Miller "torment[ed] Henry exceedingly by endeavouring to make him abandon the 'n———.'"[30] As rumors spread that Seward was considering defending Freeman, more Auburnites raged against the ex-governor. Many followed Reverend Winfield's lead to blame Freeman's crimes on Seward and his moral insanity defense of Wyatt. These Auburnites waged what Seward called "a busy war" to dissuade him from defending Freeman. They confronted Seward's law partners, demanding to know his plans. Some hurled rocks at Seward's children; others conspired to destroy the family's home. Frances Seward wrote that "all who call themselves his friends with one or two exceptions" tried to persuade her husband that defending Freeman would be "very hazardous" given "the state of public feeling in regard to the murder." At one point, Seward's friends feared so greatly for his safety that when Seward returned from a trip, they met him at the railroad station opposite the prison and served as bodyguards for his ten-minute walk home.[31]

Seward's concerns extended even beyond his person, his family, and his city. If he defended a Black man who had killed a white family, he would repel many voters. As New York's most prominent Whig, he knew his choices would affect the party, perhaps even nationally. For these reasons, Seward's trusted political adviser Thurlow Weed urged him to back away from Freeman's case.[32]

Seward listened to his political allies, but it was his wife and Austin who ultimately persuaded him. Like them, Seward sincerely believed that Freeman was not guilty by reason of moral insanity. Like them, he pitied Freeman. Like Austin, he believed that Black people were dis-

PLATE 1 *Elijah Miller*

Portrait by Chester Harding, ca. 1840–1843. Courtesy of the Seward House Museum.

PLATE 2 *Frances Miller Seward*

Portrait by Henry Inman, ca. 1843. Courtesy of the Seward House Museum.

PLATE 3 *Murder of Jane McCrea*

Ca. 1846, unidentified artist, Mastin Collection, oil on bed ticking, 84 × 104 in., Farmers' Museum, Cooperstown, NY, museum purchase, F0113.1954. Photograph by Richard Walker.

PLATE 4 *Van Nest House*

1846, unidentified artist, Mastin Collection, oil on bed ticking, 97½ × 114½ in., Farmers' Museum, Cooperstown, NY, museum purchase, F0109.1954. Photograph by Richard Walker.

PLATE 5 *Van Nest House* (detail)

William Freeman attacks Phebe Wyckoff, who defends herself, while Sarah Van Nest, already stabbed, flees into the house. 1846, unidentified artist, Mastin Collection, oil on bed ticking, 97½ × 114½ in., Farmers' Museum, Cooperstown, NY, museum purchase, F0109.1954.detail. Photograph by Richard Walker.

PLATE 6 *Freeman Stabbing Child*

1846, unidentified artist, Mastin Collection, oil on bed ticking, 84 × 107 in., Farmers' Museum, Cooperstown, NY, museum purchase, F0111.1954. Photograph by Richard Walker.

PLATE 7 *Van Nest Family after Attack*

Julia Van Nest cradles her dying brother; Helen Holmes tends to the children; Cornelius Van Arsdale, wounded but alive, lies on the floor bleeding; William Freeman, brandishing a knife, peeps in the window. 1846, unidentified artist, Mastin Collection, oil on bed ticking, 90½ × 116¼ in., Farmers' Museum, Cooperstown, NY, museum purchase, F0108.1954. Photograph by Richard Walker.

PLATE 8 *Hanging Freeman*

1846, unidentified artist, Mastin Collection, oil on bed ticking, 90 × 102 in., Farmers' Museum, Cooperstown, NY, museum purchase, F0110.1954. Photograph by Richard Walker.

proportionately prone to crime and that white neglect was a cause. In a letter to Weed, Seward explained his emerging decision to aid Freeman, despite the political and personal risks: "He is deaf, deserted, ignorant, and his conduct is unexplainable on any principle of sanity. It is natural that he should turn to me to defend him." Seward knew his involvement would "raise a storm of prejudice and passion" that would "try the fortitude of my friends." Nevertheless, he vowed, "I shall do my duty. I care not whether I am to be ever forgiven for it." By the end of May 1846, Seward decided to follow the "advice of humane persons."[33] As Whigs shuddered and white Auburnites raged, William Henry Seward announced he would defend William Freeman.

CHAPTER EIGHT

Rivals

Freeman acknowledged many impairments: his deafness, his useless right hand, his difficulty socializing with members of his community. None of his recorded words, however, suggest that he considered himself mentally compromised.[1] Nevertheless, Seward pleaded on Freeman's behalf: not guilty by reason of insanity. If Freeman was aware of the plea, and if he responded to it, that exchange went unrecorded.

Seward assembled a legal team that included David Wright (husband of the feminist and abolitionist Martha Coffin Wright) and Christopher Morgan, the attorney who had accompanied Sally Freeman to visit her son. He assembled, too, a squad of medical experts, many of whom traveled from out of town and stayed in the Sewards' home — to the chagrin of Frances Seward, who was obliged to entertain them.[2]

Seward's courtroom adversary was a Democrat, New York's attorney general, John Van Buren. Famous as the son of former president Martin Van Buren, "Prince John," as he was dubbed, was aggressive and arrogant, combining a taste for fine haberdashery, food, and liquor with an equal appetite for profanity, gambling, and philandering. A year earlier, he had gotten into a fistfight with the opposing counsel in court.[3]

As Seward and Van Buren squared off in what would soon be called the "trial of the half century," spectators jammed the courtroom. Standing rib to rib, belly to back, Auburn's townspeople competed for glimpses of Freeman. Trains delivered yet more crowds to the Cayuga Courthouse. Telegraph lines that had been completed only days earlier delivered news of the trial to distant cities. People who could not

FIGURE 8.1 *William Henry Seward*

Steel engraving by J. O. Buttre after painting ca. 1843 by Henry Inman. Private collection.

travel to Auburn followed the trial via serialized transcripts. The trial captivated readers of periodicals ranging from the salacious *National Police Gazette* to the reform-oriented *Prisoner's Friend*; from the scientific *Journal of Insanity* to Black newspapers such as the *North Star*, and later *Frederick Douglass' Paper*. By one estimate, the trial generated more than one million words of print.[4]

The proceedings began with a preliminary trial that posed a single question: was Freeman insane or not? It was the same question that had gripped Auburn and motivated so many townspeople to interrogate Freeman in his cell. If the preliminary jury declared Freeman sane, he would be tried for murder. But if the jury found him incompetent,

FIGURE 8.2 *John Van Buren*

Matthew B. Brady, Photograph of John Van Buren, three-quarter portrait, three-quarters to the left [between 1855 and 1860]. Library of Congress, https://www.loc.gov/item/2004664069.

there would be no murder trial and Freeman would be confined for life at the State Lunatic Asylum at Utica.

Van Buren argued that Freeman could distinguish right from wrong and was therefore legally responsible for his crimes. According to the prosecution, Freeman was motivated by "depravity" and an "avaricious desire for pay." Freeman's claim that he deserved wages for his prison labor, the prosecution contended, was incorrect but rational. Many other prisoners held the same belief; the fact that they were wrong did not mean they were insane. The prosecution introduced a medical expert who testified to that effect. When "the ordinary sane ... spoke of pay for being in prison," he said, "it would *appear* as an absurdity; it would *seem* to be a delusion." But in Freeman's case, the prosecution's medical witness testified, "he had argued himself into the belief that he ought to have his pay by a false course of reasoning," not insanity.[5]

In contrast, the defense claimed that Freeman was insane and mentally feeble and therefore not responsible for the murders. The crime, Seward argued in an echo of his wife, was motiveless and nonsensical; it was therefore itself a symptom of insanity. The defense's strategy was to prove that Freeman's demand for wages was delusional. Over and over the defense described Freeman's "delusion about pay": the "delusion was that certain persons had imprisoned him wrongfully, and by killing them he could get his pay," and more.[6] The defense never called Freeman to the stand; throughout the trial, he sat silently in the courtroom.

Seward argued that Freeman became insane because of excessive violence, particularly the head injury. This argument might sound like a critique of the prison, but it was, in fact, a defense. Seward, who was a reformer, invariably framed problems in the prison as abuses of a system that was fundamentally sound. Thus, when Seward blamed the prison beating for Freeman's crimes, he joined with other liberal reformers, like Dorothea Dix, who wanted to ameliorate rather than uproot the system.

To make this case, the defense marshaled family members and employers who knew Freeman both before and after his incarceration. John De Puy, Deborah De Puy, Sally Freeman, and others testified that Freeman had been sane, with normal intelligence and hearing, before his head injury but insane, deaf, and mentally dull afterward. In counterpoint, Van Buren introduced witnesses who testified that Freeman was always malevolent: as a young boy, they said, he "threw stones at white boys" and had an "ugly" temper. In a devastating move, the prosecution called to the stand Cornelius Van Arsdale and Helen Holmes, the only adult survivors of Freeman's attack.[7] Neither one was asked to comment on Freeman's sanity, which they had no basis for assessing. Their testimony was relevant to the preliminary trial only because they provided sensational descriptions of the crime, which fortified the prosecution's portrait of Freeman as vicious, not insane.

Despite these differences, the prosecution and the defense initially harmonized on one point: both posited race as only a minor factor in the murders. That changed, however, when the defense called Reverend John Austin to the stand.

Seward asked the minister to explain why he considered Freeman insane. At first, Austin's testimony differed little from that of other defense witnesses who described jailhouse conversations. He reported that Freeman said he barely knew the Van Nests; that he had killed them "to get his pay"; that he referred to murder as "work that he had to do"; and that he seemed, to Austin, mentally compromised. A "child of five or six years of age," the minister averred, "had as much mind both intellectually and morally."[8]

But when the prosecution cross-examined Austin, the trial moved in a new direction: the prosecution asked him about the columns signed by "Justice." Austin acknowledged his authorship. The prosecutor then asked Austin whether his articles said "that others are more to blame" than Freeman.

Austin replied, "I have written in regard to the improprieties of others, in this matter, but did not suggest that he was not a fit object for punishment."

"Was it the object to show that his education had been neglected?"

"Very likely I may have said so."

Quoting "Justice," the prosecution asked if Austin had "suggest[ed] that the crime was the legitimate effect of the indifference of the community to the colored population." The minister answered, "I do think so.... My opinion is, that one of the legitimate causes that led to this tragical event, is the utter neglect shown to the moral, intellectual and religious instruction of the colored people."[9]

Austin's testimony, which lasted over an hour, was a turning point because it introduced to the proceedings the notion of Freeman as a victim of white society. His crimes, Austin alleged from the stand, resulted from white failure to steward African Americans—which implied that Black people were incapable of stewarding themselves. Many of the people in the courtroom had not read "Justice," so this was a new idea. The concept that social ills such as poverty could cause crime had become widespread only in the previous decade.[10] The racialization of this idea—that white prejudice and discrimination created a defective environment, which in turn caused African Americans, as a population, to commit crimes—was, to many, unfamiliar and startling.

One week later, on the Fourth of July, the trial to determine sanity concluded. The prosecution wrapped up by painting Freeman as rational, physically powerful, and dangerous. But Seward, in a nine-hour closing, picked up on Austin's tale of victimhood: he called on the jury to pity Freeman as a *"poor, friendless, demented African!"* The courtroom audience as well as the members of the jury, Austin observed in his journal, responded emotionally, even becoming "very frequently bathed in tears."[11]

Around midnight on July 4, closing arguments ended. Judge Bowen Whiting then charged the jury with deciding whether Freeman was mentally competent to stand trial. In his instructions to the jury, Whiting identified "delusion" as a decisive factor. The judge had presided over the trial of Henry Wyatt, in which Seward's insanity defense led to a hung jury. Whiting clearly wanted to avoid repeating that scenario. He enunciated the factors that he considered germane to determining "whether the prisoner is under a delusion." The jury "should consider the proof in regard to the prisoner's uniform assertion that his conviction and imprisonment had been wrongful and unjust, because he was innocent of the crime of stealing the horse; his opinion that he ought to be paid for his time in prison; his demand of that pay of Mrs. Godfrey; her refusal of that payment; his application to magistrates for process to compel payment, and their refusal of it; his declaration that the people had taken his time and labor from him; and that there was no law for him."[12] This list replicated the prosecution's narrative of events, but it also echoed Freeman's claims. Much like Freeman himself, Whiting did not refer to anti-Black discrimination, segregation, or degradation. If Freeman's beliefs were anything other than insane delusions, Whiting implied, the jury must find him fit to stand trial.

Despite Whiting's hints, the jury split: eleven jurors thought Freeman sufficiently sane to stand trial, but one thought otherwise. In response to this deadlock, Judge Whiting clarified their charge, now naming delusion as *the* defining point. "The main question for the jury to decide," Whiting said, "is whether the prisoner knows RIGHT FROM WRONG. If he does, then he is to be considered SANE." With these instructions, Whiting restricted the jury to the McNaughton (or M'Naghten) rules, a then-emergent legal concept that defined insanity as a "defect of reason" or a "cognitive incapacity" to understand that an act was wrong.[13] By this narrow definition, if Freeman was capable of reasoning—in any circumstance, regarding any matter—he was fit to stand trial.

Throughout the preliminary trial, Seward had argued for insanity in two ways. Addressing the McNaughton rules, Seward argued that Freeman was wholly incapable of reason. Seward hedged his bets, however, by also arguing for "moral insanity," the concept that a person could be rational about some things and irrational about others.[14] Thus he gave the jury two distinct avenues by which to find Freeman insane. But Whiting closed one path when he instructed the jury to discard the concept of moral insanity and adhere only to McNaughton rules.

Before Whiting resequestered the jury, he again named Freeman's demand for back pay as the case's defining issue. "I do not believe that there is evidence of delusion, as there is proof that it is common for convicts to claim pay for being confined," Whiting said.[15] By limiting the jury to the McNaughton rules and then affirming Freeman's quest for pay as rational (but wrong), Whiting all but closed the door for the jury to find Freeman insane.

The jury returned to its deliberations. Hours passed.

Austin left the courtroom for his church, where he preached on the subject of patience.[16]

At 8 p.m. on July 5, the jury reached a verdict: Freeman was sufficiently sane to stand trial. Austin, who had returned to the courtroom, described what happened next as an "awful farce" in which the district attorney spoke "in a pompous and formal tone of voice, to a *poor, demented, idiotic* creature" and "requir[ed] him to respond."[17]

THE DISTRICT ATTORNEY approached Freeman and said—"Wm. Freeman, stand up!" Freeman stood up. He then put his mouth close to Freeman's ear and read over the indictments against him. The following dialogue then ensued:

DISTRICT ATTORNEY—Do you plead *guilty* or *not guilty* to these indictments?

FREEMAN—(in a low, slow, monotonous tone of voice) "I don't know!"

DISTRICT ATTORNEY—Are you able to supply counsel?

FREEMAN—No.

DISTRICT ATTORNEY—Are you ready for trial?

FREEMAN—*I don't know.*

DISTRICT ATTORNEY—Who are your counsel?

FREEMAN—*I don't know.*[18]

The sight roiled Austin's pity: "The wretched being had not the first glimpse of what it all meant! Or what effect it would have upon him!!"[19]

The judge then asked, "Will any one defend this man?"[20]

Austin gushed, "Gov. Seward could no longer restrain himself. He buried his face in his hands and burst into tears." Then Seward rose and responded, "I shall remain counsel for the prisoner until his death."[21]

The court clerk entered a plea of not guilty. Freeman was now set to stand trial for murder.

The Main Trial

Five days later, on a sweltering Friday, Freeman's murder trial commenced. The judge, prosecutor, and defense team remained in place, identical to those of the preliminary trial. New jurors were seated. Seward, undaunted by the first jury's finding of sanity, redoubled his claim that Freeman's demand for pay constituted a delusion and re-gathered his medical experts in support. Now, however, Seward integrated that strategy with the racialized pity that Austin had voiced. Austin's argument, introduced in the preliminary trial only through the prosecution's cross-examination and expounded on in Seward's closing argument, now became central. In the defense's opening statement, David Wright described Freeman's "isolated position amongst us, by reason of the wicked and unchristian prejudice against him and all others of his kind, by reason of their color ... the wrongs he had suffered, the hardships he had endured, and the cruelties which had been inflicted upon him." Wright expressed "amaze[ment] that we should now hold up our hands in holy horror at the result of our own treatment" of him. Freeman, the defense argued, killed because he was the outraged victim of white society. It would later be called the "first recorded black rage defense."[22]

Van Buren also repeated his arguments from the preliminary trial—and he, too, set them in a newly racialized frame. In the prosecution's opening statement, district attorney (and coprosecutor) Luman Sherwood emphasized that Freeman's "father was an African—his mother was the offspring of an African and an Indian" and then characterized Freeman as an "unlearned, ignorant, stupid and degraded negro." As before, Van Buren argued that Freeman's quest for pay was wrong but not delusional. As before, Van Buren claimed Freeman had always been vicious. Now, however, Van Buren offered an explanation for Freeman's violence: Black and Indian ancestry. The prosecution argued that these groups were savages who required white control. One witness even alleged that some Indians practiced cannibalism, which he said explained why Freeman misheard John Van Nest threaten to eat his liver.[23]

Throughout the trial, no witness quoted Freeman as saying, or even hinting, that racial denigration motivated him. When the prosecution and the defense blamed race and racism, respectively, for the murders, they asked the jury to disregard Freeman's own articulation of motive. Thus, they both distracted from Freeman's challenge to the Auburn System.

This distraction went over easily in the company town. Much as magistrate James Bostwick had a vested interest in dismissing Freeman in his law office, so too did many individuals involved in the trial. One juror ran a comb factory inside the Auburn State Prison; in 1843 he bought $2,323.65 worth of prisoners' labor. A witness for the defense sold goods to the prison's stone shop, for which he was paid $150.50 in 1841. Attorney General John Van Buren and his father, Martin Van Buren, were major architects of the Democratic Party, whose power was bound to Auburn State Prison—as Seward's gubernatorial election had shown. Coprosecutor Luman Sherwood was, in 1845, one of the Democrat-appointed inspectors of the Auburn State Prison, who were responsible for affirming its competent and responsible management—so any failing of the prison reflected on him. The defense team, too, was entangled with the prison. Christopher Morgan, Seward's law partner, was the son-in-law of Joseph Pitney, the physician in the Auburn State Prison who invented the shower-bath. David Wright, cocounsel for the defense, sold a cord of wood to the prison for $3.00 in August 1841. And no one in the court was more associated with the prison than William Henry Seward. As governor, Seward defined himself as a prison reformer who endeavored to make New York's prisons simultaneously more humane and more profitable. And Seward was closely associated with two of the prison's three founders. Not only was one, Elijah Miller, Seward's live-in father-in-law, but another, John H. Beach, had supplied Seward with financial statistics that had aided his gubernatorial campaign. Furthermore, one of Beach's sons, John Campbell Beach, was Seward's law partner in 1844–1845, while another son, William Beach, worked with Seward to develop commercial property throughout Auburn.[24]

Throughout the trial, no one commented on these conflicts of interest because they were ubiquitous and normal. They were mere background, not scandal—business as usual in the prison's city.

Auburn versus Pennsylvania

Some circumstances surrounding Freeman's case, however, were anything but ordinary. At the moment when the trial convened, the Auburn System was on the verge of losing a long-standing rivalry with the Pennsylvania System of incarceration, in which prisoners endured near-total, permanent solitary confinement and labored alone in their cells. To Auburnites' long-standing pride, their system of silent, group work in factories was prevailing nationally and prisons along the Auburn model had mushroomed throughout the United States.[25] But in spring 1846, Auburn's dominance was eroding.

Five European nations had recently sent envoys to the United States to evaluate the two systems. Four "reported warmly and decidedly in favor" of Pennsylvania, while only one ("cautiously and qualifiedly") favored Auburn. According to Dorothea Dix, Pennsylvania's "superior advantages" influenced prisons in Belgium, Prussia, Hungary, Scotland, France, Germany, England, and elsewhere. In France alone, Dix noted in 1845, "more than thirty prisons are in progress of construction, or completed, on the Pennsylvania plan." The Prison Association of New York was forced to admit that public support for the local system had been "shaken," belief in the "infallibility of the system of Auburn has been done away with," and Pennsylvania's system was "gaining ground every day." The threat to Auburn worsened when the Prison Discipline Society, which had been the Auburn System's greatest champion, splintered. Three of the Prison Discipline Society's most celebrated members — Samuel Gridley Howe, Charles Sumner, and Horace Mann — wrote a critique of the Auburn System and a blistering attack on the Prison Discipline Society for supporting it.[26]

The rivalry between Pennsylvania and Auburn centered on precisely the two issues that Freeman raised: money and morality. By the first measure, Auburn won: most people acknowledged that prisons using the Auburn System ran more cheaply and could even enrich state coffers (although, to Auburn's humiliation, other prisons using its system were showing better profits than the original). The moral high ground, however, seemed to be Pennsylvania's. The Pennsylvania System was invented by Quaker reformers with the redemption of prisoners as its primary goal. In contrast, the Auburn System was created by businessmen with capitalist goals. But Auburn strained to compete by this measure, too. In the three decades since the Auburn Prison opened, some agents, including Gershom Powers and later Henry Polhemus, tried to introduce reformist goals into the capitalist enterprise. These agents had some success, as when Polhemus improved heat, bedding, and nutrition — which benefited Freeman. Powers, who succeeded Elam Lynds in 1826, believed that Christianity and education could reform the prisoners. For that reason, he engaged chaplains, distributed Bibles, promoted literacy, lessened physical punishment, and permitted prisoners to communicate with their family (which Lynds had forbidden). Auburn's supporters used these accomplishments to claim that the profit-seeking prison, as much as its counterpart in Pennsylvania, successfully rehabilitated criminals.[27]

Freeman's case undermined these claims. As the Reverend Winfield preached at the Van Nests' funeral, Freeman had been "in the school of a state prison for five years, and yet comes out a murderer!" Newspapers jumped on board: the Auburn State Prison, they repeated, far from providing a "reforming process," only "proved to be worse than in vain."[28]

Freeman's failed redemption was especially devastating because it magnetized with another narrative: that of Jacob (or Jack) Hodges, a Black man convicted of murder who was incarcerated at Auburn during Gershom Powers's administration. In an idealized story that Christian reformist publications repeated for decades, the Auburn State Prison transformed Hodges from a "wicked, drunken … Negro" into a penitent, sober, "very humble Christian." The prison's factory labor, reformers said, helped Hodges avoid temptation. In nightly solitary confinement, Hodges "communed alone with his own heart and his Saviour, and here he was satisfied." Even the prison's architecture contributed to Hodges's conversion: his cell was a "dark abode of penitence and searchings after God, where light had broken upon his mind, [and] he had met Jesus and found peace to his soul." The stories often quoted Hodges as saying, "I love every stone of this building." Reformers said that Hodges's transformation remained stable after his release from the Auburn State Prison because he "never associated with the people of his own colour." Hodges avoided Black people, reformers claimed, to resist being "led" back to the "former habits" that had resulted in "misery and guilt." Thus he remained a "pious old colored man" until his death in 1842.[29]

Hodges's narrative—echoing across church pulpits, reprinted and recirculated by the American Sunday-School Union and many other sources—made him the nation's most famous Black prisoner throughout the 1830s and early 1840s. The story of a Black man converted by the Auburn State Prison from a remorseless murderer to a pious Christian scored ample points in the contest with Pennsylvania. The Prison Discipline Society made Hodges a prime example of Auburn's power to reform criminals. On Hodges's death, the society's founding leader, Louis Dwight, acquired the Bible by which Hodges had been converted at Auburn; Dwight then used it as a spectacular prop in public lectures about the reformatory power of the Auburn State Prison. Hodges's reformation even delivered a win to the Democrats who controlled the prison throughout his incarceration—including Martin Van Buren, then New York's Democratic governor, who pardoned Hodges.[30]

William Freeman almost perfectly duplicated, but then reversed, stories of Jacob Hodges. Freeman was said to grow up, in words used to describe Hodges, "without education or moral restraint," influenced by the "ignorance, or wickedness of his parents" as well as other "poor coloured children."[31] Freeman, like Hodges, served at Auburn under a reform-minded agent who sincerely tried to layer spiritual redemption atop the prison's profit-driven foundation. In prison, Freeman, like Hodges, had access to Bibles, church services, and chaplains. Like Hodges, he experienced the nightly isolation that could, reformers insisted, induce penitence. After their respective releases, however, the two men's paths could not have diverged more.

Neither prosecution nor defense ever whispered Hodges's name— indeed, they had every motivation not to. But the parallels between Freeman and his famous forebear were unavoidable. This raised a question: if the Auburn System's reformatory power was proven by Jacob Hodges, why did it fail with William Freeman? Did Freeman's story refute that of Hodges? Together, the prosecution and defense parried these questions by focusing on the difference between the men's stories. Hodges, his white biographers insisted, retained the redemption he found in the Auburn Prison by avoiding other African Americans.[32] In contrast, Freeman tried to rejoin the New Guinea community after his release from prison. This gave both prosecution and defense a new target.

Blaming Black Women

Seward put Sally Freeman, William's mother, on the stand. Weeping, she testified that her son changed while in prison, becoming deaf and insane. She acknowledged that he had lived with white employers from the age of nine and that she saw him infrequently from that time forward. Moreover, she did not visit him in prison, and "since he came out I don't think he has been to see me more than six times." For two months prior to the murders, she said, they had had no contact.[33]

Seward used this testimony in two distinct ways. He sentimentalized Sally Freeman as a "truthful woman" of "decency, modesty, and propriety"; a mother who "utters the voice of NATURE," the "guardian whom God assigned to study, to watch, to learn, to know what the Prisoner was, and is, and to cherish the memory of it forever." But Sally Freeman, in Seward's portrait, was no generic mother. Rather, because of her "mingled blood of the African and Indian races," she was, Seward argued, a pathetic victim who was inadequate to her God-given responsibilities. "The white man enslaved her ancestors of the one race, exiled and destroyed those of the other, and debased them all by corrupting their natural and healthful appetites"—that is, by introducing them to alcohol. Seward argued that Sally Freeman drank because of historical white misdeeds, "yet when she comes here to testify for a life that is dearer to her than her own, to say she knows her own son, the white man says she is a drunkard! May Heaven forgive the white man for adding this last, this cruel injury to the wrongs of such a mother!"[34] With this argument, Seward both did and did not blame Sally Freeman: she was an intemperate and neglectful mother, but only for the same reason that her son had killed the Van Nests: victimization by white society combined with her inherent racial weakness. A totalizing picture of a good-hearted but ultimately pathetic victim.

In contrast, Van Buren treated Freeman's mother with unmixed scorn. In his portrait, Sally Freeman left her son "utterly uncared for." He argued that Freeman, like many members of his family, was a drunkard, and that much of Freeman's erratic behavior could be explained through a combination of intemperance and racial inferiority. What one of Seward's medical experts called Freeman's "Restless nights—Insanity" should, Van Buren argued, be called "Negro Frolic—Rum."[35]

The Black community was further targeted when Deborah De Puy took the stand for the defense. In response to Seward's initial questions, she testified that her friend and brother-in-law had changed while in prison. She repeated her points from the preliminary trial, describing a boy who had been playful and smart but was transformed by prison into a man who spoke only when spoken to and who "didn't act cheerful, but very stupid" and "had a strange smile."[36] When the prosecution cross-examined Deborah De Puy, however, the trial took an unexpected turn. The prosecution asked not about Freeman, but about her husband, Hiram De Puy, the brother of John De Puy. Where, the prosecution asked, did Hiram De Puy live?

"He lives where I do, of course."

"Then you live together."

"I don't know as it is any body's business whether we do or not." At this moment, some spectators in the courtroom must have wondered where the prosecutor was heading. Why should anyone care if Deborah De Puy lived with her husband?

The prosecution continued with exaggerated politeness. "Well, Deborah, I thought that perhaps you would oblige me so much as to answer that."

"Yes we do; but I can't answer any more questions."

The prosecutor's next question seemed to move in a new direction. "Never mind, Deborah, we've got along with that, and will turn to a more agreeable subject. Do you recollect when you were married?"

By getting Deborah De Puy to acknowledge that she lived with Hiram, the prosecution had led her into a trap, because she was not, in fact, legally married. The prosecution was trying to use that fact to smear her and discredit her testimony.

Deborah De Puy deflected by answering one question with another. "Do you s'pose I'm going to answer such questions?"

"Yes; I rather supposed you would like to tell me about that."

"Suppose I couldn't tell?" A second question in response to a question.

"Suppose you should try?"

A third: "Well, s'pose I shouldn't?"

"I think you had better tell me that, Deborah."

Deborah De Puy now faced an impossible choice: she could admit on the stand that she lived with a man to whom she was not legally married, or she could claim a legal marriage and commit perjury. Having exhausted the strategy of answering questions with questions, Deborah De Puy now stalled by criticizing the prosecutor's request: "I shan't answer such foolish questions."

"Will you tell me where you were married?" the prosecution insisted.

Deborah De Puy dodged perjury: "If you'll come down to my house, I'll tell you all about it, but I won't here."

The prosecution would not relent. "It may be inconvenient for me to come, Deborah, and therefore I shall have to insist upon your answering me now."

"Well, I shall not."

At that point, the court instructed Deborah De Puy to answer the prosecution's question. But she continued to resist: "I couldn't tell you where I was married."

"Did you have a large wedding party on the occasion?"

"I couldn't tell you how large the wedding was...."

"Can you tell who performed the marriage ceremony?"

"I couldn't."[37]

The prosecution abandoned the issue, but it had made its point: Deborah De Puy was discredited, in Van Buren's racial term, as "an unchaste black" and Sally Freeman as a drunkard.[38] Both, the prosecution suggested, were immoral women who exemplified the inadequacy of Black families, Black freedom, Blackness itself.

Throughout this onslaught, however, Deborah De Puy stood strong. She neither acknowledged her unformalized marriage nor committed perjury. Thus she proved herself as resistant and unyielding as her brother-in-law and friend William Freeman.

Inventing Black Criminality

The focus on Black women enabled the prosecution and defense both to libel Black families, and by extension, communities overall, as immoral and inadequate—and therefore unfit to educate their own children. And miseducation, both sides agreed further, caused crime. As Van Buren put it, because Freeman was, as a boy, "unrestrained" by school or parents, he "naturally end[ed] by being a criminal man." Seward agreed: "Neglect of education is a fruitful cause of Crime." Freeman "was a bright, cheerful, happy child," Seward said, who became violent because "there has been no school here for children of his caste. A school for colored children was never established here, and all the common schools were closed against them."[39] Prosecution and defense agreed, then, that Black people needed white assistance and supervision—without which they would commit crimes. In both narratives, Freeman's murders proved that white people needed to control Black lives.

Importantly, neither Seward nor Van Buren suggested that poor education might cause *some* Black children to become criminals in the *future*. Rather, the prosecution and the defense agreed that *all* Black children possessed the quality of criminal potential in the *present*. Therefore, in the wake of Northern slavery, the state needed to construct new controls over *all* Black youth. If the state failed to do so, this narrative suggested, Black children's criminal potential would inevitably find expression in crimes such as William Freeman's. Thus both sides in the trial generalized from Freeman's individual crimes to imagine something broader: Black "criminality."

Weeks earlier, the abolitionist periodical the *Liberator* had fretted that because Freeman "happened to have a colored skin, no doubt the wicked persecutors of the colored people will hold them all responsible" for his crimes. The trial realized these fears. In his closing, Van Buren railed against "the crimes which this race commits." "This race"—not Freeman, the individual. The language of the courtroom reverberated with that of the newspapers, which constantly referred to "the Negro Freeman." Sometimes Freeman's race even obliterated his name, as when newspapers referred to "the Negro murderer." The newspapers, Seward, and Van Buren all associated criminality with Blackness, making Freeman representative of all Black freemen.[40]

Verdict and Sentencing

On Thursday July 23, after deliberating two hours, the jury found Freeman guilty of murder. At 6:30 a.m. on Friday July 24, Freeman was brought back to the courthouse for sentencing. Despite the early hour, the courthouse was "filled to overflowing, a large portion of the audience being ladies." Freeman kept his face impassive, which prompted different interpretations. A newspaper described him as "unconcerned as usual"; John Austin interpreted Freeman's flat affect as evidence that he could not comprehend the proceedings.[41]

Judge Whiting gestured for Freeman to approach the bench. Raising his voice, the judge asked, "Can you hear me?" In response, Freeman "turned his ear to the Judge as almost to touch his face." Whiting asked, even louder, "Do you hear me *now*?" Freeman nodded.[42]

"Do you remember John G. Van Nest?" Whiting asked.

"Yes."

"Do you know you killed him?"

"Yes."

"Do you know you have been tried for killing him?"

"I don't know."

"Do you know you have been found guilty?"

"I don't know."

At this, Whiting pointed to the jury. "The jury, there, say you did kill him, and we are going to sentence you. Do you understand that?"

"I don't know."

"Do you know you are to be hanged? Do you even know that?"[43]

At this, Freeman appeared, to some, "very sensitive."[44] He spoke a single word: "Yes."

"Have you got anything to say against it—against being sentenced?"

"I don't know!"[45]

Whiting sent Freeman back to his seat and then delivered the sentence. As Austin noted that day in his journal, the format of the sentence was unusual because it "was not addressed to the prisoner at all," but instead to the crowd in the courtroom and to the greater society reading daily newspaper reports.[46]

Whiting's sentence unfolded as a story. He described Freeman's youth and conviction for horse theft, then narrated, step by step, Freeman's preparation of weapons, his murder of the Van Nest family "with savage ferocity," and his escape.[47] Whiting commended the prosecution's medical experts, "some of whom have known him from childhood, both in and out of the prison," who "testified that they never had discovered or suspected anything like insanity in his conduct before the murder." And finally, he praised the "intelligent and conscientious jury" that heard "all the proof adduced to sustain his defense of insanity" and "decided that he was not insane, but a responsible man." Whiting registered the court's agreement with this verdict from the preliminary hearing and its affirmation in the second, noting that Freeman's "whole defense has rested on his alleged insanity. And after twenty-four men"—the juries for the preliminary and main trials—"have said upon oath he is sane, it is to be hoped that those who have heretofore doubted it, will yield to an opinion thus carefully formed and solemnly expressed."[48]

Until this point, Whiting affirmed the prosecution's case. But now, in a twist, he endorsed one of Seward's key points. "The lessons to be drawn from this tragic event are many," Whiting said. "The most impressive one is, that there is a duty upon society to see to the moral cultivation of the colored youth, now being educated for good or evil in the midst of us. This is so obvious that it needs no comment."[49] Seward's and Austin's argument that white neglect of "duty" toward Black people caused crime, which was novel and controversial at the start of the trial, became, by its end, common sense—that which is "so obvious that it needs no comment."

After delivering this judgment, Whiting condemned William Freeman to death. A "demoniacal shout issued from a portion of the immense crowd," one newspaper reported.[50] Which portion of the crowd? And what was the cry? Triumph and relief? Anger? Grief?

Freeman showed no emotion.[51] Perhaps he could not hear Whiting's words. Perhaps he expected and was prepared for them. Or perhaps he took one more opportunity to refuse the white populace a satisfying, melodramatic display.

The case seemed closed. Freeman was to die by hanging on the afternoon of September 18, eleven days shy of his twenty-second birthday. But the trial produced far more than a verdict. It distracted from Freeman's challenge to the Auburn System by unfurling two stories about Blackness: one of social deprivation, the other of inherent menace. One of a pathetic, damaged victim who deserved pity, the other of a vicious, dangerous villain who warranted contempt and punishment. These stories appeared to be rivals, but in fact they supported each other: both asserted an inherent Black inferiority and therefore the need for white control in the postslavery North. In Freeman's trial, these stories were told by the former governor and the son of the former president, confirmed by expert testimony, delivered by telegraph to tabloids across the United States, reprinted and circulated in thousands of pamphlets. These stories were now loose in the world, available as resources for other people to refashion for their own, sometimes unexpected, purposes.

CHAPTER NINE

Roads over Trails

At 7:30 p.m. on October 23, 1846, a white man stepped onto the stage of a dark auditorium. Twelve immense paintings hung on the stage's rear and side walls, forming a ring around the man's body. He was there to tell stories. Eight of the paintings—illustrations for his tales—depicted events from the Bible and US history. And four showed, scene by bloody scene, "the Murder of the Van Nest Family by the negro Freeman."[1]

Two musicians—on cornet and accordion—joined the man on stage. The audience of women, men, and children waited. Who were they? White tourists, certainly—people traveling to and from Niagara Falls, people who visited Auburn to view its famous prison and related attractions. White townspeople, certainly—the same ones who crowded the courtroom during the trial barely three months earlier. Many, likely, who pressed into the Cayuga County Jail to interrogate and taunt Freeman. Some, perhaps, who had hung nooses from trees in Fleming and Auburn or tried to wrest Freeman from the sheriff's wagon.

The musicians played a few opening notes. The audience hushed.

The man's name was George Mastin. He was white, thirty-two years old, and unmarried. While working, reluctantly, as a tailor of men's clothes, he lived with the family of his older brother, Selah, in Genoa, a small farming community twenty miles south of Auburn. But Mastin's ambitions extended beyond Genoa's farms, its sparse scattering of churches and general stores, and its only notable industry, the Stevens

Thrasher Works.[2] George Mastin longed for something grander: show business. When the Van Nests died, George Mastin saw his opportunity.

Show business was making fortunes throughout the North. New York supported a stampede of traveling entertainers—each one promising delight or fascination, edifying high culture or thrilling sensationalism. Troupes of actors lugged costumes and sets across the state, staging melodramas, classics, and minstrel shows. Lecturers traveled from town to town, arousing audiences with speeches about abolition and temperance, science and religion. Itinerant phrenologists cupped the bumps on people's heads and then delivered flattering assessments of each person's character. Circuses and traveling menageries brought New York's villagers nose to nose with elephants, monkeys, and camels.[3]

These performances were possible because they followed routes that the nations of the Haudenosaunee had engineered over centuries. The trails were among the assets that John Hardenbergh and his comrades had seized during Sullivan's Campaign and other acts of genocide. One of the most important routes was the Great Genesee Trail, which connected Haudenosaunee communities along an east–west pole from Oneida, across the Owasco Outlet, and on to the Genesee River. The Haudenosaunee designed trails for single-file foot traffic, but as non-Natives pressed westward, they felled trees and pulverized underbrush to accommodate their wagons' width.[4] By the 1830s, many trails had become well-traveled turnpikes that were vital to New York's economy—and available to roaming storytellers like George Mastin.

Mastin seized the prosecution's narrative of Freeman's inherent brutality and poured it into a theatrical format that was then as profitable as it was popular: a show-and-tell performance involving large-scale paintings, known as a *cantastoria*. He commissioned local painters to create monumental paintings—some as large as eight feet tall by ten feet wide.[5] He packed his paintings in a wagon and then traveled about New York State—first with his brother Selah and a friend, later with other family assistants. Over the next four decades, Mastin would follow a routine. He would enter a town and hang his giant paintings in a tavern, church social hall, or museum. Then, in a nighttime performance, he held a candelabra up to each painting, illuminating it in the flicker of nearly two dozen flames. While his assistants played dramatic background music, Mastin told stories of Jesus Christ's temptation, Indian attacks, and the American Revolution. The performance climaxed with scenes of William Freeman's crimes and punishment.

Previously, scenes of Black-on-white violence were nearly unknown, even taboo, on the American stage. Theaters avoided such images because they were intolerably threatening. Black-on-white violence was a daily-felt possibility: white Americans trembled in response to Denmark Vesey's attempted slave revolt of 1822, David Walker's *Appeal* to armed uprising in 1829, Nat Turner's Rebellion of 1831, Madison Washington's shipboard slave revolt of 1841, and a rush of attempted uprisings in 1846 in Florida, Louisiana, Virginia, and Tennessee.[6] The possibility of Black-on-white violence haunted white people. Most did not want to think about it, much less watch it played out by live actors. American theaters therefore took elaborate measures to avoid staging Black-on-white violence. Even in *Othello*, which traveling actors performed in Auburn in 1838 and 1840, they found ways to avoid this spectacle. During the early nineteenth century, American theaters sidestepped this play's Black-on-white violence by representing the title character as *not* Black: they costumed Othello as an "Arab" and painted the white actor's face to look not dark but rather "tawny."[7] This version of Othello was an exotic who visually asserted that he was *not* African American. White America wanted to see African Americans as they appeared in minstrel shows: comic, dim-witted, and perhaps sentimental, but never dangerous.

George Mastin upended this norm. His show drew on the story of inherent Black criminality as voiced by the prosecution and Democrat-led newspapers. But he layered this narrative over older tales of Indian-on-white attacks. The result was a shocking, three-dimensional spectacle of violence that taught white New Yorkers a new way to imagine Black people—and themselves.

Mastin before Freeman

George Mastin was born in 1814 in Ulster County—the birthplace of William Freeman's grandparents Harry and Kate, as well as the Hardenberghs who enslaved them. His family migrated from Ulster County to Genoa in about 1828, when Mastin was fourteen years old.[8] His siblings became farmers and businesspeople. But George, who was the youngest of six sons (and second youngest of eight children), was the family's free spirit. Ambitious yet distractible, with grandiose visions but little facility with details, Mastin was susceptible to enthusiasms. Spiritualism and phrenology entranced him.[9]

Sometime around 1835, long before he ever heard of William Freeman, Mastin began laying plans for a future in show business. He had the skills to entertain audiences: he knew hundreds of "jigs and reels" that he would play from memory on his fiddle "so fast you couldn't whistle and keep up with him," and he could perform phrenological examinations. Mastin was a commanding presence: tall and broad-shouldered, with dramatic eyebrows over heavy-lidded eyes. In a photograph of Mastin late in life, he appears serious, with an unfocused gaze. But those who knew him enthused about his "wonderful personality," shining cheer, exceptional powers of memory, and relish for music and dance. Mastin designed a show that incorporated all these elements: a show-and-tell with paintings on well-liked, familiar subjects, followed by phrenological demonstrations and music for social dancing.[10]

Mastin chose stories and illustrations from books and from the *Family Magazine*.[11] He hand-copied his scripts from these sources and hired folk artists to reproduce the illustrations on a large scale. The paintings and stories were calculated to arouse the pride of his targeted audience: rural New Yorkers. One painting showcased the region's grandest natural spectacle and reliable crowd-pleaser, Niagara Falls. Two celebrated military heroes of the American Revolution. And two showed Indians threatening white Americans. In this initial set of painting-stories, one was special because it united Mastin's themes of New York, the Revolution, and white resistance to Indians. This painting depicted the murder of Jane McCrea (plate 3).

Jane McCrea was a white Tory who in 1777 traveled from New Jersey to New York State to meet with a British officer she likely intended to marry. She reached her destination and waited for her man. Soon,

FIGURE 9.1 *George Mastin Late in Life*

Unidentified photographer, Mastin Collection, photographic print, Fenimore Art Museum, Cooperstown, NY.

a group of Huron-Wendat Native Americans arrived and promised to escort her to the British regiment. Because they were allied with the British, McCrea trusted them and went willingly. The Huron-Wendats then shot and scalped her. The reasons for the killing were unclear. Most likely, the shooting was accidental and the purpose of the postmortem scalping was to collect a British bounty. However, the murder-mutilation of Jane McCrea inflamed anti-Indian racism in the emerging nation. Dozens of newspapers, poems, songs, stage plays, and novels (most notably James Fenimore Cooper's *The Last of the Mohicans*) retold the story. The most critically acclaimed visual image of McCrea was John Vanderlyn's painting, *The Murder of Jane McCrea*.

FIGURE 9.2 *The Death of Lucinda*

Robert Smirke, in Joel Barlow, *The Columbiad: A Poem* (Philadelphia; Conrad, Lucas and Co., 1807), facing 238.

But the most widely circulated and often-imitated picture was an 1807 book illustration by Robert Smirke.[12] One echo of Smirke's image appeared in an 1835 issue of the *Family Magazine*, where Mastin encountered it. These retellings collectively reduced complex historical events to a story of white feminine innocence versus Indian savagery, good

FIGURE 9.3 *Murder of Miss Jane M'Crea, at Fort Edward, N.Y.*

MURDER OF MISS JANE M'CREA, at Ford Edward, N. Y

Family Magazine, June 1835, 1.

assailed by evil, trust betrayed. For many, Jane McCrea's death proved that alliances across race were impossible: racial divisions constituted an inherent, permanent threat to white life.[13]

But as the story replicated over decades, its meaning changed. By the time Mastin read about McCrea in the *Family Magazine,* the Revolution was won and the murder was more than two generations past. No longer a call for retribution, the story had become a celebration of past white heroism in the face of atrocity. Jane McCrea may have perished, the tale suggested, but white civilization endured and triumphed. For this reason, representations of past Native-on-white violence proliferated while images of Black-on-white violence—which was perceived as a *current* threat—were absent from the American stage.

Mastin narrated the story of Jane McCrea to emphasize polarized racial violence, as was standard. His script described her as "youth and innocence" destroyed by "savage" Indians who embodied "cruelty and violence." Mastin made his retelling unique, however, by pairing it with a second, amplifying tale of Native American aggression against white people: the less-known story of Milly Francis. In a story that Mastin adapted from a history by Henry Trumbull, Francis's tribe captured and attempted to kill a white man, but Francis saved his life (the story was often likened to that of Pocahontas). Soon thereafter, Francis's unnamed tribe itself crumbled: unable to care for themselves, these Indians were reduced to "a starving condition" and were forced to "surrender themselves" and become "prisoners" of the white people they had previously threatened.[14] Mastin implied that the tribe collapsed naturally, inevitably, due to inherent Indian weakness. Thus Francis's story supplied what McCrea's lacked: an ending in which white people survive while Indians quietly, bloodlessly, disappear.

Mastin designed his cycle of history paintings and scripts to tell New Yorkers a heroic story about themselves: their origins, their enemies, their victories, their destiny. He harnessed the majesty of Niagara Falls and the triumph of the American Revolution. He crossed these arousals of pride with racial melodrama. These stories teased: they aroused racial fear but then quelled it, reassuring the white audience that the danger was long past, the Revolution complete. Most of all, these obsessive revisitations of Indian-on-white violence erased the *reasons* for that violence. By cropping out the context of white-perpetrated genocide, these tales suggested that Indian-on-white attacks were unprovoked, senseless—the result of inherent Indian savagery rather than a response to settler colonialism. Thus Mastin's paintings of Jane McCrea and Milly Francis reconfigured white violence as white victimhood.

FIGURE 9.4 *Burning of American Captive at the Stake*

Milly Francis entreats her father to spare the life of a white man. Ca. 1846, un-identified artist, Mastin Collection, oil on bed ticking, H: 84 × W: 104 in., Farm-ers' Museum, Cooperstown, NY, museum purchase, F0114.1954. Photograph by Richard Walker.

Mastin collected these stories and commissioned the accompany-ing paintings one after another. The paintings accrued in his brother's home, each one rolled up inside a custom-made wooden box. For the decade following 1835, the boxes stacked up. The performance circuit beckoned to Mastin, but for reasons unknown he seems to have re-mained in Genoa, his paintings boxed and unseen. But when William Freeman killed the Van Nests, he inadvertently gave Mastin's show what it needed: a climax, and even more important, a revised message.

Mastin must have recognized the murders as compatible with the stories his history paintings told. Like Jane McCrea, the Van Nests suffered a fate that was widely known and hideous. And both events accrued meaning as tales of white vulnerability to nonwhite violence. Moreover, each incited white outrage. But the story of William Freeman was also groundbreaking: the new menace was not solely Native American but instead of mixed Native American and Black heritage. It was a story not of New York's Revolutionary past but its revolutionary present—and therefore its potential future. Most important, the new threat seemed to demand a new solution: one executed not through military decimation but instead through criminal justice.

Mastin rushed to procure source material. He lifted a script and image from a Democrat-leaning newspaper. His painters hastily created four new canvases. Through the murder of the Van Nests, Mastin would tell white New Yorkers a story about themselves that was new yet hauntingly familiar.

Mastin on Stage

Off stage, Mastin could claim few accomplishments. But when he finally mounted the stage after a decade's delay, he became sorcerer-king. He tantalized. He thundered. His written script consisted of faithfully transcribed articles and Bible verses, but Mastin, like preachers at the Spiritualist meetings he cherished, welcomed inspiration. His voice, his oratorical style, echoes through a letter Mastin wrote to his niece:

> I profess to Be a Bible Spiritualist I think The Bible is an in spired book I think that Our Spirts ar with us Garding our foot steps from day to day I believe in Healing Spirits and a Phroffisizing Spirit And a Healing spirit And a desrner of spirits.[15]

I think, I think, I believe ... Mastin's rolling repetitions welcomed healing spirits, prophesizing spirits, and more. He believed these eternal companions literally to surround him, protect him, propel him. This certainty filled his show with the rhythms, sounds, and religious ecstasy of a revival meeting.

Mastin stood before paintings of people that were, as his advertisement promised, "as large as life."[16] And indeed, the scale itself created a sense of aliveness. As Mastin stood before each painting to illuminate it by the candles' flicker, he was scaled to appear to be in the garden with Adam and Eve, alongside Jesus blessing the children, third wheel to Christ and the devil. As Mastin shifted from his paintings of religious subjects to those of American history, he slipped among Jane McCrea and her malefactors, then entered the crowd of exulting Indians as Milly Francis saved a white man from being burned. Mastin tilted his candelabra toward the characters and the candles flickered—which created the special-effect illusion of motion, of quivering, breathing life.

The setting for Mastin's performance imbued the canvases with yet more liveliness. Mastin launched his tour at Chedell's Museum, Auburn's showcase for specimens of nature and world culture. To reach the museum's auditorium, Mastin's audience walked past fossils, Chinese art, a sperm whale's lower jaw, and taxidermy reportedly including five hundred birds. At the "world in miniature" of Chedell's, potentially frightening displays such as an Egyptian mummy were commodified as entertainment. In Mastin's paintings, Indians raised two-dimensional axes and daggers against their white victims. Meanwhile, mere yards away, Chedell displayed Indian "War Clubs [and] Battle-axes": three-dimensional weapons with wear that suggested they had been used exactly as Mastin visualized.[17] Mastin's history paintings set alongside Chedell's artifacts cotestified: the Indian threat to the white race was horrific and real, but it was past—vanquished, controlled, and now confined behind museum glass. The more hyperbolic the claim of Indian savagery, the more glorious the implied white victory.

But now, Mastin intoned, a new, dark threat had arisen. Mastin's handwritten script records the words with which he introduced his next painting: "This is a Repersentation of the Murder of the Vannest family. By a Negro."[18]

The audience must have gasped as Mastin illuminated his first painting in the William Freeman sequence.[19] This was the melodrama they had come to see: Freeman on the attack; Sarah Van Nest, pregnant, stabbed, and fleeing; Phebe Wyckoff battling Freeman knife for knife (plate 4).

Many members of Mastin's Auburn audience would have recognized the painting's source: a woodcut published in their local newspaper shortly after the murders (figure 6.1). The journalistic reference affirmed the verity of Mastin's spectacle. But the twice-seen image— now in color and eight feet tall—must also have caused Mastin's first painting to trigger a shock of memory, a cognitive transportation from October back to that terrible March when each day's newspaper delivered a fresh set of shattering details.

The newspapers had pictured the Van Nests' home and Freeman in his cell, but none had visually represented the bloodshed. Even images of Indian-on-white violence, which were so familiar to Mastin's audience, seldom showed blood (Jane McCrea was typical in this way: Mastin, like Vanderlyn and Smirke, showed her in the moment *before* a bullet and a knife ruptured her white skin). But Mastin's first painting of William Freeman smashed that taboo (plate 5).

As Mastin moved his candelabra to the next painting, his assistants probably swelled their music to a crescendo. The show's climax had arrived. Candlelight flickered, and the audience saw William Freeman creeping toward George Van Nest while the boy's father lay dead on the floor (plate 6). The previous painting had shown blood from a distance, the figures miniaturized. But the bedroom scene plunged the audience back into the scale of the human body. The audience saw Mastin *in* the bedroom with the murderer and the baby.

At this point, the audience surely booed the villain, as was customary. Months earlier, Auburnites had mobbed the sheriff's wagon shouting, "Tear him limb from limb—roast him alive!" Now, when they saw Freeman's likeness on stage, large as life and quivering before Mastin's candles, they likely frothed with the same demand: "Hang him!" Mastin seemed to expect this vitriol because he warned in his advertisement, "Individuals using vulgar language in the Room will forfeit their admission."[20]

Mastin's candelabra drew audience members' eyes from Freeman's bloody knife to its quietly slumbering target: George, his face, arm, and chest an exposure of white, swaddled in the layered whiteness of sheets and nightclothes. George's luminous pale chest resembled that of Jane McCrea, who remained dimly visible to Mastin's audience even as the candelabra tilted at other paintings. George and McCrea formed a pair: each threatened by a dark-skinned man with a long knife, each pictured in the moment immediately before death. All that Jane McCrea had symbolized since 1777—white innocence in the face of Indian savagery, good versus evil, and the inevitability of racial betrayal—now flowed into the mirrored figure of George. And Mastin reminded his audience that George's fate was as brutal as McCrea's: Freeman "discovered the Little boy George W. Vanest, asleep in bed," Mastin recited, "and stabbed him with such unabated ferocity that the knife Passed Entirely through his body."[21]

George's sleep amplified the scene's horror. But the boy's obliviousness also had a second utility: it was a crucial component of his innocence. In Mastin's painting, George was not simply innocent; he was innocent *of* the dagger above him. In the mid-nineteenth century, this obliviousness had special importance because it defined childhood innocence—the child's "holy ignorance," as one writer put it.[22] Jane McCrea, a white *adult* innocent, was aware of impending violence: she looked with terror at the man who was about to kill her. But George never glimpsed his attacker. The paintings of George and McCrea equally emphasized the figures' white innocence, but the painting of George intensified that effect by locating it in an unknowing child rather than an aware adult. The painting of George Van Nest weaponized the 1840s concept of childhood ignorance-innocence by welding it to a racial claim. On this canvas, childhood innocence warped into racial innocence.

This racial innocence was what white Auburn wanted for itself. The same people who, through great effort, avoided hearing William Freeman's critique of Auburn's system of prison for profit now paid to gaze at a babe who had no misdeeds to forget. George, who was asleep, made no effort to not-see; his serene ignorance-innocence seemed as natural, as essential, as his youth, as his pale skin. The painting was a racial manifesto. It represented white Auburn's sharpest desire and fiercest fear, aquiver together in the glow of Mastin's candelabra.

Mastin's next painting raised the symbolic stakes even higher: it likened George to no less a figure than Jesus Christ (plate 7). In this third painting, which depicted the stabbing's aftermath, George and his surviving sister Julia quoted the *pietà*—the iconic scene, most famously cast in marble by Michelangelo, of Mary cradling Jesus after the crucifixion. The term *pietà* derives from the Italian word for pity or compassion. And indeed, that is what this painting called for: pity. But not for William Freeman, as Austin and the Sewards wanted. Instead, Mastin's *pietà* begged its audience for mercy for the Christlike, innocent white baby, a victim of dark savagery.

Mastin directed his audience's attention across the arrayed figures. At the painting's left, Helen Holmes attended to the suffering children. And to the right, Freeman returned to the house and peeked in the window, "still panting for Blood," Mastin recited, and brandishing his bloodstained knife. In a "show...of defiance," Freeman looked through the Van Nests' window into their home, but also, it seemed, *through* their home, into the audience.[23] A public that paid twenty-five cents to peep at Freeman in the Auburn State Prison factories now paid the identical sum to view Mastin's show in which Freeman peeped at them.

As Mastin emphasized, however, the image of Black "defiance" balanced against one of white resistance. This counteraction crystallized in the figure of Cornelius Van Arsdale, who slumped on the floor, severely wounded but alive. As Mastin regaled the crowd, Van Arsdale survived because he seized a candlestick and with it "succeeded...in driving" Freeman into retreat.[24] The painting did not depict that all-important candlestick. But it did not need to. The candlestick was present on stage: Mastin held one in his hand. Mastin's candelabra stood in for Van Arsdale's improvised weapon. He likely brandished his candelabra as he narrated Van Arsdale clubbing Freeman. Earlier in the show, when Mastin narrated his paintings of the Bible and American history, his candelabra had been a mere tool to deliver illumination and the special-effect quiver. But at this moment, the candelabra transformed into a prop, an animated element of the show, that seemed to have popped out of the painted scene and into three dimensions. And as Mastin's candleholder substituted for Van Arsdale's, Mastin himself assumed the role of the hardy farmhand—the sole person to survive Freeman's blows. In the painting, Van Arsdale appeared depleted, even half-dead. But Mastin was tall and robust. Shaking his candelabra in imitation of Van Arsdale's fight, he reminded Auburnites of the Cornelius Van Arsdale who survived and lived among them—and who might even have been in the audience. The slumped man in the painting and the dynamic man on the stage formed a before-and-after sequence: testimony to white strength and hope.

Mastin's final canvas depicted the outcome that Mastin assumed was inevitable and just: William Freeman at the gallows (plate 8). This painting took the previous work's racial terror of the Black gaze and neutralized it, relocating the power of looking both to the white figures who stared at the hooded, hanged Freeman and the white audience that inspected the painting. Mastin described the painting's characters, saying that Freeman, while incarcerated in the Auburn State Prison for horse theft, had "attempted on one occasion to durk [dirk] with a knife Mr. James E. Tyler one of the then assistant keepers." Mastin was silent, however, regarding Tyler's admitted beating of Freeman. Much as the third painting refuted Austin and the Sewards by assigning pity to George, not Freeman, the fourth painting and narration erased the violence against Freeman, including Tyler's deafening blow. Mastin then likely pointed to the smiling African American figure and identified him as Nathaniel Hersey, a friend of Freeman who asserted, without corroboration, that Freeman had "meant to kill [John] depuy." Mastin then added, in one of the very few lines not lifted from the newspaper article, "This is the character of the murderer freeman [*sic*]."[25]

Mastin's script did not mention one of the painting's most striking figures: the young white ruffian picking a pocket. Most likely, Mastin improvised some commentary. Later in the century, urban youths working as pickpockets would be considered a serious social problem. But when Mastin took the stage in 1846, they were still largely regarded as "urchins," a mostly benign, if pesky, element of metropolitan life.[26] At this moment, the pickpocket represented less a criminal threat than Auburn's success as an urban center, a city of activity and importance. And even as this painting caught the impoverished boy in the commission of a crime and thus associated him with the hanging man, it also likened the pickpocket to George Van Nest. The pickpocket's open white blouse and bare feet and chest linked him visually to the toddler in the *pietà*. As that third painting had cried out for pity and mercy, this painting, too, demanded compassion—not for William Freeman, but for yet another white boy, who was depicted as innocent *even while he committed a crime*. The pickpocket visualized, in yet another way, white Auburn's fantasy of racial innocence despite all evidence of misdeeds.

Until this moment in the show, Mastin had grafted the prosecution's story of inherent Black violence onto older tales of Indian savagery. In both stories, racialized "others" attacked innocent, vulnerable white people—for no cause beyond the attackers' inherently violent nature. But this fourth painting swerved from the familiar plot by proposing a different ending. The stories of Jane McCrea and Milly Francis defined Indians as savages and as military enemies who deserved extermination. In contrast, Mastin's fourth painting of William Freeman pictured the gallows, that ultimate symbol of criminal justice fulfilled, as the proper resolution of the murder of the Van Nests.

This solution retroactively redefined the problem. Mastin's first three paintings of Freeman, much like Attorney General Van Buren's courtroom arguments, alleged inherent Black brutality—which differed little from alleged Indian savagery. But this fourth painting proposed a *legal* remedy rather than a military one, which redefined William Freeman himself: he was not only a Black brute; he was a Black *criminal*.

And not just *one* Black criminal. Many of Mastin's paintings depicted individuals, but each carried vast symbolic weight. Adam and Eve. Jesus Christ—blessing the children, tempted by the devil. George Van Nest—first serenely asleep, the quintessential innocent white child, then sacrificed, a *pietà*. An Indian's dark fingers crunching Jane McCrea's pale wrist. Good and evil, savagery and civilization, villainy and innocence, all wedged into the "world in miniature" of Chedell's Museum. In this context where *no* character existed solely as an individual, William Freeman *could not* represent simply himself, one criminal who was Black. In this context where every character symbolized a grand concept, William Freeman, too, took on symbolic power: he represented Black *criminality*. This symbolic character enabled Mastin in turn to tell white Auburnites a tale about their own *noncriminality*: although they lived on Indian land and prospered through forced prison labor, their vulnerability and victimhood proved their essential innocence.

Mastin's first three paintings of Freeman aroused terror, which the fourth painting sought to assuage: yes, this painting murmured, Black criminality was as dangerous as Indian savagery, but the Indians were extinct, their weapons safely behind museum glass, and in parallel, Black criminality could—must—be contained, controlled, by the criminal justice system. The fourth painting pictured that hope in the white frame of the gallows. The luminous rectangle at the painting's center delivered death to one Black criminal, but even more, it confined Black criminality. The image offered the reassuring ending the audience craved.

But this reassurance failed. It failed because when Mastin debuted his show at Chedell's Museum in October 1846, William Freeman was still alive.

Life

As extravagantly as Mastin imagined the death of William Freeman, he was forced to admit the truth: the murderer lived. William Freeman "was Centanced to Bhung on the 18th day of sept 1846 But he has had a new trial Granted and was not hung."[27]

When Mastin commissioned his paintings in spring 1846, he must have assumed that his work would depict an event that would occur by the time his show opened. But then that outcome slipped away—*for the second time*. The first rush of attempts to hang Freeman occurred days after the murders, at the Van Nest home and then at the Cayuga County Jail. There, white mobs raged not only against Freeman but also against a criminal justice system that had, in their view, abandoned them and left them vulnerable. As one would-be lyncher said, "We have no law; we tried it once; justice is denied us."[28] That day, the law protected Freeman, and the mob was forced to transfer its hanging-dreams to the legal realm. Perhaps George Mastin was one man in that mob. Perhaps he was not. But his fourth painting accurately pictured the lynchers' revised hope: that the legal system would delay but then deliver Freeman's death.

In Chedell's Museum, however, this painting exposed the opposite of what Mastin wanted to show: not a historical fact but a thwarted wish, a broken promise. Not a monument to white triumph but instead testimony to white failure. The painting of Jane McCrea visualized white victimization, but it ultimately asserted white victory and subsequent security. The paintings of William Freeman would have done the same—had he hanged.

The truth was not in Mastin's painting but in a jail cell less than two blocks away (figure 4.1). There, William Freeman sat, stony and chained and resolutely alive. Chedell's Museum and the Cayuga County Jail were both on West Genesee Street, barely a two-minute walk from each other. Some people in Mastin's audience may well have stared into Freeman's eyes earlier that day. As those individuals walked up West Genesee Street from the jail to Chedell's, they trod one short segment of a road built on, and named after, the Great Genesee Trail that John Hardenbergh and other soldiers seized from the Haudenosaunee.

By picturing William Freeman's death while admitting his ongoing life, Mastin inadvertently staged Freeman's triumphant escape—from the lynching tree *and* the state-sanctioned gallows. The show whispered ominously into white ears: *The Black predator kicks at your door. He peeks in your window. He escapes justice. What will you do?*

And then, George Mastin invited his audience to move.

He invited audience members to rise, to submit their own heads for phrenological examinations to confirm their fine characters, and finally, to dance. Mastin picked up his fiddle. His assistants stepped forward with accordion and cornet. Jigs and reels streamed from the trio—fast, lively, joyous. The audience flowed out of their seats and onto the stage. They danced. But their dancing, their pleasures, were framed by the paintings of William Freeman and his crimes, which still hung on the stage's walls. The paintings were scaled to admit Mastin into their scenes; now, the dancers saw each other enter the Garden of Eden, join the American Revolution, survive Indian savagery. They danced among George and John, Sarah and Phebe, Helen and Cornelius. They danced with a corpse that lived. They danced into a scene of white justice that never happened. They danced themselves into starring roles in an emerging drama: of Black criminality, of Black life as itself an escape from justice, of law as a new day's necessary tool of racial control. On a stage in a museum on a road built over a trail, they danced into a new old story about themselves as vulnerable and innocent and racially threatened.

CHAPTER TEN

Freedom after Freeman

After Freeman's trial, as newly crystallized stories of Black criminality and white victimhood traveled across New York and beyond, Black Auburnites faced hard questions: How to move forward? How could they live with these narratives? What could freedom be after Freeman?

Schools

On August 3, 1846—ten days after Freeman's trial ended—Joseph Pascal Thompson, the minister of Auburn's AME Zion Church, called on John Austin. He came because "Justice" had defined what Judge Whiting called the "lesson" to be drawn from Freeman's crime: that "there is a duty upon society to see to the moral cultivation of the colored youth."[1] AME Church leaders had forged a strategy: rather than repudiate this condescension, they would use it in a petition to the town government for funding for a schoolhouse for Black children. Thompson knocked on Austin's door to challenge him to back up his words with action: if Austin could blame Freeman's crimes on a lack of Black education in Auburn, then he could help fund a Black school.

The Black community astutely nominated one minister to represent the cause to another, clergy to clergy. But Thompson's call on Austin suggests an even more complex game. Thompson asked Austin for assistance drafting the petition. The request might seem surprising because Thompson was a well-educated physician and theologian who surely did not need Austin's help writing up the petition.[2] But it was

FIGURE 10.1 *Bishop Joseph P. Thompson, M.D., D.D.*

BISHOP JOSEPH P. THOMPSON, M.D., D.D.

J. W. Hood, *One Hundred Years of the African Methodist Episcopal Zion Church, or, The Centennial of African Methodism* (New York: AME Zion Book Concern, 1895).

canny for Thompson to flatter Austin, thus confirming the white minister's self-image as Black people's protector. Furthermore, Austin's court testimony had revealed he had the ear of the ex-governor. This association created opportunities for Black Auburnites: Austin could potentially attract other white elites to the fundraising effort.

Austin promised to help his fellow clergyman. Two days later, he conferred with Seward, and then, on the same day, drafted the petition to fund a school for Black children, as well as a new edifice for the AME Zion Church.[3]

With this strategically obtained white support, the Black community secured public funds. Auburn's Black school opened in September 1846, only two months after the end of Freeman's trial. Its initial Black leaders were all founders of Auburn's AME Zion Church. They included Jacob Jordan, an abolitionist, and Joseph W. Quincy, the barber who refused to shave Freeman and later testified for the prosecution. Among the school's first trustees was Charles Griffin, who would later write a powerful antiracist pamphlet that argued, in terms consonant with Freeman's, that every person, regardless of race, has "the right to eat the bread ... which his own hand earns." Black women, too, were surely involved with the mission and management of the school—either directly as fundraisers, educators, or administrators or indirectly as home-based workers who enabled husbands and sons to do public-facing work. Joseph P. Thompson's wife, Catherine Thompson, for example, was "deeply interested her husband's lifework." Known as a "great organizer" with "wonderful executive abilities," Catherine Thompson's "greatest delight was in Sunday school work."[4]

Members of the AME Zion Church also recruited white supporters beyond—and likely through—Austin and Seward. Of the school's white cofounders, all were in Seward's orbit and several contributed to his defense of Freeman. The school was authorized, for example, by Auburn's superintendent Charles A. Parsons, Seward's clerk, who testified at Freeman's trial. Alongside Charles Griffin, the school's initial trustees included three white men: John R. Hopkins, an abolitionist who called on Freeman in jail and then testified for the defense; Daniel Hewson, a neighbor and "warm personal friend" of Seward; and Israel F. Terrill, a businessmen associated with David Wright, the co-counsel in Freeman's defense.[5]

Soon, the idea to transform Austin's and Seward's narrative of victimhood into a tool for Black institution building reached as far north as Ontario, Canada. There, Josiah Henson—the abolitionist, minister, and self-freed man whom Harriet Beecher Stowe would soon cite as her model for Uncle Tom—was raising funds for a Manual Labour Normal School to serve the Black community. In January 1848 he traveled to Auburn and, like Thompson before him, knocked on Austin's door.

Henson might have heard about Auburn's new Black school. Auburn was a hub on the Underground Railroad, and fugitives from slavery, as well as their allies, traveled frequently between the city and points in Canada, including Dawn Township, where Henson lived.[6] These travelers could have carried news of Black Auburnites' success in raising a school. But Henson might also have conceived the idea independently, because Austin's and Seward's argument that miseducation caused

FIGURE 10.2 *Josiah Henson*

Frontispiece to Josiah Henson, *Truth Stranger Than Fiction: Father Henson's Story of His Own Life* (Boston: John P. Jewett and Company, 1858).

Black crime was disseminating widely. The Freeman trial elevated Austin to the national stage, and he became sought after as a speaker, consultant, and author. Seward's closing argument was published in pamphlet form and went through four reprints in as many months. Austin appointed himself a distributor of Seward's argument and people contacted him to obtain it.[7] As Austin spread his and Seward's ideas, he burnished his reputation and underscored his association with the ex-governor. But he also identified himself as a potential source of support for Black education—and therefore attracted people like Henson.

When Henson called, Austin invited him inside for lunch. The two ministers talked for four hours. Henson left, but he returned three months later. This time, he asked Austin for significant support: he wanted him to turn over his church the next Sunday for the purpose of a fundraising sermon. He also wanted to leave the money he had already raised with Austin for safekeeping. Clearly Henson viewed Austin as trustworthy (at least with a bundle of money) and as a gateway to white potential donors. Austin granted both requests. Henson delivered a sermon that took the form of an abolitionist lecture: he narrated his escape from slavery in Maryland and described life in his Canadian community of self-freed people. He raised $18.32. Henson remained in Auburn for four days and gave a second sermon at the First Presbyterian Church. As he raised more funds, he deposited the cash with Austin and ate more meals with him. He then collected his money and moved on. A year later, Henson published his autobiography, in which he described his fundraising efforts in New York and other states: during these "journeys ... I have found or made some friends to the cause, and, I hope, some personal friends," he wrote, adding, "I have received many liberal gifts, and experienced much kindness of treatment."[8] Henson, Thompson, and other members of the Black community chose not to refute the argument that poor education produces Black criminality. Instead, they challenged the minister to match his claims with "liberal gifts." Thus they fashioned Austin into a lever by which to raise Black schools.

Black Abolitionist Lecturers

Josiah Henson was not the only Black abolitionist to gravitate to Auburn after Freeman's trial. In the three years following 1846, at least eight Black abolitionists spoke in Auburn, some multiple times. They included some of the movement's brightest stars: not only Henson but also Henry Highland Garnet, Charles Lenox Remond, Samuel Ringgold Ward, and most of all, Frederick Douglass, who from 1847 through 1849 lectured annually in Auburn, despite apparently never having done so before. On a single day in 1848, Douglass, Remond, and Henson all spoke in Auburn simultaneously.[9]

This convergence constituted a striking change: prior to 1846, only one Black abolitionist—Samuel Ringgold Ward—seems to have lectured in Auburn. In contrast, many white abolitionists—most notably

Gerrit Smith—spoke in Auburn during the first half of the 1840s. The city even hosted a convention of white abolitionists in 1842. Meanwhile, Black abolitionists such as William Wells Brown, Charles Lenox Remond, J. C. Hathaway, and E. D. Hudson lectured all around Auburn—but not within its borders.[10] Prior to Freeman's crimes and trial, then, white Auburnites constituted a ready audience for abolitionist lectures and Black abolitionists lectured regularly *near* Auburn—but Black abolitionists showed little interest *in* Auburn.

Douglass and his colleagues never explained why Auburn suddenly became a priority for Black abolitionists. What is certain, however, is that shortly after Auburn's courthouse resounded with stories about Freeman as a vicious savage or a helpless lunatic, Frederick Douglass and other Black abolitionists chose Auburn as a site in which to tell their own stories. In Auburn, they narrated their lives on their own terms, describing their oppression in the context of their agency, their suffering as a force toward their political agenda.

Black Suffrage

In 1846, suffrage topped the political agenda for Black New Yorkers. They had organized around this issue since 1821, when an amendment to the New York State Constitution introduced a new requirement that Black men—but not white ones—must own $250 in property to qualify to vote. Before then, most free Black men had held the right to vote in New York. But the 1821 amendment revoked voting rights from almost all Black men; in the immediate Freeman family, for example, Luke alone was enfranchised.[11] In a massive organizing effort that intensified during the early 1840s, Black people petitioned to recover their voting rights. Largely due to Black activism, an amendment was advanced to reverse the 1821 measure and thus equalize voting rights for men regardless of race.[12] The amendment was scheduled for a vote in November 1846.

When Freeman murdered the Van Nests in March 1846, the impending vote was already subject to angry debate in Auburn.[13] One day before the murders, the Democrat-leaning *Cayuga Patriot* published a withering column against Negro suffrage. "Unfortunately," the columnist wrote, "we have in our midst a race of men" who are "far less virtuous and intelligent than our white population." For that reason, he claimed, "the negroes are not qualified for the privilege" of voting.[14]

For many Auburnites, such debates over Black male suffrage were the context for the murder of the Van Nests. Newspapers reported on the murders and their aftermath alongside coverage of the suffrage debate.[15] Seward worried that Freeman's crime would tip public sentiment against Black male voting. He wrote that the Democrats in Auburn "are playing on the prejudices of the Whigs against Negro Suffrage, now roused by the late tragedy in which a Negro murdered a white family."[16] Seward's assessment was accurate: by claiming in court that Freeman's violence resulted from his immutable racial characteristics, Van Buren created an opportunity to gain ground for the Democratic Party—and take ground from the Whigs—by defining it as a unifier of white people *against* people of color.[17]

The New York State Constitutional Convention met in fall 1846. The delegates—all white—debated Black voting rights. Not surprisingly, the Freeman trial's narratives of Black villains and victims now found voice in the halls of government. An important factor in these debates was the alleged association between Blackness and crime. One delegate cited the overrepresentation of African Americans in prison to argue that Black people's "aggregate moral character," their "nature," and the "criminal disposition in the race" disqualified them from voting. Using statistics from the Auburn State Prison and others, he claimed that "the relative proportion of infamous crime is nearly thirteen and a half times as great in the colored population as in the white." In response, another white delegate parroted Seward's argument that racism caused Black criminality: "The wonder," this delegate suggested, was not that Black people committed crimes, but instead "that all the colored people were not degraded so low by the treatment they met with, as to make the number of criminals *greater*."[18]

Finally, on November 3, 1846, after more than a decade of Black organizing and petitioning, New York voted on whether to reinstate Black male suffrage. The results were devastating. The amendment failed by a margin of 2.6 to 1. Across the state, 72 percent voted against equal enfranchisement. In Auburn, the numbers were worse: almost

78 percent against, 22 percent for. And in Fleming, the numbers were overwhelming: only 6 percent supported equal suffrage, while 94 percent voted against it. The defeat "crushed hope," as Black abolitionist James McCune Smith put it. One writer in the Black newspaper the *North Star* described it as a humiliation: the property requirement for voting, wrote "J.C.," "disgraces the constitution of our State, degrades our manhood and belittles" us.[19]

Less than a year later, in 1847, Black people convened in Troy, New York. They needed to reenergize a community after these blows. They needed to collectively conceive a path forward.

"A Press of Our Own": The 1847 Colored Convention in Troy

The gathering in Troy was known as a "colored convention." From the 1830s through the late nineteenth century, across the United States and Canada, Black men and women organized colored conventions to debate current issues, present and vote on resolutions designed to advance civil rights, and strategize ways to improve the lives of free and enslaved African Americans. Colored conventions laid the foundations for many Black institutions, including the school for which Josiah Henson raised funds in Auburn. That school was incubated in 1838 when Josiah Henson called a convention in London, Upper Canada. During the three-day meeting, Henson rallied financial support and goodwill to build a school. When he went knocking on Austin's door nearly a decade later, he extended a process that had launched through the colored convention movement.[20]

In the half-decade before Freeman's trial, colored conventions met across New York in cities ranging from Buffalo and Rochester to the west, Syracuse and Schenectady to the east, and closest to Auburn, Geneva. At these conferences, conversation focused overwhelmingly on voting. But in Troy in 1847, delegates spoke little of voting rights. That ship had sunk.

Instead, the delegates discussed a range of Black priorities: commerce, economic independence, education, and temperance. Two issues, however, towered above the others: violence and publishing. For the convention's first three days, discussions of publishing and violence spanned the

FIGURE 10.3 *Henry Highland Garnet*

Albumen silver print by James U. Stead, ca. 1881. Object number NPG.89.189, National Portrait Gallery, Smithsonian Institution. Creative Commons.

morning, afternoon, and evening sessions. Thus the delegates in Troy confronted a question: should they move forward by pen or by sword?

Violence had been a much-debated topic at colored conventions since 1843. That year, at a convention in Buffalo, Henry Highland Garnet delivered "An Address to the Slaves of the United States of America." In this speech, Garnet suggested that moral suasion should receive a fair try, but that when it fails, "there is not much hope of Redemption without the shedding of blood." It is better, Garnet intoned, to "DIE FREEMEN, THAN LIVE TO BE SLAVES." The speech met with "great applause" but also controversy; Frederick Douglass said that Garnet's speech relied on "too much physical force" and "that it would lead to insurrection." The text of the ninety-minute speech was omitted from the official minutes, but it inspired Black politics for decades.[21]

Garnet attended the colored convention in Troy and restaged his 1843 address.[22] Now, in the wake of the failed constitutional amendment, the conditions Garnet had described seemed fulfilled: a coordinated, lawful, lengthy grassroots effort at rational persuasion had failed. What remained was Garnet's call to physical resistance—but now, after Freeman's crimes, that call, too, resonated anew. Freeman had physically resisted, and the backlash was devastating.

Concerns about violence and backlash spilled into a debate the next day about the "Report of the Committee on Abolition," which Frederick Douglass authored with three others. In words that could have described Freeman, Douglass and his coauthors condemned the "shedding of blood" as "suicidal in the extreme." Pointedly criticizing any "argument put forth in favor of insurrection and bloodshed, however well intended," they called for a total rejection of "such absurd, unavailing, dangerous and mischievous ravings."[23]

Were the delegates thinking of Freeman as they debated the efficacy and dangers of violence? The convention minutes do not explicitly refer to Freeman, and none of the delegates represented Auburn or even Cayuga County.[24] His rebellion must have been on delegates' minds, however, because throughout 1847, newspapers continued to publish wave after wave of articles about Freeman. One delegate, James McCune Smith, read of the case and became incensed at Seward's defense. He excoriated Seward for using "an expression about 'inferiority of race.'" That perspective, McCune Smith wrote later, "I can forgive in no man; and I gave up all hope of him [Seward] when I read that sentence, because no man can fight the true Anti-Slavery fight who does not believe that all men are equal socii."[25]

Delegates in Troy must also have been aware of Freeman because many had recently traveled through or near Auburn, where townspeople still could not stop talking about the case. Frederick Douglass, for example, attended the Troy convention two weeks after lecturing in Auburn's Town Hall. Henry Highland Garnet was at the convention, and he, too, had lectured in Auburn weeks earlier. William Wells Brown was at the Troy convention, and he lectured frequently in Cayuga County in 1846–1847.[26] All these men visited Auburn and its vi-

FIGURE 10.4 *Dr. James McCune Smith*

DR. JAMES McCUNE SMITH,
First regularly-educated Colored Physician in the United
States. (See page 325.)

Daniel Alexander Payne, *Recollections of Seventy Years* (Nashville, TN: Publishing House of the AME Sunday School Union, 1888).

cinity, passed through the ongoing chatter about Freeman, and then converged in Troy.

There, they confronted a dilemma. New York's vote on suffrage marked the limits of moral persuasion. But Freeman had proved that violent resistance incurred dangers—not only physical but narrative, not only for the individual but for the collective. What, then, to do?

James McCune Smith led a committee that proposed a solution: a Black-owned, Black-run national printing press. The committee envisioned a press for which the "thinking writing-man, the compositors, pressman, printers' help, all, all" would be "men of color." The press would exceed the scope of any Black newspaper by publishing both weekly and quarterly. It would unify Black communities by providing a "rallying point, toward which the strong and the weak amongst us would look with confidence and hope." And it would pose a "burning rebuke and overwhelming argument upon those who dare impede our way." The proposal that McCune Smith coauthored echoed his denunciation of Seward: "Our friends sorrow with us, because, they say we are so unfortunate! We must ... command something manlier than sympathies. We must command the respect and admiration due men, who, against fearful odds, are struggling steadfastly for their own rights." This extirpation of a Sewardian narrative of Black victimhood "can only be done through a Press of our own."[27]

The proposal sparked both enthusiasm and hesitation among convention-goers. Henry Highland Garnet welcomed it in terms consonant with his "Address to the Slaves": a Black-run national press, he said, would "send terror into the ranks of our enemies."[28] But Douglass and William Wells Brown doubted the practicality of the proposal. What if a press started with national aspirations but then dwindled for lack of funding? In place of a national press that would publish on multiple schedules, Douglass contended, the community should focus on sustaining individual Black newspapers. The recommendation carried more than a touch of self-interest: Douglass himself was in the final stages of planning a newspaper of his own.

After two days' debate, the resolution to establish a national Black press passed 27–9.[29] Douglass and Brown abstained, and their hesitations proved prophetic: the Black national press never secured the sufficient funding to launch. But the publishing agenda forged in Troy soon framed a newspaper with its own lofty ambitions: Douglass's *North Star*.

Douglass had been planning for at least seven months to launch a newspaper, but he seems to have made his final decisions—and commitments—in the three weeks following the Troy convention. On October 28, 1847, Douglass wrote that he "finally decided on publishing the *North Star* in Rochester."[30] By the end of October 1847, he had bought type and other necessary equipment. The *North Star* published its first issue five weeks later. In the wake of the failed suffrage amendment and under the penumbra of Freeman's violence and the ignition of pernicious libels, a premier Black newspaper was born.

In Troy, Douglass inveighed against violence, declaring calls to physical resistance "ravings." But perhaps Garnet's argument influenced him. Perhaps Douglass's visits to Auburn did as well. Half a year later, Douglass's newspaper published one of the only articles to seriously consider Freeman's demand for wages. When Freeman was released from prison, the *North Star* reported, he "insisted on having payment for the time that the State had robbed him of; but asking nothing for the brutalities to which he had been subjected. Never was there a more righteous demand than this." Extracting Freeman's story from narratives of contempt and pity, the *North Star* heard the challenge to the Auburn State Prison—and affirmed it.[31]

The Great Emancipator in the Prison's City

In the years following Freeman's trial, Black abolitionists continued to stream into Auburn. Many lectured and then moved on. One, however, stayed: Harriet Tubman. As the "Great Emancipator," Tubman was unique, but when she settled in Auburn, she became entangled, as all Auburnites did, with the prison. Thus Tubman faced the same questions as all Black people in Auburn, and New York, and the North: how to build freedom after Freeman? How to live free alongside carceral servitude?

Tubman seems to have first passed through Auburn soon after she liberated herself from slavery in 1849. Over the next decade, she ran about thirteen missions between Canada and the South to free some seventy people, including members of her family. Along her travels, Tubman met Auburn's white elites, including William Henry Seward and Frances Miller Seward, as well as Freeman's codefender David Wright and his wife, the feminist and abolitionist Martha Coffin Wright.[32]

By the mid-1850s, Tubman had led her parents out of slavery and settled them in Canada—but they wanted to return to the United States. For this purpose, Tubman's relationship with Frances Seward proved pivotal. Frances Seward's father, Elijah Miller, had recently died, leaving extensive real estate that he had developed as cofounder of the Auburn State Prison.[33] Because of the Married Women's Property Act of 1848, Frances Seward, not her husband, inherited this land.

One of the lots lay a mile south of the Sewards' home, just over the border between Auburn and Fleming. The seven acres of farmland included a house, a barn, and more. It was a place where Tubman could settle her family and find sanctuary between missions. The prospect was risky, however, because the Fugitive Slave Act of 1850 determined that anyone who escaped slavery could be legally captured and reenslaved. Auburn was home to about two hundred self-liberated people who slid quietly into free life, but the well-known Tubman and her relatives could not pass for freeborn. Despite these dangers, Tubman bought the land on good terms from Frances Seward in 1859 (later, Tubman bought adjacent land by borrowing from the Auburn Bank, which John Beach had established concurrently with the prison to manage state capital flowing into Auburn). The fact that Tubman trusted her family's safety to Auburn testifies to the strength of the Black community. She apparently relied on Auburn's Black citizens (and some white ones) to protect her elderly parents when she was not physically present.[34]

Soon, Tubman collaborated with a local white woman, Sarah Bradford, and an Auburn-based publisher, W. J. Moses, to publish *Scenes in the Life of Harriet Tubman*. This autobiography, like Tubman's land and everything else in Auburn, tied to the prison. The book was published with funding from Josiah Barber, owner of the carpet factory for which Freeman dyed fiber. The book was also financially supported by Freeman's defense team of Seward, Wright, and Christopher Morgan, as well as other white men who had prospered along with Auburn. Sarah Bradford was the daughter of Samuel Miles Hopkins Sr., an early champion of the Auburn System and of Elam Lynds (later, as evidence of Lynds's corruption and cruelty emerged, Hopkins became one of Lynds's most vociferous critics).[35]

Surely the Great Emancipator had thoughts about the famous prison two miles north of her home. Surely she had opinions about the Auburn System on which her city's economy depended. But if she connected Southern slavery to the toil of incarcerated "slaves of the

FIGURE 10.5 *Harriet Tubman*

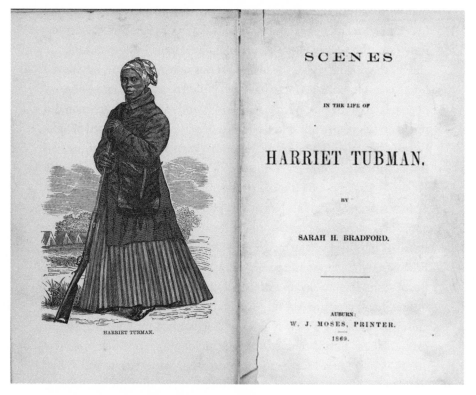

Frontispiece and title page, Sarah H. Bradford, *Scenes in the Life of Harriet Tubman* (Auburn, NY: W. J. Moses, Printer, 1869).

state," she never said so in print. Nor did she speak publicly about William Freeman and his demand to benefit from his own labor. But Tubman must have been aware of Freeman, because she knew his family. Tubman worshipped at Auburn's AME Zion Church along with Sally Freeman, Luke Freeman, Deborah De Puy, and other family members. Tubman's brother, John Stewart, became treasurer of the Auburn Suffrage Club, which met in the Shaving Saloon owned by Burget Freeman, Luke's son and William's first cousin. John Stuart and Burget Freeman had a long relationship, working together into the 1860s to recover voting rights for Black men.[36] What did Harriet Tubman say, in quiet, private moments, about the system William Freeman challenged— and her own connections to it?

A lone clue appears in Tubman's narrative. There, she described "a man who was put in State Prison for twenty-five years." The man served five times Freeman's sentence, but his experiences on release could have described Freeman's: "At last the day comes," Tubman said. He "leaves the prison gates—he makes his way to his old home, but his old home is not there. The house has been pulled down, and a new one has been put up in its place; his family and friends are gone." Tubman did not liken forced prison labor to slavery, or prisoners to enslaved people. But she did liken the man's release to her own self-emancipation: "So it was with me," Tubman continued. "I had crossed the line" into the North. "I was free" but "I was a stranger in a strange land."[37]

It was true. Tubman's North was strange: as the region gradually abolished slavery, it planted a new form of unfreedom. The slavery-based economy transformed into state-funded, carceral capitalism. Freeman's challenge incited new stories that provided narrative infrastructure for racialized incarceration. By the time Tubman arrived in Freeman's city, the Auburn System had marched from one state to another, spreading a new regime of discipline, a modern method to extract labor in exchange for nothing, an ideology in which prisoners are an economic resource, a social contract that leaves no individual untouched. In this sense, all the North, and later all America, became Auburn. It was—is—strange indeed, this life of freedom in prison land.[38]

Afterlives

William Freeman never did hang. Seward, citing irregularities in jury selection and other technicalities, petitioned for him to be granted a new trial. He succeeded, and Freeman was set to return to court in fall 1847.[1] During the summer, however, Freeman sickened with tubercular phthisis. His jailors, in what some thought a deliberate attempt to worsen his illness, alternated between overheating his cell and letting the temperature plummet. He developed a severe cough. A discharge leaked from his ear. The artist George Clough, who had sketched Freeman twice before, returned to the cell for one more sitting. This time, however, Freeman took charge of the image's production. He told Clough that he was "too weak to sit up" and instructed the artist to "draw him lying down." After Clough finished, Freeman asked to see the image. Clough showed him, and, according to one witness, Freeman "seemed much pleased with it." But the image was apparently never published. Days later, Freeman sickened further. One side of his face became paralyzed, and he went blind in his left eye. His mouth drew to the right. On August 21, 1847, William Freeman died.[2] He was twenty-two years old.

After Freeman died, his family surely tried to collect his body. But white Auburnites—with "an almost unanimous impulse"—demanded an autopsy to determine whether he had been insane. A preliminary autopsy was conducted in Freeman's cell. Lansingh Briggs, the doctor who had been implicated in the death of a prisoner during one of Elam Lynds's scandals, removed Freeman's brain and took it to his office. There, while a "large number of lawyers and other persons" watched, seven physicians dissected it. The procedure revealed advanced disease—most likely the result, a doctor concluded, of a head injury. For many, the autopsy vindicated Seward, proving that Freeman was incapable of rational thought. And equally, the results seemed to vindicate the prison, as per Seward's argument: excessive punishment was a problem to be remedied, but the Auburn System itself was sound. After the autopsy, William Freeman was laid to rest in the North Street Cemetery, not far from his grandfather Harry Freeman, in an unmarked grave.[3]

In 1859, Luke Freeman suffered a stroke that paralyzed him and rendered him speechless. His son Burget then took over his barbershop, renaming it "B. C. Freeman's Shaving Saloon." Burget extended his father's practice of using the business as a hub for antiracist activism: it was there that Harriet Tubman's brother and others gathered to organize the Auburn Suffrage Club to try, yet again, to regain voting rights. (Black men in New York gained equal voting rights only with the ratification of the Fifteenth Amendment to the federal Constitution in 1870; Black women became legally enfranchised along with non-Black women through an amendment to the New York State Constitution in 1917.) When Luke died in 1863, five ministers preached at his funeral, and fourteen carriages were reportedly necessary to transport the mourners, Black and white, to the North Street Cemetery. There, he was buried along with his nephew William. Luke's five children scattered: Burget to Cleveland, two other sons to Philadelphia and New Orleans, and a daughter to St. Catharines, Canada. Only one daughter, Helen Elizabeth Freeman, remained in Auburn.[4]

Shortly after testifying in William Freeman's defense, John De Puy got into a fight with a white man named Glenn. De Puy "drew a knife in self-defence," and a mob cried, "kill the d——d n——s." De Puy struck Glenn with a stone. A mob took off after De Puy, who ran for his life. The thwarted mob then rushed to De Puy's home and destroyed it. De Puy seems to have died one year later at the age of thirty-six.[5]

Deborah De Puy bought land next to the AME Zion Church in 1857; she lived there until her death in 1879.[6] Her husband, Hiram De Puy, disappears from the records and may have died by 1850. The fates of

Sally Freeman, Caroline Freeman De Puy, Kate Freeman, and many other members of the Freeman family are currently unknown.

In the decade following Freeman's trial, Black abolitionist energy transformed Auburn into a publishing hub for an emerging form of literature: the slave narrative.[7] Frederick Douglass published the first edition of *My Bondage and My Freedom* simultaneously in Auburn and New York City in 1855. Solomon Northup chose Auburn, along with Buffalo and London, for the first edition of *Twelve Years a Slave* in 1853. Kate E. R. Pickard followed with *The Kidnapped and the Ransomed: Being the Personal Recollections of Peter Still and His Wife "Vina," after Forty Years of Slavery*, published in Auburn and elsewhere in 1856. This Black genre, characterized by the opening three words, "I was born," declared the right to narrate one's own life.

William Henry Seward became a US senator and then Abraham Lincoln's secretary of state. In 1867 he brokered the purchase of Alaska (later called "Seward's Folly"). Contra the fears of his political allies, the Freeman trial did not end Seward's career. But it did provide his epitaph. Seward chose three words for his own headstone: "HE WAS FAITHFUL." This summating phrase quotes his closing argument in William Freeman's preliminary trial.[8] During that emotional nine-hour speech, Seward imagined his own death:

> In due time, gentlemen of the jury, when I shall have paid the debt of Nature, my remains will rest here in your midst, with those of my kindred and neighbors. It is very possible they may be unhonored, neglected, spurned! But, perhaps, years hence, when the passion and excitement which now agitate this community shall have passed away, some wandering stranger, some lone exile, some Indian, some negro, may erect over them a humble stone, and thereon this epitaph, "He was faithful!"[9]

In court, Seward said he wanted "some Indian, some negro" to admire him as a faithful ally. In death, he got the praise he wanted—in his own words.

John Austin parlayed his prominence in Freeman's trial into ever-wider professional opportunities. He resigned from his Auburn ministry in 1851 to become editor of the *Christian Ambassador*, a Universalist newspaper. He continued to benefit from his close friendship with Seward: in 1862, through Seward's influence over Lincoln, Austin became paymaster for the Union Army. When Seward died, Austin wrote effusively of his friend and ally.[10]

Elam Lynds retired to Brooklyn with wealth of obscured origin. Prison doctor Blanchard Fosgate, who treated Freeman in jail and participated in the autopsy, published a book arguing that interracial contact causes social disorder. Henry Polhemus spent his postprison life combating lawsuits against him and promoting hemorrhoid ointment. James E. Tyler, the guard who beat William Freeman with a board, became agent of the Auburn State Prison in 1849. In 1868, he became mayor of Auburn.[11]

In Freeman's trial, white Auburnites incubated libels of larger-than-life Black villains and victims—and they did so decades before other white masses did. These stories gained power as they metastasized. The prosecution's allegations of innate Black viciousness spread through George Mastin's show (which he performed for forty years) and a serialized novel about Freeman called *A Night of Blood*.[12] The anonymously authored novel, like Mastin's show, claimed that Freeman's motives were purely racial: a "cross of the Indian and negro, with all the restless malice of the latter and none of his talent," Freeman "looks upon the whites as his oppressors" and seeks revenge against them all. The novel combined facts with invented scenes in which Freeman attempts to murder a white bartender, stalks and tries to kill a white mother and baby, and creeps into a white orphan girl's bedroom, implicitly to rape her (the racist idea of Black men as sexual threats to white women was nearly unheard of in the 1840s; *A Night of Blood* constitutes one of its earliest manifestations).[13] During the second half of the nineteenth century, the defense's story of Freeman as the powerless victim of totalizing racism also repeated and expanded. When Seward died in 1872, newspapers, magazines, and books celebrated the man, often highlighting his defense of Freeman and republishing excerpts from his closing argument.[14]

As stories about Freeman as villain or victim spread, they pooled into the respective branches of racist thought that historian Ibram X.

Kendi calls "segregationist" and "assimilationist" and historian Daryl Michael Scott calls "contempt and pity." Contemptuous "segregationists" (like John Van Buren and George Mastin) argue that Black people are inferior for reasons based on biology or "plain old common sense." In contrast, pitying "assimilationists," of which Seward was an exemplar, assert that "Black people *and* racial discrimination [are] to blame for racial disparities."[15]

These stories ripped through American culture, causing incalculable damage both separately and together. The libel of innate Black criminality grew into what historian Khalil Gibran Muhammad calls "the most significant and durable signifier of black inferiority in white people's minds since the dawn of Jim Crow." Threading through political speeches, legal discourse, the novels of Thomas Dixon Jr. and other writers, the 1915 film *Birth of a Nation*, and beyond, this narrative justifies police violence, including lethal violence, against Black people. It makes mass incarceration seem necessary and inevitable.[16] And starting in 1848, in the immediate wake of Freeman's trial and death, the "environmentalist" theory of criminology—that is, that racism, poverty, and inadequate education cause crime—became central in New York. One of the most important amplifiers of this argument was the *Northern Christian Advocate*, which was published in Auburn at 16 Clark Street, one block north of the courthouse where Freeman was tried (see figure 4.1). By the turn of the twentieth century, conservative and liberal forces both leveraged this argument, asserting that racism and discrimination create a toxic environment that psychologically damages African Americans. Liberals especially used this claim to support paternalistic interference in Black communities. The practice crested in 1965 with the Moynihan Report, which notoriously described Black culture—in an echo of Freeman's trial—as a "tangle of pathology." The Moynihan Report in turn became, as historian Elizabeth Hinton shows, a tool by which the Lyndon B. Johnson administration and others built the prison industry.[17] Thus two distinct forms of American racism, each voiced in Auburn decades before they resounded nationally, led to the same conclusion: mass incarceration.

Today, profit-driven, racialized incarceration is often called "slavery by another name." This phrase can refer to the Thirteenth Amendment

FIGURE 11.1 *The Auburn Correctional Facility on State St. in Auburn, N.Y.*

Photo by Corey Sipkin/NY Daily News Archive via Getty Images.

to the US Constitution, which abolished slavery "except as a punishment for crime." But as William Freeman's life reveals, profit-driven, penal slavery emerged fifty years before the Thirteenth Amendment, and in the context of Northern, not Southern, abolition. The South did not invent convict leasing, but instead adapted the Auburn System. As Heather Ann Thompson has pointed out, Southern prison labor often involves more agricultural than factory work, but this variation should be understood as a "difference ... of form but not necessarily of substance" from Northern carceral practices.[18] With the "loophole" clause allowing carceral slavery, the Thirteenth Amendment worked to preserve an old system of unfree labor rather than authorize a new one.

The Auburn State Prison still exists—and factory labor continues to define it. Now called the Auburn Correctional Facility and holding approximately thirteen hundred men, it is the oldest continually operating maximum security prison in the United States. Today, Auburn prisoners manufacture all New York State license plates—2.5 million pairs annually. Unlike William Freeman, these workers receive compensation. But at $.65 per hour, they do not earn the life-supporting wage Freeman demanded.[19]

William Freeman challenged the triangulation of incarceration, capitalism, and slavery by insisting he was a worker who deserved to benefit from his labor. He demanded fair payment along with everything that it conferred: economic stability, dignity, justice. Self-definition as a free man—his name itself. In short, he sought a foundation on which he could build his life. Today, these values comprise a vital part of the prison abolition movement. Prison abolition, as Ruth Wilson Gilmore has famously said, is "about presence, not absence. It's about building life-affirming institutions."[20] The prison abolition movement organizes around no single plan for the future, but instead a process of imagining a world in which justice, freedom, and life flourish—without prisons. Prison abolition is a commitment to a simple, powerful idea: prisons do not foster justice. Together, we can build something better.

Author's Note

Much of William Freeman's story is astounding, but every event, person, and claim in this book reflects historical evidence. The primary sources are massive: over forty thousand pages of unpublished diaries, letters, genealogical records, newspaper articles, court documents, governmental reports, pamphlets, travel accounts, maps, and more. To research this book, I obtained the previously unexamined diary of an 1830s prison guard; entered a dark storage facility to view paintings with a flashlight; and met and talked with men currently serving time in the prison that held William Freeman almost two centuries ago. My goal: to represent history accurately.[1]

Within the ocean of evidence, two currents required especially careful navigation. First, every document was biased. This is a book about a profit-driven prison, a young Afro-Native man who violently challenged it, and white and Black people's efforts to manage the aftermath. Every person involved in the case had an agenda. Their biases raise questions: When members of William Freeman's family testified on his behalf, did they say what they believed? Or what they thought would save his life? Or both? Some of the individuals in this book deliberately created misleading documents. Corrupt prison administrators, for example, wrote voluminous, highly detailed reports that were designed to camouflage their own crimes.

I negotiated these problems by reading across sources. As I read the words of dozens of different people who described the same set of events, I tuned into the overall music that incorporated but also exceeded individual notes. This technique was especially important for hearing William Freeman's voice. Freeman never wrote or dictated his own story, nor did he testify in his trials. But many people, both Black and white, some friendly and some hostile, described their encounters with him. Across these sources, Freeman emerges: acerbic and taciturn, strategic but also quick to cry, laugh, or fight. Sometimes witty, sometimes stoic, often confident, and always unyielding. A young man who had his own ideas and refused to compromise.

A second problem I confronted was that almost all the texts that were published or preserved in archives are white authored. As Saidiya Hartman points out, evidence of nineteenth-century Black lives entered the archive most often in situations of white violence—for example, through the legal system or the recordkeeping of slavery.[2] That is the case here. The stoutest records of William Freeman's life attend to his imprisonment and his trials. His family appears in more records: legal documents, yes, but also newspapers and censuses, plus a few passing references in memoirs by white authors. But almost none of Freeman's relatives left their own written texts.

The failures of archives to preserve Black women's voices is especially painful. Freeman had two sisters: one named Caroline and another whom family members and friends mentioned without a name, and usually with the adjective "foolish."[3] She may have been mentally disabled. I found no trace of this second sister in any other records, even censuses. What remains is but a wisp of a Black woman's life: an adjective and nothing more. Another example: in 2016, early in the process of researching this book, I found a thrilling fragment from the life of William Freeman's grandmother, Kate Freeman. Deep in the archive of the Cayuga Museum of History and Art was an 1829 deed recording the sale of land on which Kate Freeman had been formerly enslaved. The deed included an extraordinary stipulation: the property was "subject ... to a lease of a small part of said premises ... to Catherine Freeman, for her life."[4] Kate Freeman had secured the right to permanent housing. I held the deed in my hands, stared at the handwritten name of this Black woman who successfully negotiated a legal system designed to exploit her. I photographed the deed and carefully returned it to its archival box. When I returned to the Cayuga Museum six years

FIGURE 12.1 "Deed—John Hardenbergh and his wife to Allen Warden and Asaph Leonard, July 23, 1829"

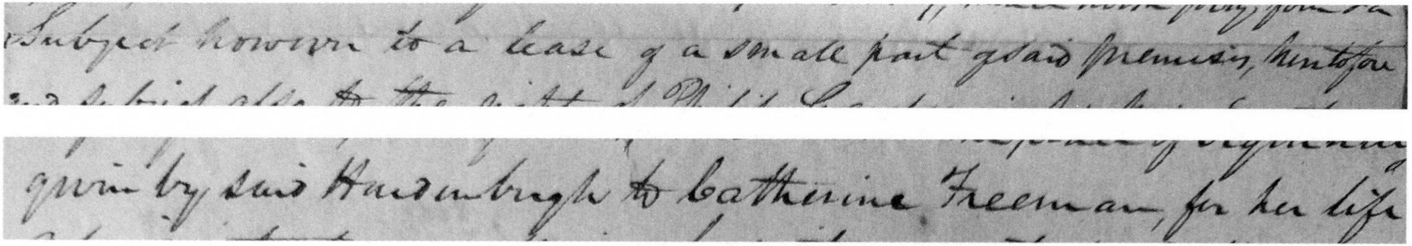
subject however to a lease of a small part of said premises, heretofore
given by said Hardenbergh to Catherine Freeman, for her life

Details, 1829 deed providing that Catherine (Kate) Freeman could continue to rent "a small part of said premises . . . for her life." Hardenbergh Archives, file "Hardenbergh, Deeds and Land Grants," item 141, Cayuga Museum of History and Art, Auburn, NY. Photograph by Robin Bernstein.

later, at the end of my research, I opened that box again. But the deed was gone.

How to deal with the ravages of archives? Hartman famously proposes "critical fabulation": a Black method of reparative historiography that speculates through the spaces of irreversible loss. I respect this approach but it is not mine, nor should it be. Instead, my process has been inspired by Tiya Miles's technique of reconstructing the textures of Black individuals' lives through parallel figures. For example, in *All That She Carried: The Journey of Ashley's Sack, a Black Family Keepsake*, Miles reads the autobiographies of Harriet Jacobs and Elizabeth Keckley to recover possibilities about an enslaved woman named Rose and her daughter Ashley. With cues from Miles, I looked to the experiences of African Americans who were in central New York State around Freeman's time: Frederick Douglass, Sojourner Truth, Harriet Tubman, William Wells Brown, and others.[5] Henry Highland Garnet was crucial to my understanding of Freeman's use of violence to challenge the Auburn System of incarceration. By far, William Freeman's most important parallel was Austin Reed, a Black youth who was incarcerated in the Auburn State Prison alongside Freeman. Reed wrote a book-length memoir in the 1850s, which Caleb Smith edited and published in 2016. Reed provided rich information about the prison as seen through the eyes of a young Black prisoner. Because Auburn's leaders aimed to subject prisoners to identical routines (the prison valued consistency to the point of "fetish," as one historian put it), Reed's narrative provides extensive and reliable evidence of Freeman's circumstances.[6]

This book also draws inspiration from the work of literary scholars, most importantly Koritha Mitchell. Across her scholarship and popular writing, Mitchell argues for an understanding of white violence as a response to Black success.[7] In Mitchell's framework, the primary actors are Black and the reactive or resistant actors are white. This perspective enables one of the core claims of this book: that white Auburnites rose so adamantly against Freeman because he successfully threatened the Auburn State Prison. The threat was effective not only because it took the form of violence, but also because the Auburn State Prison had pre-existing vulnerabilities due to the misjudgment, amorality, and ineptitude of its white leaders. In other words, the white people who made the prison strong simultaneously made it weak—a fact that Freeman's actions had the potential to expose. White Auburnites responded to this threat by collectively contriving the larger-than-life Black criminal—an early moment in the making of this national myth. In short, a devastating formation of white supremacy was, at one point of origin, essentially defensive: white people criminalized African Americans to avoid confronting their own shortcomings.

Another crucial frame for this book came from philosopher and activist Angela Y. Davis. In 1998, Davis posed a question: why was Frederick Douglass "consistently silent" about postbellum Southern convict leasing? *Freeman's Challenge* responds to this question by expanding its scope: I show that because profit-driven incarceration began long before the Civil War, Douglass's reticence lasted longer than Davis stated; furthermore, Harriet Tubman and other abolitionists made a similar choice not to oppose carceral slavery. Thus Freeman's story gives Davis's question even more gravity. To answer that question, I turned to literary scholars Kevin Quashie and Derrick Spires. Quashie enables us to understand Douglass's choice not as silence but instead as *quiet*, an expression of Black interiority that is not defined by resistance or protest. Quashie prompted me to ask what African Americans did *instead of* directly engaging Freeman or organizing in opposition to the rise of carceral slavery. My answer: Black New Yorkers' collective quiet made room for what Spires calls "practices of citizenship." Spires argues that nineteenth-century African Americans defined citizenship not exclusively through governmental recognition such as voting, but also through quotidian activities. Everyday practices—of writing and reading, collective organizing, and neighborliness—theorized Black citizenship.[8] This, I have argued, is exactly what Freeman's community did instead of organizing against the rising prison system.

As a white historian writing a multiracial story with an Afro-Native youth at its center, I constantly asked myself, How can I grapple with Freeman's ideas and experiences? How can I do justice to him and his family? Ultimately, this book is not about William Freeman's individual psychology or his emotional life. I do not have access to that. I focus on the external: what he experienced, what he said and did, and how white and Black people responded to his actions. I tried never to underestimate the differences between me and the people I wrote about—differences in race as well as gender, class, culture, and century. I tried, equally, to honor the bravery of Black Auburnites who took precipitous risks to talk with white people about William Freeman. Friends and family members testified on his behalf in court—and some suffered life-altering retribution. Their courage motivates me to amplify their sworn testimony, treating it with gratitude and respect.

Acknowledgments

I wrote this book with the generous support of a Public Scholars Fellowship from the National Endowment for the Humanities and a Radcliffe Fellowship and Joy Foundation Fellowship from the Radcliffe Institute for Advanced Study at Harvard University. My residency at Radcliffe in 2018–2019 conferred many joys. Among the sweetest was the formation of a brilliant writing group: Corinne T. Field, Tanisha C. Ford, Malick W. Ghachem, Dana Sajdi, and Katherine Turk. Thank you, fellow travelers, for reading many chapter drafts and thinking with me through every stage of this project. The entire Radcliffe community, especially Meredith Quinn, made the year as warm as it was intellectually thrilling.

Many friends helped me develop this project. Elizabeth Maddock Dillon, Marah Gubar, Judith Hamera. Elizabeth Hinton, Martha Hodes, Rebecca Schneider, Caleb Smith, and Kyla Wazana Tompkins read portions of the manuscript and provided vital comments. I especially thank Bruce Dorsey and Amy Kittelstrom, who read the full manuscript and responded with generosity and acumen. This book benefited from conversations with Michael Awkward, Stephanie Batiste, Elizabeth Bernstein, andré carrington, Jeannine DeLombard, Jim Downs, Anna Mae Duane, Nick Fesette, Ellen Gruber Garvey, Nicole Gonzalez Van Cleve, Leslie Harris, Hendrik Hartog, Brian Eugenio Herrera, Amy Hughes, Rebecca Kastleman, Kareem Khubchandani, Deborah Korn, Betsy Leondar-Wright, Gail Leondar-Wright, Jill Lepore, Sarah Lewis, Dianne Lior, David Lobenstine, Suzanne McCarthy,

Derek Miller, Koritha Mitchell, Durba Mitra, Khalil Gibran Muhammad, John Muse, Phil Nel, Charmaine Nelson, Janet Penn, Tina Post, Chanda Prescod-Weinstein, Kevin Quashie, Robert Reid-Pharr, Joe Rezek, Seth Rockman, Karen Sánchez-Eppler, Bethany Schneider, Rebecca Schneider, Sarah Schulman, Evie Shockley, Manisha Sinha, Cynthia Verba, Priscilla Wald, Sara Warner, Mary Jo Watts, and Crystal Lynn Webster. A conversation with Dwight McBride, Colleen S. Boggs, and Paul Erickson at the American Antiquarian Society remains a fond memory. I never stop learning from my colleagues and students at Harvard University in the Department of African and African American Studies, the Program of Studies in Women, Gender, and Sexuality, and the Program in American Studies.

I presented portions of this book at Brown University, Cornell University, Duke University, Harvard University, Princeton University, Rutgers University at Camden, the University of Buffalo, the University of Chicago, the University of Maryland–College Park, the University of Massachusetts–Amherst, the University of Michigan–Ann Arbor, the University of Pittsburgh, and Yale University, as well as the conferences of the American Society for Theatre Research and the Society for the History of Children and Youth. The audiences in all these venues taught me a great deal. I especially thank Keith Green and Jodi Schorb for including me in the seminar "Carceral Pasts/Abolitionist Futures" at the conference C19: The Society of Nineteenth-Century Americanists. That seminar, which included Julia Dauer, Anna Mae Duane, Jess Goldberg, Sean Gordon, Lindsey Grubbs, Allison Hanna, Caleb Smith, Jordan Stein, and Ali Tal-mason, was nothing short of paradigm shifting for me.

The research of Mary Jo Watts, the "Database Whisperer," always dazzles me and fills me with gratitude. I thank Kim Marra for teaching me about horses, Tara Rodman for explaining japanning to me, Jonathan Senchyne for answering my questions about printing technologies, Paul Erickson for helping me understand land indentures, and Heather Nathans for spotting and sharing David P. Hillhouse's travel journal.

This book could not have been written without the collaboration of many excellent archivists, librarians, and curators. In Auburn, I dove into the records of the Cayuga County Historian's Office with county historians Linda Frank and then Ruth Bradley, along with Jessica Armstrong (who has done astounding detective work on Auburn's early deeds) and Nancy Assmann. Dori Gottschalk-Fielding, at the Seymour Library, was a joy to work with. I thank Eileen McHugh, Karyn Radcliffe, and Kirsten Wise at the Cayuga Museum of History and Art; Phyllis Catalfano and Renee Schmidt at the Norman F. Bourke Memorial Library, Archives and Manuscript Collections at Cayuga Community College; and Emma Dailey and Emily Kraft at the Seward House Museum. I was fortunate to learn from many people in Auburn, especially Laurel Auchampaugh, Karen Bove, David Connelly, Bill Hecht, Sean Lattimore, and Tanya Warren. I thank Bill Hecht for sharing his astonishing map collection and allowing me to publish images from it. My profound gratitude goes to Bruce Levitt, a facilitator of the Phoenix Players Theatre Group inside the Auburn Correctional Facility. Bruce welcomed me into that community, and it is because of his hard work that I was able to enter the prison and speak with men who are incarcerated there. I am equally grateful to Rob Scott, executive director of the Cornell Prison Education Program, for the opportunity to connect with Auburn's incarcerated students and their families.

Beyond Auburn, I thank Joe Festa, Jennifer Griffiths, and Erin Richardson at the Fenimore Art Museum (formerly the New York State Historical Association); Melinda Wallington at the River Campus Libraries at the University of Rochester; Gina Modero at the New-York Historical Society; Fred Burchsted at Harvard's Widener Library; and Matt Wittmann at the Harvard Theatre Collection. The American Antiquarian Society has been one of my intellectual homes since 2008; I thank Brianne Barrett and Dan Boudreau for their assistance toward this book. Claire Gallagher provided excellent clerical support. Amy Parker enabled me to hire brilliant assistants: proxy researchers Joni Christel (who also double-checked endnotes and contributed to the index) and John Vsetecka, as well as research assistant Huey Hewitt. At Radcliffe, I benefited from the work of Radcliffe Research Partners Samantha Gamble and Marshall Sloane.

I thank Tim Mennel, executive editor of the University of Chicago Press, for his vision and support. I also thank Carrie Olivia Adams,

Nicole Balant, Susannah Engstrom, and Tamara Ghattas. Dennis Mc-Clendon prepared Auburn's maps for publication. Roz Foster believed in this project from its earliest stages, and I am very grateful.

During the COVID-19 lockdown, I began writing in community with friends online. Our group eventually swelled to include over fifty people who gathered virtually to do timed writing sets, or "pomodoros." This community gave me collegiality, solace, focus, and accountability during the pandemic's loneliest moments and beyond. It is not possible to list all the pomodorians, but I especially thank Ryan Bunch, andré carrington, Shahar Colt, Elizabeth Maddock Dillon, Ellen Gruber Garvey, Nancy Grey, Ora Grodsky, Brian Herrera, Karen Jaime, Lorrie Kim, Susan King, Amy Kittelstrom, Roberta Klarreich, Dana Luciano, Patrick McKelvey, Susan Messina, Ariel Nereson, Shirley Samuels, Jonathan Shandell, LaKisha Simmons, Alisa Solomon, Jaime Tessler, Heidi Voskuhl, Patricia Ybarra, and Mary Zaborskis. You kept me going. Deb DeCelles, Moby, Sofia, Dan: you are a joy. For years of friendship, love, and overall awesomeness, I thank Ellen Gruber Garvey, Brian Herrera, and Laura Wexler. Congregation Dorshei Tzedek sustains my soul. Lyn Swirda, acupuncturist extraordinaire, was my treasured guide. I wish I could share this book with her. Matthew Frye Jacobson and Jill Lane have profoundly influenced me as a thinker and writer. I inadvertently omitted them from the acknowledgments for my previous book, *Racial Innocence: Performing American Childhood from Slavery to Civil Rights*. I am glad for this opportunity to express my gratitude for all they continue to teach me. I thank my parents, Joanne and Michael Bernstein; my brother, Andy Bernstein; my in-laws, David, Janis, and Mike Townsend; and my chosen family, Elisa and Gavin Michel, for their love and support. Most of all, again and again, I turn with love to Maya Townsend. This book would not exist without her. Thank you, Maya, for sharing your life with me. Thank you, Maya, for everything.

Notes

Preface

1. American Civil Liberties Union and the University of Chicago Law School Global Human Rights Clinic, "Captive Labor: Exploitation of Incarcerated Workers," 2022, 5–6, 8, 10, https://www.aclu.org/sites/default/files/field _document/2022-06-15-captivelaborresearchreport.pdf.

2. This popular impression derives from readings of Michelle Alexander, *The New Jim Crow: Mass Incarceration in the Age of Colorblindness*, rev. ed. (New York: New Press, 2010); Douglas A. Blackmon, *Slavery by Another Name: The Re-Enslavement of Black People in America from the Civil War to World War II* (New York: Doubleday, 2008); and David Oshinsky, *Worse Than Slavery: Parchman Farm and the Ordeal of Jim Crow Justice* (New York: Free Press, 1996; hereafter Oshinsky); as well as viewings of Ava DuVernay's 2016 film *13th*. None of these important works claims that the South invented profit-driven incarceration. However, the vivid description of the postbellum South has led many readers to draw that conclusion. This book shows how the North innovated a system that later enabled the practices described by Alexander, Blackmon, Oshinsky, and DuVernay. For a critique of the idea that the Thirteenth Amendment enabled or even caused the reenslavement and mass incarceration of Black people, see Daryl Michael Scott, "The Scandal of Thirteentherism," *Liberties* 1, no. 2 (Winter 2021): 273–93.

3. The term *capitalism* entered the lexicon in the second half of the nineteenth century and became widespread only after Karl Marx published *Das Kapital* in 1867. Long before that, however, the Auburn State Prison was structured through a set of practices and relationships that define capitalism. Simultaneously with slavery (which was rising in the South, diminishing but not gone in the North), the Auburn System developed and proliferated techniques of accounting; disciplined, efficient, alienated labor; and interdependence with financial institutions such as banking. Like capitalist formations of slavery, the

Auburn System forced people into what Elizabeth Maddock Dillon calls *bare labor*. Building on Giorgio Agamben's concept of *bare life*—that is, lives that are deemed disposable and can be ended with impunity—Dillon defines bare labor as "the reduction of the human, in the words of Sylvia Wynter, to 'so many units of labour power.'" The "conscription of Africans into capitalist modernity," Dillon writes, "functions by way of stripping sociality from the labor force through technologies of social death." Dillon's argument about capitalist slavery is apt to the Auburn System, which used silence to destroy sociality and augment production—all through unpaid workers. Another hallmark of capitalism (in and beyond slavery) is the process of positioning things and people so they can function as *assets*—that is, investments toward future growth and expansion. The Auburn State Prison reconfigured as assets the current of the Owasco River, the land, its own building, and most of all, its prisoners. On the Auburn State Prison as a capitalist endeavor, see Dario Melossi and Massimo Pavarini, *The Prison and the Factory: Origins of the Penitentiary System, 40th Anniversary Edition* (London: Palgrave Macmillan, 2018), especially 179, 185–88, 218–23. On hallmarks of capitalism, see Jonathan Levy, *Ages of American Capitalism: A History of the United States* (New York; Random House, 2021), introduction (especially xiii–xxvi) and chap. 6, "Between Slavery and Freedom" (especially 154). On debates about the definition of capitalism, see Sven Beckert and Christine Desan, "Introduction," in *American Capitalism: New Histories*, ed. Beckert and Desan (New York: Columbia University Press, 2018), 4–5. On capitalism and slavery, see Sven Beckert and Seth Rockman, eds., *Slavery's Capitalism: A New History of American Economic Development* (Philadelphia: University of Pennsylvania Press, 2016); Walter Johnson, *River of Dark Dreams: Slavery and Empire in the Cotton Kingdom* (Cambridge, MA: Belknap Press of Harvard University Press, 2013); Edward E. Baptist, *The Half Has Never Been Told: Slavery and the Making of American Capitalism* (New York: Basic Books, 2014); and Sven Beckert, *Empire of Cotton: A Global History* (New York: Knopf, 2014). On bare labor as a defining aspect of capitalist slavery, see Elizabeth Maddock Dillon, "Zombie Politics," *American Quarterly* 71, no. 3 (November 2019): 626–27; and Sylvia Wynter, "Jonkonnu in Jamaica: Towards the Interpretation of Folk Dance as Cultural Process," *Jamaica Journal* 4, no. 2 (1970): 36.

4. The Auburn State Prison was not the first American prison in which prisoners were forced to manufacture goods for sale to consumers. A few others, such as the Charlestown Prison in Massachusetts, did so earlier. Reform-oriented Pennsylvania prisons briefly instituted prison contracts to offset costs, but these efforts met with swift and successful opposition. These earlier prisons instituted limited factory work with the main goals of reforming prisoners and teaching vocational skills. In contrast, Auburn's innovation was to build in-

prison factories without regard to prisoners' spiritual or physical well-being. In other words, the Auburn Prison, unlike earlier American prisons, was founded not as a capitalist means to reformist ends, but instead as a profit-driven venture. Furthermore, Auburn codified its system, which then spread to prisons across the United States. For this reason, I describe the Auburn State Prison as America's original prison for profit.

In the years following the establishment of the Auburn System, some prison leaders attempted to layer redemptive goals on top of the capitalist infrastructure. Gershom Powers, agent and keeper from 1826 to 1829, was the best known of these administrators. Thomas Eddy and Louis Dwight, reformers who cared about prisoners' souls, believed the Auburn System could redeem prisoners and therefore supported the prison. These secondary efforts have caused some scholars, most notably David Rothman and Jennifer Graber, to describe redemption as fundamental to Auburn's mission. See David J. Rothman, "Perfecting the Prison: United States, 1789–1865," in *The Oxford History of the Prison: The Practice of Punishment in Western Society*, ed. Norval Morris and David J. Rothman (New York: Oxford University Press, 1995), 117; and Jennifer Graber, *The Furnace of Affliction: Prisons & Religion in Antebellum America* (Chapel Hill: University of North Carolina Press, 2011).

However, as I show in Chapter 1, the Auburn State Prison, unlike its predecessors, was profit-driven from its inception. Capitalism, not Christianity, was Auburn's founding principle. In concert with W. David Lewis, Rebecca McLennan, H. Bruce Franklin, and Caleb Smith, I emphasize differences between Auburn and earlier US carceral systems. See W. David Lewis, *From Newgate to Dannemora: The Rise of the Penitentiary in New York, 1796–1848* (1965; reprint, Ithaca, NY: Cornell University Press, 2009); Rebecca M. McLennan, *The Crisis of Imprisonment: Protest, Politics, and the Making of the American Penal State, 1776–1941* (New York: Cambridge University Press, 2008), 53–54; and Caleb Smith, "Editor's Introduction," in Austin Reed, *The Life and Adventures of a Haunted Convict*, ed. Caleb Smith (New York: Random House, 2016), xlv–xlvi.

For an analysis of the interplay among redemption, work, and profits in early Massachusetts prisons, particularly Charlestown, see Adam Jay Hirsh, *The Rise of the Penitentiary: Prisons and Punishment in Early America* (New Haven, CT: Yale University Press, 1992). The distinction between Auburn's and Charlestown's uses of contract labor registers in *Description and Historical Sketch of the Massachusetts State Prison* (Charlestown, MA: printed by S. Etheridge, Jr. by Order of the Board of Directors, 1816). This document outlines the use of labor contracts at Charlestown to offset the expenses of incarceration and punish criminals. Describing the prison as a "benevolent institution," the prison's directors defend its expenses to the public—that is, its failure to generate profits—on the basis that the prison provokes "repentance and reformation" (15). On the use of contract labor in Pennsylvania prisons, see Jen Manion, *Liberty's Prisoners: Carceral Culture in Early America* (Philadelphia: University of Pennsylvania Press, 2015), 43; and Ralph S. Herre, "The History of Auburn Prison from the Beginning to about 1867" (PhD diss., Pennsylvania State College, 1950), 116–17 (hereafter Herre).

On the general history of prison labor in United States, see Genevieve LeBaron, "Rethinking Prison Labor: Social Discipline and the State in Historical Perspective," *WorkingUSA: The Journal of Labor and Society* 15 (September 2012): 327–51; Glen A. Gildemeister, *Prison Labor and Convict Competition with Free Workers in Industrializing America, 1840–1890* (1977; reprint, New York: Garland Publishing, 1987) (hereafter Gildemeister); and Rosalind P. Petchesky, "At Hard Labor: Penal Confinement and Production in Nineteenth-Century America," in *Crime and Capitalism: Readings in Marxist Criminology*, ed. David F. Greenberg (New York: Mayfield Publishing, 1993), 569–611.

The Auburn State Prison had some international precedents, most notably the Maison de Force at Ghent, where prisoners worked collectively and in isolation to produce goods for public sale. See Herre, 8, 45, 48; Gildemeister, 10; and Michael Ignatieff, *A Just Measure of Pain: The Penitentiary in the Industrial Revolution, 1750–1850* (New York: Pantheon Books, 1978), 31–32.

5. Gershom Powers, *A Brief Account of the Construction, Management, & Discipline &c, &c, of the New-York State Prison at Auburn, Together with a Compendium of Criminal Law* (Auburn, NY: U. F. Doubleday, 1826), 68.

6. "Trial of Wm. Freeman, On the Preliminary Issue of Present Insanity," *Cayuga Patriot*, 8 July 1846, 2.

7. Ruth Wilson Gilmore, with Craig Gilmore, "Restating the Obvious," in Ruth Wilson Gilmore, *Abolition Geography: Essays towards Liberation*, ed. Brenna Bhandar and Alberto Toscano (London: Verso, 2022), 273.

8. For a cogent summary of Davis and Gilmore on this point, see Brett Story, *Prison Land: Mapping Carceral Power across Neoliberal America* (Minneapolis: University of Minnesota Press, 2019), 9. Also useful are the terms "carceral archipelago" and "carceral matrix," as defined, respectively, by Michel Foucault and by Liat Ben-Moshe, Chris Chapman, and Allison C. Carey. See Michel Foucault, *Discipline & Punish: The Birth of the Prison*, trans. Alan Sheridan (1977; reprint, New York: Vintage Books, 1995), 297; Ben-Moshe, *Decarcerating Disability: Deinstitutionalization and Prison Abolition* (Minneapolis: University of Minnesota Press, 2020), 1; and Liat Ben-Moshe, Chris Chapman, and Allison C. Carey, eds., *Disability Incarcerated: Imprisonment and Disability in the United States and Canada* (New York: Palgrave Macmillan, 2014).

Chapter One

1. Brian Rice, *The Rotinonshonni: A Traditional Iroquoian History through the Eyes of Teharonhia:wako and Sawiskera* (New York: Syracuse University Press, 2013), 181; John L. Hardenbergh, *Journal of Lieut. John L. Hardenbergh of the Second New York Continental Regiment from May 1 to October 3, 1779, in General Sullivan's Campaign against the Western Indians*, ed. and introduction by John S. Clark (Auburn, NY: Knapp & Peck, 1879), 19 (hereafter Clark); Joseph R. Fischer, *A Well-Executed Failure: The Sullivan Campaign against the Iroquois, July–September 1779* (Columbia: University of South Carolina Press, 1997); Bruce Elliott Johansen and Barbara Alice Mann, *Encyclopedia of the Haudenosaunee (Iroquois Confederacy)* (Westport, CT: Greenwood Press, 2000), s.v. Sullivan, John, 1740–1795; "Part of Colonel Dearborn's Journal, 1779," in Clark, 77–78; "Part of George Grant's Journal, 1779," in Clark, 74; "John L. Hardenbergh," in Clark, 15. The land now called Cayuga County, which includes the city of Auburn, is the unceded territory of the Cayuga Nation, a member of the Haudenosaunee. For a brief history of the Cayuga Nation and its land claims, see Cayuga Nation: People of the Great Swamp, "Tribal History," accessed 4 July 2023, https://cayuganation-nsn.gov/tribal-history.html.

2. Henry Hall, *The History of Auburn* (Auburn, NY: Dennis Bro's & Co., 1869), 39–42 (hereafter H. Hall). Harry Freeman reportedly died at the age of ninety-two in 1845; therefore, he was born in 1753. "Uncovering the Freedom Trail in Auburn and Cayuga County, New York," Judith Wellman, project coordinator, sponsored by the City of Auburn Historic Resources Review Board and the Cayuga County Historian's Office, 2005, 81, citing Cayuga County poorhouse records (hereafter "Uncovering").

3. H. Hall, 46–47, 53, 70. "Aurelius" originally referred to a large area that included the town of Auburn. Auburn formally separated from Aurelius in 1823. Oliver Goldsmith, *The Deserted Village* (1770; reprint, Arbroath, Scotland: printed by J. Findlay, and sold by the book-sellers, 1807); John W. Barber, *Pictorial History of the State of New York* (Cooperstown, NY: H. & E. Phinney, 1846), 60 (hereafter Barber). See also Charles Williamson, *Description of the Settlement of the Genesee Country, in the State of New-York, in a Series of Letters from a Gentleman to His Friend* (New York: T. & J. Swords, 1799), 1188.

4. DeWitt Clinton, "Private Canal Journal, 1810," in William W. Campbell, *The Life and Writings of De Witt Clinton* (New York: Baker and Scribner, 1849), 169; H. Hall, 66, 92, 121–22, 126–27; Elliot G. Storke, *History of Cayuga County, New York* (Syracuse, NY: D. Mason & Co., 1879), 144 (hereafter Storke); Barber, 60.

5. Jane was also known as Betty, Luke as Lewis or Morgan, and Sidney

as Hannibal (see *Aurelius NY Town Government Minutes Book*, 441–45, accessed 24 June 2023, https://www.cayugagenealogy.org/books/; and "John Hardenbergh—Inventory Personal Property, Sept. 12, 1806," Cayuga Museum of History and Art & Case Research Laboratory, Auburn, NY. It was common for Black and white people in this region to go by their middle names, which seems to have been the case with three of Kate and Harry's children (as an example among whites, William Henry Seward went by "Henry" and several of his children also used their middle names in everyday life). It is possible that Kate and Harry had children in Rosendale from whom they were separated. Some later census records refer to another son, Platt R. Freeman, born in 1800. Ted Freeman, a pastor and descendant of Platt Freeman, has self-published a "historical presentation guided by God" that describes Platt as the son of Harry and Kate Freeman. Ted Freeman, *God's Free-Man: An American Tale of Perseverance: A Life in Service* (Pittsburgh, PA: Dorrance Publishing Co., 2021), rear cover. Platt is absent from other records, including the *Aurelius NY Town Government Minutes Book*, which recorded the birth of Luke and his siblings. It is possible that Platt was not born to Harry and Kate but was instead a relative or friend who was later informally adopted into the Freeman family. Another tantalizing but unverified possibility is that Platt was born prior to 1793—and thus a baby whom Kate and Harry were forced to leave behind in Rosendale. Platt seems to have also been called Harry Freeman Jr.—which would make sense if he were the first son, born before James. If Platt was born before 1793, a claimed birth date of 1800 could have provided some protection from enslavement.

6. See Patrick Rael, "The Long Death of Slavery," in *Slavery in New York*, ed. Ira Berlin and Leslie M. Harris (New York: New Press, 2005), 111–46; Leslie M. Harris, *In the Shadow of Slavery: African Americans in New York City, 1626–1863* (Chicago: University of Chicago Press, 2003), 96–133; David N. Gellman and David Quigley, eds., *Jim Crow New York: A Documentary History of Race and Citizenship, 1777–1877* (New York: New York University Press, 2003), 19–23, 52–55, 67–72; and David N. Gellman, *Emancipating New York: The Politics of Slavery and Freedom 1777–1827* (Baton Rouge: Louisiana State University Press, 2006).

7. See "1820 Federal Census: African Americans of Cayuga County, New York," compilation developed as part of the "Survey of Sites Relating to the Underground Railroad, Abolitionism, and African American Life in Auburn and Cayuga County, 1820–1870," Judith Wellman, coordinator, in cooperation with the Cayuga County Historian's Office, Auburn, NY, n.d., accessed 30 June 2023, https://www.cayugagenealogy.org/census/1820/africana.html (hereafter Wellman, "1820 Federal Census"). In 1820, Auburn was still subsumed under the name "Aurelius." *Aurelius NY Town Government Minutes Book*, 443–45.

8. "Guinea" was used in eighteenth-century America as a generalized reference to Africa, and several African American neighborhoods were called

"New Guinea." Black people on Nantucket and in New Bedford, for example, called their neighborhoods New Guinea. See David N. Gellman, *Emancipating New York: The Politics of Slavery and Freedom 1777–1827* (Baton Rouge: Louisiana State University Press, 2006), 103; Tiya Miles, "Nantucket Doesn't Belong to the Preppies," *Atlantic*, 30 August 2021, https://www.theatlantic.com/ideas/archive/2021/08/nantucket-doesnt-belong-to-the-preppies/619874/; and Russell G. Handsman, Kathryn Grover, and Donald Warrin, "New Bedford Communities of Whaling: People of Wampanoag, African, and Portuguese Island Descent, 1825–1925" (US Department of the Interior, National Park Service, Northeast Regional Ethnography Program, Boston, MA, 2021), 197–98, https://www.nps.gov/nebe/learn/historyculture/upload/NEBE_Ethnographic_1825-1925_FY22_508.pdf. Auburn's New Guinea neighborhood was also occasionally called "the Settlement" or "the Colony."

9. Wellman "1820 Federal Census"; Benjamin F. Hall, *The Trial of William Freeman for the Murder of John G. Van Nest, Including the Evidence and the Arguments of Counsel, with the Decision of the Supreme Court Granting a New Trial, and an Account of the Death of the Prisoner, and of the Post-Mortem Examination of his Body by Amariah Brigham, M.D. and Others* (Auburn, NY: Derby, Miller & Co. Publishers, 1848), 46–48, 235, 248, 286 (hereafter B. F. Hall); H. Hall, 150–51.

10. "The Case of Luke Freeman," *Auburn Daily Union*, 27 July 1859; B. F. Hall, 17, 285, 387, 333.

11. William Freeman had two sisters, one named Caroline and another whose name is no longer known. When Freeman's family and friends referred to this sibling, they called her "foolish" or said she was not "very smart," which suggests she may have been developmentally disabled. See, for example, B. F. Hall, 286, 259.

12. B. F. Hall, 264.

13. B. F. Hall, 18, 58, 61, 273–74, 321–22, 325, 383; "Trial of Wm. Freeman, on the Preliminary Issue of Present Insanity," *Cayuga Patriot*, 15 July 1846, 1.

14. "Trial of Wm. Freeman, on the Preliminary Issue of Present Insanity," 1; B. F. Hall, 292, 331; "Trial of Wm. Freeman," *Cayuga Patriot*, 8 July 1846, 2.

15. David Dimon, *The Freeman Trial: Presenting the Testimony Given in this Remarkable Case, with Comments* (Auburn, NY: Dennis Bro's & Thorne, 1871), 32 (hereafter Dimon).

16. Cayuga Gen. Sessions, "The People vs Sidney Freeman, Indict. for Obtaining Goods under False Pretenses," 23 May 1832, Cayuga County Records Office, Auburn, NY; Cayuga Gen. Sessions, "The People vs Sidney Freeman, Indictment for Petit Larceny, 2nd Offense," 19 September 1832, Cayuga County Records Office, Auburn, NY; *Auburn Prison, Registers of Male Inmates Discharged (ca. 1816)–1894, 1908–1942,* New York State Archives, Albany, NY, and Ancestry.com; B. F. Hall, 350.

17. As Tiya Miles and Sharon P. Holland have shown, many African Americans viewed Native land as a "refuge," which may explain why Freeman ran there. See Tiya Miles and Sharon P. Holland, "Introduction: Crossing Waters, Crossing Worlds," in *Crossing Waters, Crossing Worlds: The African Diaspora in Indian County*, ed. Miles and Holland (Durham, NC: Duke University Press, 2006), 4. "$25 Reward," *Auburn Journal and Advertiser*, 8 September 1840, 3; *Cayuga Patriot*, 8 July 1846, 2; B. F. Hall, 60, 326. In the years 1846–1851 in New York's seventh judicial district, which includes Cayuga County, fifty-one people were convicted of grand larceny; only 5.8 percent of those convictions resulted in sentences of five years or longer. See Documents of the Assembly of the State of New York (hereafter Doc. Assembly), 75th sess., vol. 1, no. 20, 7 January 1852, 48. Some believed Freeman's jailbreak accounted for his longer-than-average sentence. See William Henry Seward Jr., "William Freeman," 1886, 4; unpublished manuscript in file, "Articles and Speeches," William Henry Seward Papers 1801–1872, Box 121, River Campus Libraries, Special Collections, University of Rochester, Rochester, NY.

18. Documents of the Senate of the State of New-York (hereafter Doc. Senate), 63rd sess., vol. 2, no. 37, 15 February 1840, 3; Gershom Powers, *Report of Gershom Powers, Agent and Keeper of the State Prison, At Auburn* (Albany: Croswell and Van Benthuysen, 1828), 12 (hereafter Powers 1828); H. Hall, 361.

19. Many secondary sources claim that in 1848, this wooden statue was replaced by a copper one that then became known as "Copper John." However, the diary of prison guard David Mervin Bagley shows that the term "Copper John" was in use as early as 1839. Diary of David M[ervin] Bagley, 28 August 1839, 84, Bagley Family Papers, Collection 18, Box 1, Folder 11, Michigan State University Archives, Michigan State University (hereafter Bagley).

20. Bagley, 29 July 1839, 60; Powers 1828, 12; Anonymous, *A Peep into the State Prison, at Auburn, N.Y. with an Appendix, By One Who Knows* (n.p.: pub. for the author, 1839; copyrighted, 1838), 10; Austin Reed, *The Life and Adventures of a Haunted Convict*, ed. Caleb Smith (New York: Random House, 2016), 135 (hereafter Reed).

21. Scott W. Anderson, *Auburn, New York: The Entrepreneurs' Frontier* (Syracuse, NY: Syracuse University Press, 2015), 110, 112 (hereafter Anderson).

22. On the importance of the Erie Canal to New York's development of state-funded capitalism, see Brian Phillips Murphy, *Building the Empire State: Political Economy in the Early Republic* (Philadelphia: University of Pennsylvania Press, 2015), esp. chap. 5. See also Carol Sheriff, *The Artificial River: The Erie Canal and the Paradox of Progress, 1817–1862* ([New York:] Hill and Wang, 1996); and Gerard Koeppel, *Bond of Union: Building the Erie Canal and the American Empire* (Cambridge, MA: Da Capo Press, 2009).

23. Ralph S. Herre, "The History of Auburn Prison from the Beginning to

about 1867" (PhD diss., Pennsylvania State College, 1950), 32–33 (hereafter Herre). On Newgate, see W. David Lewis, *From Newgate to Dannemora: The Rise of the Penitentiary in New York, 1796–1848* (1965; reprint, Ithaca, NY: Cornell University Press, 2009), 29–53 (hereafter Lewis).

24. Quoted in Brian Phillips Murphy, *Building the Empire State: Political Economy in the Early Republic* (Philadelphia: University of Pennsylvania Press, 2015), 207.

25. Anderson, 111–12; "Legislative Acts/Legal Proceedings," *Republican Farmer* (Bridgeport, CT), 17 April 1816, 2. See also Herre, 34, citing Laws of the State of New-York, Passed at the Thirty-Ninth, Fortieth and Forty-First Sessions of the Legislature. From January 1816 to April 1818, 39–41 Sessions (Albany, 1818), 4:79–80.

26. H. Hall, 130–31, 524; "New York 1816 Assembly, Cayuga County," A New Nation Votes: American Election Returns 1787–1825, Tufts University, 11 January 2012, https://elections.lib.tufts.edu/catalog/ns0646175.

27. "Samuel Dill David Hyde to The People of the State of New York 46 Aurelius 6 Acres," *Cayuga County Deed Book S*, 22 June 1816, Cayuga County Clerk's Office, Courtesy of Cayuga County Historian's Office, Auburn, NY, 101, 102.

28. Anderson, 111; Storke, 178. On the rise of Auburn's banking industry, especially in relation to the Auburn State Prison, see Anderson, 125–31.

29. Scott Christianson, *With Liberty for Some: 500 Years of Imprisonment in America* (Boston: Northeastern University Press, 1998), 110; H. Hall, 132; Herre, 37, 42.

30. H. Hall, 132.

31. H. Hall, 133.

32. Herre, 45, 54–55, 65–66; Lewis, 86.

33. The "Pennsylvania System" was defined by total solitary confinement combined with labor inside individual cells (this labor was intended to reform prisoners and offset costs of running the prison, not to render profits). David J. Rothman, *The Discovery of the Asylum: Social Order and Disorder in the New Republic* (rev. ed.; Boston: Little, Brown, and Company, 1990), 79–88 (hereafter Rothman 1990); Rothman, "Perfecting the Prison: United States, 1789–1865," in *The Oxford History of the Prison: The Practice of Punishment in Western Society*, ed. Norval Morris and David J. Rothman (New York: Oxford University Press, 1995), 117; Herre, 60–63, 71.

34. Herre, 180–82. Herre notes that much of the income from these early contracts likely ended up in the pockets of Lynds, who was notoriously corrupt, and later wardens. Herre, 83–84.

35. Jen Manion, *Liberty's Prisoners: Carceral Culture in Early America* (Philadelphia: University of Pennsylvania Press, 2015), 32–41.

36. Edward Livingston, *Letter from Edward Livingston, Esq., to Roberts Vaux,*

on the Advantages of the Pennsylvania System of Prison Discipline for the Application of which the New Penitentiary has been Constructed Near Philadelphia, &c. &c (Philadelphia: Vesper Harding, Printer, 1828), 7.

37. Doc. Senate, 69th sess., vol. 4, no. 120, 11 April 1846, 6.

38. Levi Burr, *A Voice from Sing-Sing, Giving a General Description of the State Prison* (Albany: n.p., 1833), 16 (Burr refers to Lynds's administration of Sing Sing, during which he replicated his practices at Auburn); Doc. Assembly, 69th sess., vol. 4, no. 138, 3 March 1846, 2; Doc. Senate, 63rd sess., vol. 2, no. 37, 15 February 1840, 18.

39. Lewis, 92; Herre, 60, 71. Stripes and other clownishly humiliating uniforms had been previously used at Newgate and in some prisons in Australia and England. It was through Lynds and the Auburn State Prison, however, that horizontally striped clothing spread to other American prisons and became iconic of incarceration. See Juliet Ash, *Dress behind Bars: Prison Clothing as Criminality* (London: I. B. Tauris, 2010), 23–27; and Philip Klein, *Prison Methods in New York State* (New York: Columbia University, 1920), 152–53.

40. Edward E. Baptist, *The Half Has Never Been Told: Slavery and the Making of American Capitalism* (New York: Basic Books, 2014), 130, 139–42.

41. Charles Bulfinch, "The Subscriber Most Respectfully Requests Permission to Present to the President of the United States a Concise Statement of the Construction and of the Physical and Moral Effects of Penitentiary Prisons, On the Auburn Principle: Compiled from Authentic Documents in the Possession of his Humble Servant, Charles Bulfinch, Present Architect Capitol United States" (D. Green, Publisher, 1829), 3; "Annual Report of the Inspectors of the State Prison at Auburn, for the Year Ending 30 Sept., 1843," 12 January 1844, in Doc. Senate, 67th sess., vol. 1, no. 18, 1844, 7. Prisons using contract labor opened in Louisiana in 1835, Missouri in 1836, Alabama in 1841, and Texas in 1848. Herre, 218–19. See also Rebecca M. McLennan, *The Crisis of Imprisonment: Protest, Politics, and the Making of the American Penal State, 1776–1941* (New York: Cambridge University Press, 2008), 65–66 (hereafter McLennan), on the spread of the Auburn System in the South. The "Walls," a particularly notorious 1836 prison in Jackson, Mississippi, was modeled on Auburn. Oshinsky, 6–7.

42. On the rivalry between the Auburn and Pennsylvania Systems, see Adam Jay Hirsch, *The Rise of the Penitentiary: Prisons and Punishment in Early America* (New Haven, CT: Yale University Press, 1992), 65–66; McLennan, 62; and Rothman 1990, 81–88.

43. Gustave de Beaumont and Alexis de Tocqueville, *On the Penitentiary System in the United States and Its Application in France*, trans. Francis Lieber (1833; reprint, Carbondale: Southern Illinois University Press, 1964), xv; Herre, 89, citing *Third Annual Report of the Board of Managers of the Prison Discipline Society, Boston, 1828* (Boston, 1830), 11, 42; George Combe, *American Notes* (New

York: Cassell Publishing Co., 1894), 132–33; Harriet Martineau, *Retrospect of Western Travel* (London: Saunders and Otley, 1838), 2:123–24; Dorothea Dix, *Remarks on Prisons and Prison Discipline in the United States*, 2nd ed. (Philadelphia: Joseph Kite & Co., 1845), 10; Henry Hall, *The History of Auburn* (Auburn, NY: Dennis Bro's & Co., 1869), 260; George Combe, *Notes on the United States of North America During a Phrenological Visit in 1838–9-40* (Philadelphia: Carey & Hart, 1841), 2:71–72.

44. See, for example, David P. Hillhouse, "1826 Travel Journal," Special Collections, Wilson Library, University of North Carolina, 103–4; Maria Denny Fay, "Diary of Maria Denny Fay, 1835, May 19–June 18," Schlesinger Library, Radcliffe Institute, Harvard University, Cambridge, MA; James Stuart, *Three Years in North America, In Two Volumes*, vol. 1 (Edinburgh: printed for Robert Cadell, Edinburgh, 1833); A. M. Maxwell, *A Run Through the United States, During the Autumn of 1840, Vol. I* (London: Henry Colburn, Publisher, 1841); and Joseph Sturge, *A Visit to the United States in 1841* (Boston: Dexter S. King, 1842).

45. William Crawford, "Report on the Penitentiaries of the United States," 1835; reprinted and introduction by Norman Johnson (Montclair, NJ: Patterson Smith, 1969), 17; "A. C. F. A. History Books (A–Z), Newspapers, Periodicals," Seymour Library, Auburn, NY; Reed, 199; Anonymous, *Sketch of the Life of George Washington. Also a Journey to Niagara Falls* (Auburn, NY: Henry Oliphant, Printer, Exchange Building, 1842), 6, 22–23.

46. Doc. Assembly, 64th sess., vol. 2, no. 28, 13 January 1841, 70. The actual number of tourists may have been higher because admitting officers were sometimes suspected of pocketing admission fees. Herre, 208.

47. Anderson, 132–33; Wheeler Chapin Case, *Owasco: The "Osko," or "Was Kough" of the Cayuga-Iroquois* (n.p.: privately printed, 1950), 6.

48. Herre, 174–75.

49. Edward C. Atwater, "The Protracted Labor and Brief Life of a Country Medical School: The Auburn Medical Institution, 1825," *Journal of the History of Medicine and Allied Sciences* 34, no. 3 (July 1979): 334–52; Reed, 213; James Stuart, *Three Years in North America, In Two Volumes* (Edinburgh: printed for Robert Cadell, Edinburgh, 1833), 1:69.

50. Doc. Assembly, 64th sess., vol. 2, no. 28, 13 January 1841, 14; Phyllis F. Field, *The Politics of Race in New York: The Struggle for Black Suffrage in the Civil War Era* (Ithaca, NY: Cornell University Press, 1982), 36, quoting *Census of the State of New York for 1875* (Albany, 1877), xiv (hereafter Field).

51. On Black men's voting rights in New York before and after 1821, see Sarah L. H. Gronningsater, "'Expressly Recognized by Our Election Laws': Certificates of Freedom and the Multiple Fates of Black Citizenship in the Early Republic," *William and Mary Quarterly* 75.2 (July 2018): 465–506; Sarah L. H.

Gronningsater, "Practicing Formal Politics without the Vote: Black New York- ers in the Aftermath of 1821," in *Revolutions and Reconstructions: Black Politics in the Long Nineteenth Century*, ed. Van Gosse and David Waldstreicher (Philadel- phia: University of Pennsylvania Press, 2020), 116–38; Field, 37, 61–64, 220–21; Van Gosse, "We Think for Ourselves: Making the Battleground, 1822–1846," in *The First Reconstruction: Black Politics in America from the Revolution to the Civil War* (Chapel Hill: University of North Carolina Press, 2021), 377–434; and Paul Finkelman, "The Protection of Black Rights in Seward's New York," *Civil War History* 34, no. 3 (September 1988): 211–34.

52. Leslie Harris, "'Pressing Forward to Greater Perfection': Radical Aboli- tionists, Black Labor, and Black Working-Class Activism after 1840," in *In the Shadow of Slavery: African Americans in New York City, 1626–1863* (Chicago: University of Chicago Press, 2003), 217–46.

53. Derrick Spires, *The Practice of Citizenship: Black Politics and Print Cul- ture in the Early United States* (Philadelphia: University of Pennsylvania Press, 2019), 256n5; Jeannine Marie DeLombard, *In the Shadow of the Gallows: Race, Crime, and American Civic Identity* (Philadelphia: University of Pennsylvania Press, 2012) (hereafter DeLombard).

54. *The Present State and Condition of the Free People of Color, of the City of Philadelphia and Adjoining Districts, as Exhibited by the Report of a Committee of the Pennsylvania Society for Promoting the Abolition of Slavery, &c.* (Philadel- phia: published by the Society, 1838); DeLombard, 217–18, 223–24; see also *Re- view of a Pamphlet, Entitled an Appeal to the Public on Behalf of a House of Ref- uge for Colored Juvenile Delinquents* (Philadelphia: W. H. Brisbane, 1847), 53–54.

55. Angela Y. Davis suggests that such manipulations created an "analyti- cal impasse" for Frederick Douglass and his contemporaries. "If slavery," or ra- cial oppression more broadly, "produced criminals," Davis wrote, "then black people had to be acknowledged as criminals." Davis, "From the Prison of Slav- ery to the Slavery of Prison: Frederick Douglass and the Convict Lease Sys- tem," in *The Angela Y. Davis Reader*, ed. Joy James (Oxford: Blackwell Publish- ers, 1998), 74–95.

56. Field, 36, quoting *Census of the State of New York for 1875*, xiv.; Doc. As- sembly, 64th sess., vol. 2, no. 28, 13 January 1841, 14. African Americans were also incarcerated in Newgate Prison in New York City and in jails and juvenile reformatories throughout the state in proportions similar to that in the Auburn State Prison.

57. "Auburn, Cayuga County, New York," *Colored American*, 31 October 1840, 4, accessed 25 June 2023, Gale Primary Resources.

58. "To the Shaving Public," *Auburn Daily American*, 1856, Fulton History database, accessed 24 June 2023, https://fultonhistory.com/Fulton.html; "The Case of Luke Freeman," *Auburn Daily Union*, 27 July 1859; "A Bypath in Bygone

Cayuga. Memories of Auburn c 1901. Author Unknown. Read before CCHS. Manuscript," Cayuga Museum of History and Art & Case Research Laboratory, Auburn, NY; "Funeral of Luke Freeman, *Auburn Advertiser and Union,* 11 April 1863, clipping in Cayuga County Historian's Office, Auburn, New York; Deed Book 75, 93, and Deed Book 77, 470, Cayuga County Clerk's Office, Auburn, NY. Cited in "Uncovering," 81–84.

59. "Death of Luke Freeman," *Auburn Daily Advertiser & Union,* 10 April 1863, 12; "The Case of Luke Freeman," *Auburn Daily Union,* 27 July 1859. See also "Uncovering," 25, 28, 85–86. And see William Still, *The Underground Rail Road: A Record of Facts, Authentic Narratives, Letters, &c.* (Philadelphia: Porter & Coates, 1872), 104 and possibly 176; other references to Auburn appear on pages 54, 323, and 517.

60. "Uncovering," 83, 112–14.

61. See "1830 Federal Census: African Americans of Cayuga County, New York," compilation developed as part of the "Survey of Sites Relating to the Underground Railroad, Abolitionism, and African American Life in Auburn and Cayuga County, 1820–1870," Judith Wellman, coordinator, in cooperation with the Cayuga County Historian's Office, Auburn, New York, accessed 24 June 2023, https://www.cayugagenealogy.org/census/1830/africana.html.

Chapter Two

1. Five sources, four authored by white men and one by a Black man, provide primary evidence for Freeman's process of intake. These sources are Gershom Powers, *Report of Gershom Powers, Agent and Keeper of the State Prison, At Auburn* (Albany: Croswell and Van Benthuysen, 1828), 27 (hereafter Powers 1828); James Stuart's *Three Years in North America, In Two Volumes* (Edinburgh: printed for Robert Cadell, Edinburgh, 1833), 68–69 (hereafter Stuart); Horace Lane, *The Question What Did You Do to Get There? Answered; or, Five Years in State's Prison, Revised* (New York: privately printed, 1836); the anonymously authored *A Peep into the State Prison, at Auburn, N.Y. with an Appendix, By One Who Knows* (n.p.: pub. for the author, 1839; copyrighted, 1838), 10–12 (hereafter *Peep*); and Austin Reed, *The Life and the Adventures of a Haunted Convict,* ed. and introduced by Caleb Smith (New York: Random House, 2016), 135–37 (hereafter Reed). These sources and their authors had contrasting perspectives and goals. Powers, the agent and keeper of the Auburn State Prison from 1826 to 1829, wrote pamphlets to publicize the prison and his accomplishments. *Peep* was written by someone who was either incarcerated or worked in the prison for the purpose of contesting Powers's self-glorifying writing. Stuart was one of many white foreign visitors to the prison. Lane, also white, was imprisoned a decade before Freeman. And Reed was an African American man who was

imprisoned there simultaneously with William Freeman (Reed's lightly fictionalized memoir was likely completed in 1858, but he states that the intake process he describes is specific to 1840—the same year he and Freeman entered the prison). Although written by diverse authors with conflicting goals over a period of twenty-two years, these five narratives are consistent in their factual claims. They differ in their assessments of the intake process and highlight different details, but not one significant fact is inconsistent across the five narratives. This corroboration suggests, first, that the five narratives are accurate. Second, it evidences an intake process that was stable between 1826 and 1840 and that proceeded regardless of the prisoner's race, crime, or age. This stability is not surprising, because the Auburn State Prison valued factory-like consistency and interchangeability in all matters. W. David Lewis described "undeviating regularity" and "unchanging routine" as a "fetish among defenders of the Auburn system." W. David Lewis, *From Newgate to Dannemora: The Rise of the Penitentiary in New York, 1796–1848* (1965; reprint, Ithaca, NY: Cornell University Press, 2009), 122–23, 90 (hereafter Lewis). Since the intake process was stable and consistent, it is reasonable to assume that Freeman's experience of intake resembled the process described by Reed, Powers, Stuart, Lane, and *Peep*'s author. My description of Freeman's intake is based on a composite of these sources.

2. The locomotive in the machine room captivated the attention of first-time visitors including A. M. Maxwell, who viewed it fifteen days before Freeman entered the prison. See A. M. Maxwell, *A Run Through the United States, During the Autumn of 1840* (London: Henry Colburn, Publisher, 1841), 1:241; and Joseph Sturge, *A Visit to the United States in 1841* (Boston: Dexter S. King, 1842), 142. In general, a machine shop is a site where machining, or the cutting and shaping of raw materials, occurs; it is not a place where machines are manufactured. However, in the Auburn State Prison in 1840, men in the machine shop built threshing machines, locks, and stove furniture, in addition to the locomotive. Documents of the Senate of the State of New-York (hereafter Doc. Senate), 63rd sess., vol. 2, no. 37, 15 February 1840, 4.

3. Documents of the Assembly of the State of New York (hereafter Doc. Assembly), 64th sess., vol. 2, no. 31, 12 January 1842, 3; Doc. Assembly, 63rd sess., vol. 1, no. 18, 15 January 1840, 10; Doc. Assembly, 60th sess., vol. 1, no. 31, 13 January 1837, 12; Lewis, 117; Ralph S. Herre, "The History of Auburn Prison from the Beginning to about 1867" (PhD diss., Pennsylvania State College, 1950), 84 (hereafter Herre).

4. Basil Hall, quoted in Charles Bulfinch, "The Subscriber Most Respectfully Requests Permission to Present to the President of the United States a Concise Statement of the Construction and of the Physical and Moral Effects of Penitentiary Prisons, On the Auburn Principle" (n.p.: D. Green, Publisher, 1829), 6.

The machine shop employed thirty to thirty-two prisoners in 1840. Doc. Senate, 63rd sess., vol. 2, no. 37, 15 February 1840, 4, 26.

5. In 1840, twelve prisoners died, seven from tuberculosis. Doc. Assembly, 64th sess., vol. 2, no. 28, 13 January 1841, 16–17. From 1817 to 1843, half of all deaths in the Auburn State Prison were attributed to lung disease. Doc. Senate, 67th sess., vol. 1, no. 18, 12 January 1844, 81–83. In 1851, one doctor ascribed "nearly one half" of deaths in the prison since its founding to tuberculosis. Doc. Assembly, 75th sess., vol. 1, no. 20, 7 January 1852, 87.

6. Doc. Assembly, 64th sess., vol. 2, no. 28, 13 January 1841, 14. Seven women were incarcerated at Auburn over 1840, but they were sequestered in an attic. Women prisoners did not enter the factories and were exempt from forced silence. William Freeman likely saw women prisoners seldom or never. See Doc. Senate, 63rd sess., vol. 2, no. 37, 15 February 1840, 3; and David P. Hillhouse, "1826 Travel Journal," 106, Special Collections, Wilson Library, University of North Carolina.

7. For example, Anthony Houck, age sixty-eight, was released from Auburn in 1841, and John Wilson was listed as fourteen when he was released in 1842—after completing a sentence of five years. Houck was white; Wilson was Black. List of Convicts Discharged by Expiration of Sentence and Pardon from the Auburn and Mount-Pleasant Prisons, During the Year 1841, n.p. [p. 5]. River Campus Libraries, Special Collections, University of Rochester, Rochester, NY; List of Convicts Discharged by Expiration of Sentence and Pardon from the Auburn and Mount-Pleasant Prisons, During the Year 1842, n.p. [p. 4], River Campus Libraries, Special Collections, University of Rochester, Rochester, NY.

8. Harriet Martineau, *Retrospect of Western Travel* (London: Saunders and Otley, 1838), 2:123–34; Charles A. Murray, *Travels in North America during the Years 1834, 1835, and 1836* (New York: Harper & Brothers, 1839), 1:63.

9. Reed, 135; *Peep*, 10.

10. *Peep*, 11; Benjamin F. Hall, *The Trial of William Freeman for the Murder of John G. Van Nest, Including the Evidence and the Arguments of Counsel, with the Decision of the Supreme Court Granting a New Trial, and an Account of the Death of the Prisoner, and of the Post-Mortem Examination of his Body by Amariah Brigham, M.D. and Others* (Auburn, NY: Derby, Miller & Co. Publishers, 1848), 82, 191 (hereafter B. F. Hall); Reed, 136. If a prisoner arrived at night, his irons were cut off in the machine shop and then he was confined in a dungeon overnight. The intake process then continued in the morning. Reed, 135–36; Powers 1828, 27; *Peep*, 11. Because there is no evidence that Freeman arrived at night, his intake likely followed the standard daytime process, which bypassed the dungeon.

11. Gershom Powers, *Letter of Gershom Powers, Esq., In Answer to a Letter of the Hon. Edward Livingston, in Relation to the Auburn State Prison, Read in the*

Legislature of Pennsylvania, Jn. 23, 1829, And Ordered to be Printed (Albany: Croswell & Van Benthuysen, 1829), 12–13 (hereafter Powers 1829); *Peep*, 10–11. The narrator states that uniforms were always flung at, not given to, the prisoners. Reed, 136; Samuel Gridley Howe, *An Essay on Separate and Congregate Systems of Prison Discipline* (Boston: n.p., 1846), 43, qtd. in Lewis, 113–14; Lewis, 113, citing *Northern Christian Advocate*, 11 February 1846.

12. B. F. Hall, 332, 403; "Trial of Wm. Freeman the Negro," *Daily Cayuga Tocsin*, 4 July 1846, 3.

13. Abraham Gridley was clerk in September 1840. Doc. Assembly, 64th sess., vol. 2, no. 28, 13 January 1841, 66.

14. The clerk's questions are quoted from Reed, 136. The italicized answers reflect factual information or lightly paraphrase Freeman's answers to similar questions (see, for example, B. F. Hall, 40, 43–44, 54, 226, 234, 258, 273, 292, 294, 331–33, 358, 400; and "Trial of Wm. Freeman," *Cayuga Patriot*, 15 July 1846, 1. On the clerk measuring prisoners, see *Peep*, 11. The New York State Archives holds the *Register of Commitments of Prisoners to the Auburn State Prison after 1849*; the volume containing Gridley's notes during Freeman's intake is not extant. New York State Education Department, New York State Archives, Albany, New York, Series Number A0603.

15. B. F. Hall, 48, 75–76, 326–27.

16. Doc. Assembly, 75th sess., vol. 1, no. 20, 7 January 1852, 7.

17. On Polhemus, see *Auburn Journal and Advertiser*, 11 December 1839; "A Reptile," *Auburn Journal and Advertiser*, 15 September 1841; *Auburn Daily Advertiser*, 4 October 1858 (Card Catalog of Cayuga County Historian's Office, Auburn, New York); *Ithaca Journal and Advertiser*, 31 March 1830; Doc. Assembly, 75th sess., vol. 3, no. 128, 7 April 1852, 27; A New Nation Votes: American Election Returns 1787–1825, Tufts University, 11 April 2012, https://elections.lib.tufts.edu/catalog/cn69m500p and https://elections.lib.tufts.edu/catalog/9z903090v. See also "Henry Polhemus," Seward Family Digital Archive, University of Rochester, accessed 25 June 2023, https://sewardproject.org/person-public-fields/5975; Eric J. Greenfield, "Losing Local Power: The Coevolution of Social and Biophysical Forces in Cayuga County, New York, 1800 to 1900" (PhD diss., State University of New York College of Environmental Science and Forestry, Syracuse, New York), 99 (hereafter Greenfield); *Auburn Journal and Advertiser*, 17 May 1837, 3; Henry Hall, *The History of Auburn* (Auburn, NY: Dennis Bro's & Co., 1869), 71, 359, 508 (hereafter H. Hall).

18. *An Account of the Proceedings of the Meeting at Auburn, on the 23rd Day of August, 1828: In Relation to the Measures Taken to Enforce the Observance of the Sabbath, and the Attempt to Establish a Christian Party in Politics* (Auburn, NY: printed by Richard Oliphant, 1828); *Address Delivered by William H. Seward; at the Commencement of the Auburn and Owasco Canal, October 14, 1835: With*

the Proceedings of the Celebration (Auburn: H. Ivison & Co., 1835), 25; William Henry Seward, *Autobiography of William H. Seward from 1801 to 1834: With a Memoir of his Life and Selections from his Letters from 1831 to 1846* (New York: D. Appleton, 1877), 294; Greenfield, 277. Polhemus was also, in 1839, chairman of the powerful Cayuga County Board of Canvassers, which ran elections. *Auburn Journal and Advertiser*, 20 November 1839, 4.

19. Doc. Senate, 63rd sess., vol. 2, no. 37, 15 February 1840, 41.

20. In 1830, a scandal forced Lynds out of Sing Sing. He retreated to Syracuse to run a hardware store and manufacture high-speed rotary steam engines. Frederic A. Lyman, "A Practical Hero," *Mechanical Engineering*, February 2004, 37–38; Letter to the Editor, *Mechanics' Magazine, and Journal of the Mechanics' Institute* 5, no. 3 (March 1835): 141; "From Mr. Felt, to Messrs. Lynds," *Mechanics' Magazine, and Journal of the Mechanics' Institute* 5, no. 6 (June 1835): 303.

21. Gershom Powers, *A Brief Account of the Construction, Management, & Discipline &c, &c, of the New-York State Prison at Auburn, Together with a Compendium of Criminal Law* (Auburn, NY: U. F. Doubleday, 1826), 17; Willet Lounsbury, "The Auburn Prison," *Cayuga Patriot*, 11 July 1838, 2. For more on Powers's efforts to redeem prisoners, see Jennifer Graber, "Engaging the Trope of Redemptive Suffering: Inmate Voices in the Antebellum Prison Debates," *Pennsylvania History: A Journal of Mid-Atlantic Studies* 79, no. 2 (Spring 2012): 214–17.

22. The title "inspectors" implies that the board monitored the prison and checked its administrators' power. In fact, however, the Board of Inspectors and the prison administration, which were appointed together by the same political party, worked together. As a later report put it, "It is an abuse of terms to call them Inspectors. They are in fact governors of the prison." Doc. Assembly, 75th sess., vol. 1, no. 20, 7 January 1852, 8. Lounsbury countered the structure of governance when he opposed Lynds.

23. Willet Lounsbury, "The Auburn Prison," *Cayuga Patriot*, 11 July 1838, 2.

24. Van Gosse, *The First Reconstruction: Black Politics in America from the Revolution to the Civil War* (Chapel Hill: University of North Carolina Press, 2021), 311. In 1840, Van Buren did not win reelection, losing to William Henry Harrison, the first Whig president.

25. "To the Public," *Auburn Journal and Advertiser*, 8 August 1838, 5.

26. "To the Public," *Auburn Journal and Advertiser*, 8 August 1838, 5. The *Cayuga Patriot* also published rejoinders to its own editor. *Cayuga Patriot*, 25 July 1838, 2; "Auburn State Prison," *Auburn Journal and Advertiser*, 23 May 1838, 2; "Auburn State Prison," *Auburn Journal and Advertiser*, 20 March 1839, 5.

27. *Auburn Journal Extra, Auburn Journal and Advertiser*, 16 October 1839, 5, 6; Doc. Senate, 63rd sess., vol. 2, no. 48, 17 February 1840, 74. In 1837, when prisoners ate in the dining hall, prison doctor Leander Bigelow reported 99 to-

tal cases of diarrhea for that year. However, when dining was moved to cells, Bigelow recorded 138 cases of diarrhea in the month of June 1838 alone. Willet Lounsbury, "The Auburn Prison," *Cayuga Patriot*, 11 July 1838, 2.

28. For example, in spring 1838, an anonymous Auburn insider—possibly a former prisoner or a factory foreman—authored *A Peep into the State Prison, at Auburn, N.Y.*, which exposed extreme violence inside the prison. That summer, a circular titled *Chronicles* was published under the pseudonym "Ezra the Scribe." In mock-biblical language, it accused Lynds, or "Elam the Ishmaelite," of corruption and immorality—while celebrating his heroic antagonist, "Willet the Beautiful." Ezra the Scribe [Silas N. Shepherd, Willet Lounsbury, and Oramel Bliss], *Chronicles*, vol. 1, no. 1, 10 August 1838, Rare Book and Manuscript Library, Columbia University, New York, NY. These anonymous publications excited intrigue—especially after an author of *Chronicles* was revealed to be Willet Lounsbury. Lounsbury was arrested for criminal libel, and his hearing exposed yet more sordid facts about Lynds's administration. *Auburn Journal and Advertiser*, 15 May 1839, 3.

29. Doc. Senate, 63rd sess., vol. 2, no. 38, 15 February 1840, 5; *Auburn Journal Extra, Auburn Journal and Advertiser*, 16 October 1839, 5; Ezra the Scribe [Silas N. Shepherd, Willet Lounsbury, and Oramel Bliss], *Chronicles*, vol. 1, no. 3, 1839, 12–13; *Peep*, 68–69; Appendix to *Peep*, 10–13; "Auburn Prison," *Auburn Journal and Advertiser*, 10 April 1839, 2. Newspapers frequently reported on the public indignation caused by newspaper reports. See, for example, "A Peep into the State Prison at Auburn," *Evangelical Magazine and Gospel Advocate*, 15 February 1839, 10.

30. *Cayuga Tocsin*, 22 April 1840, 2; H. Hall, 225.

31. "From the Auburn Journal," *New York Spectator*, 7 February 1839; "Auburn Prison," *Auburn Journal and Advertiser*, 10 April 1839, 2. Polhemus took his role seriously, inspecting the prison eight and nine times in November 1839 and May 1849, respectively. Doc. Assembly, 64th sess., no. 28, 13 January 1841, 42, 49. On Polhemus's failed attempt to pass a measure to feed prisoners in the mess halls, see Doc. Senate, 63rd sess., vol. 2, no. 37, 15 February 1840, 41. Whig-backed pressure did, however, succeed in forcing Lynds's immediate Democratic successor, Noyes Palmer, to reinstate congregate meals.

32. "State Prison Cruelties," *New York Spectator*, 18 April 1839; Doc. Assembly, 63rd sess., vol. 1, no. 18, 15 January 1840, 19; "Auburn Prison," *Auburn Journal and Advertiser*, 10 April 1839, 2; "Auburn Prison," *Hudson River Chronicle*, 23 April 1839, 3; "Auburn State Prison Inquest," *Albany Evening Journal*, 25 April 1839.

33. Doc. Senate, 63rd sess., vol. 2, no. 37, 15 February 1840, 39–40. For more on the role of the von Eck scandal in Lynds's downfall, see Jeffrey A. Mullins,

"Shifting Our Focus on New York's Rural History: Politics, Prisons, and Social Reform," *New York History* 97, nos. 3–4 (Summer–Fall 2016): 427–49.

34. Diary of David M[ervin] Bagley, 4 November 1839, 142, Bagley Family Papers, Collection 18, Box 1, Folder 11, Michigan State University Archives, Michigan State University (hereafter Bagley); Bagley, 11 November 1839, 150; Bagley, 2 March 1840, 215; Bagley, 20 April 1840, 231–32. Bagley was among the non-Whigs to be fired immediately before Palmer became agent. After Lynds resigned, the Democrats retained enough power to appoint Noyes Palmer. Palmer was a Hunker (a faction of the Democratic Party that favored state capitalism, especially in alliance with business interests) and was loyal to Lynds and the Democrats; he vowed to continue Lynds's policies. *Auburn Journal and Advertiser,* 9 April 1844; *Auburn Journal and Advertiser,* 15 May 1839. As the Whigs gained power, they dismissed Palmer and installed a Whig, Robert Cook, as agent and keeper. Cook held the position one month; then the New York State Legislature split his position into two: the agent (a financial and administrative role) and the keeper (with responsibility for prison security). The new role of keeper went to Cook, and Polhemus became the agent.

35. *Corrector* (Auburn, NY) 1, no. 2 (24 May 1839): 4; *Corrector* (Auburn, NY) 1, no. 1 (1 May 1839): 3, 4.

36. *Auburn Journal and Advertiser,* 17 February 1841.

37. Under Whig pressure, Noyes Palmer reopened the dining room. David M. Bagley, a Lynds-appointed guard, first saw the prisoners in the mess hall on June 1, 1839, and commented that he was "well pleased with the change." Bagley, 1 June 1839, 11. Later that month, the phrenologist George Combe visited the prison in the company of Governor Seward and commented on the incarcerated diners "seated at narrow tables arranged like the seats in a theatre." Combe, *Notes on the United States of North America During a Phrenological Visit in 1838–9-40* (Philadelphia: Carey & Hart, 1841), 2:72.

38. Doc. Assembly, 64th sess., vol. 2, no. 28, 13 January 1841, 11–12. Throughout this section of the chapter, "Polhemus's predecessors" refers to Lynds and Palmer. Doc, Assembly, 64th sess., vol. 2, no. 28, 13 January 1841, 10–11.

39. Horace Lane, *Five Years in State's Prison; or, Interesting Truths Showing the Manner of Discipline in the State Prisons at Singsing [sic] and Auburn,* 4th ed. (New York: printed for the author by Luther Pratt & Son, 1835), 18; Ezra the Scribe [Silas N. Shepherd, Willet Lounsbury, and Oramel Bliss], *Chronicles* 1, no. 3 (1839): 13; *Peep,* 67–73.

40. Doc. Assembly, 64th sess., vol. 2, no. 28, 13 January 1841, 1–2, 9. Polhemus neglected to acknowledge that he, as inspector, had approved Noyes Palmer's report for 1838–1839—the very report Polhemus decried in his report of 1839–1840. On Polhemus's self-declared attempts to right his predecessors' wrongs,

see also Doc. Assembly, 62nd sess., vol. 1, no. 11, 7 January 1839, 8; Doc. Assembly, 63rd sess., vol. 1, no. 18, 15 January 1840, 8; Doc. Assembly, 64th sess., vol. 2, no. 28, 13 January 1841, 12, 15–16; Doc. Assembly, 64th sess., vol. 2, no. 31, 12 January 1842, 11–12. Polhemus also inherited financial woes that his predecessors' malfeasance had exacerbated but did not cause. The Panic of 1837 made it hard for some contractors to pay their fees, so previous agents leased prisoners' labor on credit. As a result, the cash-strapped prison sometimes could not pay the guards and other officers on time. Bagley, 18 November 1839, 153–54.

41. Polhemus and Freeman may have recognized each other because Polhemus was a landlord in New Guinea and he lived barely a quarter mile away from the Black neighborhood (see figure 1.2). But their new relationship as prisoner and agent eclipsed any previous association. On Polhemus's land in New Guinea, see, for example, deed of 16 September 1834, Book UU, 116, Cayuga County Historian's Office, Auburn, New York. See also vertical file "Polhamus" [sic], Cayuga County Historian's Office, Auburn, NY. For the location of Polhemus's home, see figure 1.2. Polhemus also owned land adjacent to the Hardenbergh tract, where Freeman's grandmother Kate Freeman lived. See "Deed— John H. Hardenbergh and wife to Allen Warden and Asaph Leonard, July. 23, 1829," Item 141 in file "Hardenbergh, Deeds and Land Grants," Box "Hardenberg Archives," Cayuga Museum of History and Art & Case Research Laboratory, Auburn, NY.

42. Henry Polhemus, "Manufacture of Silk at Auburn," *Cultivator*, August 1841, 129; Doc. Senate, 63rd sess., vol. 2, no. 48, 17 February 1840, 2.

43. Like the intake process of which it was a part, the agent's speech was notably stable over the decades. The content varied little, although some agents emphasized threats while others emphasized opportunities for reformation. Six primary sources corroborate the elements of this speech: Reed (which describes the speech during Polhemus's administration), *Peep* (which describes the speeches of Levi Lewis and Gershom Powers), Stuart (which describes intake under Powers), Gershom Powers, *A Brief Account of the Construction, Management, & Discipline &c, &c, of the New-York State Prison at Auburn, Together with a Compendium of Criminal Law* (Auburn, NY: U. F. Doubleday, 1826) (hereafter Powers 1826), Powers 1828, and Powers 1829 (all of which describe Powers's practices). As with the primary texts that describe the intake process overall, this harmony across sources is extraordinary because their authors differ in race, nationality, and perspective on the prison; and they describe the ritual as enacted by three Agents across fifteen years. My description of Polhemus's speech to Freeman is based on a composite of these six sources.

44. Powers 1829, 13.

45. Powers 1829, 13–14.

46. *Peep*, 12, emphasis in original.

47. *Peep*, 12–14.

48. *Peep*, 13; Reed, 145.

49. Slight paraphrases of Reed, 145, 144.

50. Reed, 144.

51. Reed, 144; *Peep*, 13–14, emphasis in original.

52. *Peep*, 12; Beaumont and Tocqueville, 164.

53. Herre, 57–59; H. Hall, 361–62.

54. Herre, 81, 185; Lewis, 125.

55. Powers 1828, 113; Stuart, 66; Doc. Assembly, 75th sess., vol. 1, no. 20, 7 January 1852, 67.

56. Camphine was a brand of lamp oil that was also used to combat bedbugs and other insects. It had little effect on the vermin, but it caused in prisoners "a great lassitude, and even faintness in the morning." Doc. Assembly, 75th sess., vol. 1, no. 20, 7 January 1852, 88. See also Stuart, 69; Herre, 58–59; Doc. Assembly, 64th sess., vol. 2, no. 28, 13 January 1841, 11; Doc. Assembly, 72nd sess., vol. 6, no. 243, 8 March 1849, 216; Doc. Senate, 94th sess., vol. 2, no. 21, 26 January 1871, 187–88.

57. *Report of the Trial of Henry Wyatt, A Convict in the State Prison at Auburn, Indicted for the Murder of James Gordon, Another Convict Within the Prison* (Auburn, NY: J. C. Derby & Co., 1846), 23.

58. Freeman's birthday was September 29. "Trial of Wm. Freeman on the Preliminary Issue of Present Insanity," *Cayuga Patriot*, 15 July 1846, 1.

Chapter Three

1. Horace Lane, *The Question What Did You Do to Get There? Answered; or, Five Years in State's Prison, Revised* (New York, privately printed, 1836), 28 (hereafter Lane 1836). The time of the morning bell varied slightly by season, and the respective use of left and right hands could vary based on the location of the jailor. The lockstep was instituted by Lynds but likely invented by Cray. W. David Lewis, *From Newgate to Dannemora: The Rise of the Penitentiary in New York, 1796–1848* (1965; reprint, Ithaca, NY: Cornell University Press, 2009), 93 (hereafter Lewis).

2. A Massachusetts Man, *Letters on the Comparative Merits of the Pennsylvania and New York Systems of Penitentiary Discipline* (Boston: Perkins & Marvin, 1836), 38; Harriet Martineau, *Retrospect of Western Travel* (London: Saunders and Otley: Harper & Brothers, 1838), 2:123, 124; Austin Reed, *The Life and Adventures of a Haunted Convict*, ed. Caleb Smith (New York: Random House, 2016), 151 (hereafter Reed); Anonymous, *A Peep into the State Prison, at Auburn, N.Y. with an Appendix, By One Who Knows* (pub. for the author, 1839; copyrighted 1838), 57

(hereafter *Peep*); Fred Packard, *Memorandum of a Late Visit to the Auburn Penitentiary* (Philadelphia, PA: J. Harding, Printer, 1842), 6 (hereafter Packard).

3. Gershom Powers, *Report of Gershom Powers, Agent and Keeper of the State Prison, At Auburn* (Albany: Croswell and Van Benthuysen, 1828), 28 (hereafter Powers 1828); Reed, 141–42. This paragraph describes the hame shop as Freeman first encountered it in 1840. By January 1842, Polhemus had ordered thirty-three prisoners, under the direction of a master builder, to construct a new brick building that would hold the hame shop and other factories. Documents of the Assembly of the State of New York, 64th sess., vol. 2, no. 31, 12 January 1842, 2–3, 13 (hereafter Doc. Assembly); Doc. Assembly, 64th sess., vol. 4, no. 65, 15 February 1842, 24–25; Documents of the Senate of the State of New-York, 64th sess., vol. 2, no. 54, 25 March 1841, 15 (hereafter Doc. Senate); *Peep*, 31. In 1841, $32,000 was worth about $1 million today.

4. Doc. Assembly, 64th sess., vol. 2, no. 31, 12 January 1842, 7. The sum refers to the total revenue from the hame shop's contractor from October 1, 1840, through September 3, 1841. On daily rates for prisoners' labor in the hame shop, see Doc. Assembly, 64th sess., vol. 4, no. 65, 15 February 1842, 49. Contractors paid half the contracted amount for the labor of disabled, or "half-price" men. Contractors manipulated the system to place as many men as possible in that category. In 1852, for example, 184 out of 636 prisoners worked at half-price. Doc. Assembly, 75th sess., vol. 1, no. 20, 7 January 1852, 10–11. In 1843, thirty men worked in the hame shop—but only six at the full rate. *Documents in Relation to State Prison Competition*, (Albany, NY[?]: n.p., 1843), American Antiquarian Society, Worcester, MA), 4. William Freeman was a half-price man. Benjamin F. Hall, *The Trial of William Freeman for the Murder of John G. Van Nest, Including the Evidence and the Arguments of Counsel, with the Decision of the Supreme Court Granting a New Trial, and an Account of the Death of the Prisoner, and of the Post-Mortem Examination of his Body by Amariah Brigham, M.D. and Others* (Auburn, NY: Derby, Miller & Co. Publishers, 1848), 388 (hereafter B. F. Hall).

5. Doc. Senate, 64th sess., vol. 2, no. 54, 25 March 1841, 19; Doc. Assembly, 64th sess., vol. 4, no. 65, 15 February 1842, 38; B. F. Hall, 263; "Trial of Wm. Freeman, On the Preliminary Issue of Present Insanity," *Cayuga Patriot*, 15 July 1846, 1; Powers 1828, 28–30; Horace Lane, *The Wandering Boy, Careless Sailor, and Result of Inconsideration* (Skaneateles, NY: printed for the author by Luther A. Pratt, 1839), 191. See also Lane 1836, 15. The morning meal consisted of meat, bread, hominy, potatoes, and rye coffee; dinner was meal-thickened broth, bread, potatoes, and water. *Peep*, 66.

6. *Daily Punishment Reports of the Auburn State Prison*, 1 November 1840, New York State Archives, New York State Education Department, Albany (hereafter *Punishment Reports*); Reed, 150.

7. Auburn prisoners' strategies for reducing labor shared much with the strategies of enslaved people. On resistance to slavery through slowed and spoiled work, see Stephanie M. H. Camp, *Closer to Freedom: Enslaved Women & Everyday Resistance in the Plantation South* (Chapel Hill: University of North Carolina Press, 2004), as well as older sources such as Eugene Genovese, *Roll, Jordan, Roll: The World the Slaves Made* (New York: Vintage Books, 1976).

8. *Peep*, 40; Reed, 167.

9. *Punishment Reports*, 2–10 November 1840.

10. *Punishment Reports*, 1 November 1840.

11. Powers 1828, 30–31. In some of the years while Freeman was incarcerated, prisoners ate a third, evening meal in their cells. John W. Barber, *Pictorial History of the State of New York* (Cooperstown, NY: H. & E. Phinney, 1846), 62.

12. B. F. Hall, 63, 262, 326–27. See also "Trial of Wm. Freeman," *Cayuga Patriot*, 15 July 1846, 1.

13. "Samuel P. Hopkins [Obituary]," *Democrat and Chronicle* (Rochester, NY), 23 December 1907, 4; "Supreme Court," *Auburn Journal and Advertiser*, 16 October 1839, 5. Hoskins, like so many of the prison's employees, owed his job to nepotism: he was hired by his father, Joshua Hoskins, who was a member of the Board of Prison Inspectors and a vociferous defender of Lynds. Doc. Senate, 63rd sess., vol. 2, no. 37, 15 February 1840, 34–35; "The Auburn Prison," *Cayuga Patriot*, 11 July 1838, 2; *Auburn Journal and Advertiser*, 16 October 1839, 6; *Corrector* (Auburn, NY) 1, no. 2 (24 May 1839), 4; Edwin R. Hoskins, "A Hoskins Family Record," Scipio Center [?], New York, privately printed, 1963, 32, https://archive.org/details/hoskinsfamilyrec00hosk.

14. B. F. Hall, 263–64; *Auburn Journal and Advertiser*, 16 October 1839, 5; *Cayuga Tocsin*, 22 April 1840, 2. James E. Tyler, a Democrat, was a holdover from the Lynds administration. In the brief period after Lynds was ousted but before the Whigs took control of the Auburn State Prison, Tyler reportedly lobbied for promotion to agent. When the Democrats instead appointed Noyes Palmer, Tyler became a "renegade" who turned on Lynds, testifying against him. *Auburn Journal Extra, Auburn Journal and Advertiser*, 16 October 1839, 5. The Whigs rewarded Tyler by retaining him as one of Auburn's few higher officers who was a Democrat. *Cayuga Tocsin*, 20 May 1840, 2; see also *Cayuga Tocsin*, 29 April 1840, 2. In contrast with Freeman, Austin Reed described Tyler in positive terms. See Reed, 148–49.

15. Doc. Assembly, 75th sess., vol. 1, no. 20, 7 January 1852, 172; *Auburn Journal Extra, Auburn Journal and Advertiser*, 16 October 1839, 5; B. F. Hall, 326–27, 241; *Cayuga Patriot*, 8 July 1846, 1.

16. B. F. Hall, 236; *Cayuga Patriot*, 8 July 1846, 1.

17. David Dimon, *The Freeman Trial: Presenting the Testimony Given in this Remarkable Case, with Comments* (Auburn, NY: Dennis Bro's & Thorne, 1871),

38 (hereafter Dimon); B. F. Hall, 64–65, 236, 262–64; *Cayuga Patriot*, 15 July 1846, 1. Benjamin Van Keuren, who witnessed the beating, did not support Tyler's claim that Freeman had attacked him. B. F. Hall, 65–66.

18. B. F. Hall, 20, 66, 236, 248, 286–87, 393, 498–99, 505. After this beating, Freeman lost all his hearing in his left ear and most of his hearing in his right ear. Blanchard Fosgate, "Case of William Freeman, the Murderer of the Van Nest Family," *American Journal of the Medical Sciences*, October 1847, 29.

19. B. F. Hall, 235–36; Bagley, 15 July 1839, 46. Bagley's diary records the tourists he observed in 1838–1839 (he did not, of course, observe all tourists). In 1839, at least 8,916 tourists were admitted. Doc. Assembly, 63rd sess., vol. 1, no. 18, 15 January 1840, 7. Bagley did not distinguish between personal visitors and tourists, likely because family members, like tourists, were required to pay the entrance fee and forbidden from speaking with the prisoners.

20. Powers 1826, 68. As support for abolition rose, parallels between enslaved and nonenslaved workers also became disturbing for other categories of people, including Northern white workers and navy men. As Martha Hodes notes in chapter 2 of *The Sea Captain's Wife*, white women workers in the North sometimes protested their working conditions by comparing them to those of enslaved Southerners or by likening "Corporation Tyranny" to "Southern Slavery." In later years, however, white women workers rejected parallels between themselves and enslaved African Americans on the grounds that the comparison "detracts from the dignity of the laborer." Martha Hodes, *The Sea Captain's Wife: A True Story of Love, Race, and War in the Nineteenth Century* (New York: W. W. Norton & Company, 2006), 49, 74. Campaigns against the whipping of US sailors arose alongside resistance to whipping in prison, and the US Navy outlawed the practice in 1850. On campaigns against the whipping of sailors and of prisoners in relation to Southern slavery, see Myra C. Glenn, "The Naval Reform Campaign against Flogging: A Case Study in Changing Attitudes toward Corporal Punishment, 1830–1850," *American Quarterly* 35, no. 4 (Autumn 1983): 408–25; and Myra C. Glenn, *Campaigns against Corporal Punishment: Prisoners, Sailors, Women, and Children in Antebellum America* (Albany: State University of New York Press, 1984), 39–40, 113–14.

21. *Report of the Trial of Henry Wyatt, a Convict in the State Prison at Auburn, Indicted for the Murder of James Gordon, Another Convict within the Prison, before the Court of Oyer and Terminer Held at Auburn, N.Y., Commencing Wednesday, February Eleventh, Eighteen Hundred Forty-Six* (Auburn, NY: J. C. Derby & Co., 1846), 11, 19.

22. Doc. Senate, 66th sess., vol. 1, no. 9, 16 January 1843, 72–74.

23. Doc. Assembly, 75th sess., vol. 1, no. 20, 7 January 1852, 141; Blanchard Fosgate, *Crime and Punishment* (Auburn, NY: W. J. Moses, 1866), 21 (hereafter Fosgate 1866).

24. Doc. Senate, 69th sess., vol. 3, no. 9, 16 January 1843, 74, emphasis in original. At the time, the application of running water to the body was associated with health more than cleanliness. See Kathleen M. Brown, *Foul Bodies: Cleanliness in Early America* (New Haven, CT: Yale University Press, 2009).

25. Levi Burr, *A Voice from Sing-Sing, Giving a General Description of the State Prison* (Albany: n.p., 1833), 16. Burr referred to Lynds's administration of Sing Sing, during which Lynds replicated his practices from Auburn. Packard, 4–5; Doc. Assembly, 75th sess., vol. 1, no. 20, 7 January 1852, 27, 98. In the late 1830s, two water-cure establishments opened near Auburn. H. Hall, 219.

26. Reed, 202–3; see also Reed, 212; Doc. Assembly, 75th sess., vol. 1, no. 20, 7 January 1852, 77.

27. Blanchard Fosgate, "State Prison Water Cure," *Cayuga Chief*, 11 March 1851, clipping, Seymour Library, Auburn, NY; Lewis, 271; Doc. Assembly, 75th sess., vol. 1, no. 20, 7 January 1852, 128–29; Fosgate 1866, 22. See also Reed, 202. Typically, three or four barrels were used. Doc. Assembly, 75th sess., vol. 1, no. 20, 7 January 1852, 141. A standard American barrel holds about thirty-one gallons.

28. Fosgate 1866, 22–23.

29. B. F. Hall, 326.

30. Doc. Assembly, 75th sess., vol. 1, no. 20, 7 January 1852, 87; B. F. Hall, 326–27; "Trial of Wm. Freeman," *Cayuga Patriot*, 15 July 1846, 1; Reed, 202.

31. Dorothea Dix, *Remarks on Prisons and Prison Discipline in the United States*, 2nd ed. (Philadelphia, PA: Joseph Kite & Co., 1845), 24–25. Fosgate condemned both showering and whipping, favoring the Pennsylvania System of permanent solitary confinement, combined with labor, for all prisoners. His condemnation of all pain-based punishment was based in white supremacist ideology: the "confiding, imitative, and delicately organized African [cannot] be brought up by physical pain to our highest standard of energy, any more than the proud spirited son of the forest, in whose breast the Almighty has implanted a deep hatred to all our forms of civilization, can be made to see things as we perceive them." Doc. Assembly, 75th sess., vol. 1, no. 20, 7 January 1852, 78–79.

32. David R. Roediger, *The Wages of Whiteness: Race and the Making of the American Working Class* (London and New York: Verso, 1991); Leslie Harris, "'Pressing Forward to Greater Perfection': Radical Abolitionists, Black Labor, and Black Working-Class Activism after 1840," in *In the Shadow of Slavery: African Americans in New York City, 1626–1863* (Chicago: University of Chicago Press, 2003), 217–46.

33. Doc. Assembly, 64th sess., vol. 4, no. 65, 15 February 1842, 40, 68; Doc. Assembly, 63rd sess., vol. 3, no. 339, 30 April 1840, 2, 8.

34. Doc Assembly, 64th sess., vol. 2, no. 54, 25 March 1841, 2.

35. On ongoing attacks from Democrats, see, for example, "A Reptile," *Auburn Journal and Advertiser*, 15 September 1841. New York legislators advocated

silkmaking in prisons in 1835, and a few mulberry trees were then planted in Auburn—but without an in-prison champion, the venture withered. Doc. Assembly, 64th sess., vol. 2, no. 31, 12 January 1842, 14; Lewis, 194. When Polhemus restarted silkmaking in Auburn, he took every opportunity to credit Seward with the idea, and Seward did not demur. Denise Nicole Green and Nancy Breen, "Silk Mania in the Auburn Prison, 1841–1844," *Dress: The Journal of the Costume Society of America* 2021, 1, doi:10.1080/13612112.2021.1877975 (hereafter Green and Breen), citing "Chapter III, Article 1" of *The Revised Statutes of the State of New York* (Albany, NY: Packard, 1835), 2:639. See also Henry Polhemus, "The Silk Business at Auburn," *Cultivator*, March 1843, 43.

36. Emily Pawley, *The Nature of the Future: Agriculture, Science, and Capitalism in the Antebellum North* (Chicago: University of Chicago Press, 2020), 104–30; "Silk in State Prisons," *Auburn Journal and Advertiser*, 25 May 1841, 2.

37. "Manufacture of Silk at Auburn," *Cultivator*, August 1841, 129, emphasis in original. In 1841, $350 would have been worth more than $11,000 today.

38. "The Prisons—Mechanical Labor—Manufacture of Silk," *Auburn Journal and Advertiser*, 19 May 1841, 2; "Manufacture of Silk at Auburn," *Cultivator*, August 1841, 129. By eliminating contractors, silkmaking addressed the contractors' threat to the power of agents. Many people who were associated with the prison observed that because Auburn's administration turned over frequently but contractors stayed for decades, the "contractors rule the prisons." Doc. Assembly, 75th sess., vol. 1, no. 20, 7 January 1852, 4–5, 79. Silkmaking promised to shift power to Agent Polhemus.

39. Doc. Assembly, 64th sess., vol. 2, no. 31, 12 January 1842, 14.

40. Abraham Gridley, "Silk Manufacture at Auburn," *Cultivator*, January 1842, 13; Doc. Senate, 66th sess., vol. 1, no. 9, 16 January 1843, 12; Green and Breen, 9; Doc. Assembly, 64th sess., vol. 2, no. 31, 12 January 1842, 13–14; William Seward, "Governor's Message," *New York Tribune*, 5 January 1842, 1; H. Hall, 250.

41. Doc. Senate, 66th sess., vol. 1, no. 23, 4 February 1843, 4; Green and Breen, 1; L. P. Brockett, *Silk Industry in America: A History Prepared for the Centennial Exposition* (New York: George Nesbitt & Co for the Silk Association of America, 1876), 121; Doc. Senate, vol. 2, no. 63, 9 March 1843, 38; Doc. Senate, 66th sess., vol. 1, no. 23, 4 February 1843, 4.

42. "Trial of Wm. Freeman," *Cayuga Patriot*, 15 July 1846, 1; Abraham Gridley, "Silk Manufacture at Auburn," *Cultivator*, January 1842, 13; B. F. Hall, 284, 327. For the practices of dyeing silk that were likely used in the Auburn State Prison, see E. G. Storke, ed., *The Family and Householder's Guide* (Auburn, NY: Auburn Publishing Company, 1859), 83–86; and Thomas Packer, *The Dyer's Guide; Being a Compendium of the Art of Dyeing Linen, Cotton, Silk, Wool, Muslin, Dresses,*

Furniture, &c., &c. 2nd ed. (London: printed for Sherwood, Gilbert, and Piper, 1830), 63–68.

43. Doc. Senate, 67th sess., vol. 1, no.18, 12 January 1844, 9; Doc. Senate, 66th sess., vol. 1, no. 23, 4 February 1843, 4, 7.

44. Elliot G. Storke, *History of Cayuga County, New York* (Syracuse, NY: D. Mason & Co., 1879), 422. On Seward not seeking reelection in 1842, see Walter Stahr, *Seward: Lincoln's Indispensable Man* (New York: Simon & Schuster, 2012), 83.

45. Doc. Senate, 67th sess., vol. 1, no.18, 12 January 1844, 16.

46. Green and Breen, 11. Surprisingly, Beardsley did not seek political gain from his predecessor's illegal neglect of the *Punishment Reports.* The day he became agent, however, Beardsley reactivated the ledger. Doc. Senate, 67th sess., vol. 1, no. 18, 12 January 1844, 9; Abraham Gridley, "Silk Manufacture at Auburn," *Cultivator,* January 1842, 13; Green and Breen, 10, citing *Daily Punishment Reports* and "Manufacture of Silk at Auburn," *Cultivator,* August 1841, 129.

47. B. F. Hall, 338; *Punishment Reports,* 5 June 1843; *Punishment Reports,* 18 July 1843; Dimon, 21.

48. Holograph trial transcript, Box A20, folder "Account of Freeman Trial?," 9, Cayuga Museum of History and Art & Case Research Laboratory, Auburn, NY; B. F. Hall, 42–43, 71–72, 282–83; *Punishment Reports,* 10 November 1843, 23; *Punishment Reports,* 22 December 1843. The Andrew Aiken identified in the *Punishment Reports* is likely Andrew Agan (also spelled Agun and O'Gan), a man from Scotland, born in 1817, who was imprisoned alongside Freeman from 1841 to 1844. New York State Archives, Albany, NY; *Auburn Prison, Registers of Male Inmates Discharged (ca. 1816)–1894, 1908–1942;* Ancestry.com. I thank Mary Jo Watts for her identification of Aiken.

Chapter Four

1. Images of US half-dollars, including half-dollars coined between 1839 and 1845, are available from the American Numismatic Society at http://numismatics .org/.

2. List of Convicts Discharged by Expiration of Sentence and Parole, from the Mt. Pleasant, Auburn and Clinton Prisons, During the Year 1845, n.p. [p. 7], River Campus Libraries, Special Collections, University of Rochester, Rochester, NY.

3. See Benjamin F. Hall, *The Trial of William Freeman for the Murder of John G. Van Nest, Including the Evidence and the Arguments of Counsel, with the Decision of the Supreme Court Granting a New Trial, and an Account of the Death of the Prisoner, and of the Post-Mortem Examination of his Body by Amariah Brigham,*

M.D. and Others (Auburn, NY: Derby, Miller & Co. Publishers, 1848), 338, 389 (hereafter B. F. Hall); Documents of the Senate of the State of New York (hereafter Doc. Senate), 69th sess., vol. 2, no. 46, 30 January 1846, 75; Ralph S. Herre, "The History of Auburn Prison from the Beginning to about 1867" (PhD diss., Pennsylvania State College, 1950), 193–94; Documents of the Assembly of the State of New York, 64th sess., 1842, vol. 4, no. 65, 105 (hereafter Doc. Assembly); and Gershom Powers, *A Brief Account of the Construction, Management, & Discipline &c, &c, of the New-York State Prison at Auburn, Together with a Compendium of Criminal Law* (Auburn, NY: U. F. Doubleday), 1826, 17. See also W. David Lewis, *From Newgate to Dannemora: The Rise of the Penitentiary in New York, 1796–1848* (1965; reprint, Ithaca, NY: Cornell University Press, 2009), 129.

4. B. F. Hall, 338, 389, 404; "Copy Amendments to the Bill of Exceptions Luman Sherwood DA for David Wright Defense," n.d. [July 1846], 10–11, Box A20, Cayuga Museum of History and Art & Case Research Laboratory, Auburn, NY. The names of the agent and clerk at the time of Freeman's release are recorded in the *Annual Report of the Inspectors of the State Prison at Auburn, 30 January 1846*, Doc. Senate, 69th sess., vol. 2, no. 46, 30 January 1846, 76.

5. B. F. Hall, 236.

6. "Rail Road Depot," *Auburn Journal and Advertiser*, 24 March 1841, 2. Auburn would formally incorporate as a city in 1848.

7. Michael S. Myers, "Recollections of Auburn: A Paper Read before the Cayuga County Historical Society, November 19, 1878," in *Collections of Cayuga County Historical Society Number Seven* (Auburn, NY: Knapp, Peck & Thompson, 1889), 124. Prior to 1840, visitors often remarked on the poor quality of Auburn's roads. See, for example, George Combe, *Notes on the United States of North America During a Phrenological Visit in 1838–9-40* (Philadelphia: Carey & Hart, 1841), 2:73–74.

8. Diary of David M[ervin] Bagley, Bagley Family Papers, Collection 18, Box 1, Folder 11, Michigan State University Archives, Michigan State University, 2 August 1839, 62; Henry Hall, *The History of Auburn* (Auburn, NY: Dennis Bro's & Co., 1869), 260–61 (hereafter H. Hall); John W. Barber, *Pictorial History of the State of New York* (Cooperstown, NY: H. & E. Phinney, 1846), 59; New York State, Secretary's Office, *Census of the State of New-York, for 1845*, 11, https://nysl .ptfs.com/data/Library1/06042012/88797.PDF; United States, Bureau of the Census, and Leslie T. C. (Leslie Tse-chiu) Kuo, *Census of New York State by Counties, Cities & Towns, 1840–1940* (Ithaca, NY, 1941), 55.

9. B. F. Hall, 236. A newspaper report about a fire at Elijah Applegate's Carriage Shop on July 4, 1845 locates the shop on State Street in a building owned by J. M. Sherwood. See figure 4.1. See also the advertisement in *Auburn Herald*, 2 January 1841, 1. I thank Mary Jo Watts for identifying Applegate's location.

10. B. F. Hall, 45, 235, 420. Peter Wyckoff died on May 5, 1840, shortly after De Puy and Freeman left. See *The Wyckoff Family in America, a Genealogy; Pre-*

pared from the Manuscript Genealogical Collections of the Late William F. Wyckoff of Jamaica, New York, ed. And pub. By Mr. and Mrs. M. B. Streeter (Rutland, VT: Tuttle Company, 1934), 69, https://archive.org/details/wyckofffamilyina 00wyck_0/page/n9/mode/2up.

11. B. F. Hall, 76, 277, 328, 393; "Trial of Wm. Freeman," *Cayuga Patriot*, 8 July 1846, 1.

12. B. F. Hall, 236–37, 241, 248. Jack Furman, also known as John Willard, was convicted of bigamy in 1844 and sentenced to two years in the Auburn State Prison. He was discharged on September 18, 1846. *Cayuga General Sessions: The People vs. John Willard Indict. For Bigamy*, 17 September 1844, Cayuga County Historian's Office, Auburn, NY; *Auburn Prison, Registers of Male Inmates Discharged (ca. 1816)–1894, 1908–1942*, New York State Archives, Albany, NY; Ancestry.com.

13. B. F. Hall, 63, 237. Freeman voiced the same idea to former employer Ira Curtis (B. F. Hall, 37), postprison employer Levi Hermance (B. F. Hall, 275), and others. The fact that Freeman never sought compensation for his injuries is significant because such a suit was an option. Kimberly Welch describes contemporaneous cases in which African Americans sued white people who had beaten them, demanding—and sometimes receiving—monetary compensation for bodily injuries. See Welch, *Black Litigants in the Antebellum American South* (Chapel Hill: University of North Carolina Press, 2020), 3–6 (hereafter Welch). See also Melissa Milewski, *Litigating across the Color Line: Civil Cases between Black and White Southerners from the End of Slavery to Civil Rights* (New York: Oxford University Press, 2018).

14. Nell Irvin Painter, *Sojourner Truth: A Life, a Symbol* (New York: W. W. Norton, 1996), 34.

15. I thank Bethany Schneider for pointing out the connection between Elizabeth Freeman and Sally Freeman.

16. Sojourner Truth was born (and named Isabella Baumfree) after Harry and Kate left Rosendale, so she never knew them. However, Harry and Kate likely knew Truth's parents, James and Betsey Baumfree (or Bomefree). The Hardenberghs worked together to become one of the most powerful enslavers in New York State. Given the coordination among white enslavers, it is very likely that the enslaved also communicated. Furthermore, many of the enslaved, like their enslavers, may have been related by blood. If either Harry or Kate was a sibling to either James or Betsey Baumfree, then Sojourner Truth was William Freeman's first cousin once removed. On the enslaving practices of the Hardenbergh family, see Margaret Washington, *Sojourner Truth's America* (Urbana: University of Illinois Press, 2009), 14–15.

17. B. F. Hall, 237. It may seem surprising that Freeman appealed directly to a magistrate rather than a lawyer, but this strategy had been used successfully

by many other African Americans. Welch documents more than one thousand cases in which African American southerners sued non-Blacks in all-white courts; in many of these cases, the litigants, like Freeman, brought their initial complaint directly to a judge.

18. The Bostwicks, the Freemans, and John Hardenbergh all arrived at the banks of the Owasco Outlet within six years of each other, at the close of the 1700s. Shortly after Hardenbergh bought Tract 47, the 450-acre plot of land to the west, Military Tract 46, was sold in pieces. One portion went to Robert Dill, who eventually sold the land to build the Auburn State Prison. Most of the rest of Tract 46 went to William Bostwick, the father of Magistrate James H. Bostwick. Scott W. Anderson, *Auburn, New York: The Entrepreneurs' Frontier* (Syracuse, NY: Syracuse University Press, 2015), 50, 57 (hereafter Anderson).

19. B. F. Hall, 45, 291–92, 444.

20. "Trial of Wm. Freeman," *Cayuga Patriot*, 8 July 1846, 1; B. F. Hall, 291, 292–93.

21. B. F. Hall, 237.

22. B. F. Hall, 237.

23. Slight paraphrase from B. F. Hall, 258–59.

24. 1860 Federal Census, "Deb De Puy"; "A Bypath in Bygone Cayuga. Memories of Auburn c. 1901, Author Unknown. Read before CCHS. Manuscript," Cayuga Museum of History and Art & Case Research Laboratory, Auburn, NY, 17; "Local Necrology," *Collections of Cayuga County Historical Society, Number Nine* (Auburn, NY: Knapp, Peck & Thomson, 1891), 72; "Trial of Wm. Freeman," *Cayuga Patriot*, 8 July 1846, 1; B. F. Hall, 44–47, 285–87.

25. B. F. Hall, 288. Deborah De Puy similarly observed that Freeman "would laugh very hearty without any thing to laugh at. He wouldn't know what he was laughing at." B. F. Hall, 287.

26. "Trial of Wm. Freeman," *Cayuga Patriot*, 8 July 1846, 1, 2; B. F. Hall, 47, 288.

27. "Trial of Wm. Freeman," *Cayuga Patriot*, 8 July 1846, 1; "Trial of Wm. Freeman, On the Preliminary Issue of Present Insanity," *Cayuga Patriot*, 15 July 1846, 1; "Trial of Wm. Freeman the Negro on the Preliminary Issue of Present Insanity," *Daily Cayuga Tocsin*, 1 July 1846, 3; B. F. Hall, 237–38, 240–41, 390. On the rise of the temperance movement in Auburn 1841–1842, see H. Hall, 254–55.

28. B. F. Hall, 259, 238.

29. B. F. Hall, 259, 239.

30. "Trial of Wm. Freeman," *Cayuga Patriot*, 8 July 1846, 1.

31. "African Methodist Zion's Church," *Northern Christian Advocate*, 10 November 1847, 127; "Uncovering the Freedom Trail in Auburn and Cayuga County, New York," Judith Wellman, project coordinator, sponsored by the

City of Auburn Historic Resources Review Board and the Cayuga County Historian's Office, 2005, 81, citing Cayuga County poorhouse records, 55 (hereafter "Uncovering").

32. The near-60 percent increase in the Black population between 1840 and 1845 was sudden and unprecedented in Auburn. For comparison, from 1835 to 1840 the Black population of Auburn rose only 20 percent, from 116 to 140. The rise in Auburn's African American population from 1840–1845 is also notable in relation to changes in the city's population. In this five-year span, Auburn's overall population increased by 545 people, of whom 83 were Black. In other words, African Americans, who in 1840 constituted just under 2.5 percent of Auburn's population, accounted for 15 percent of the city's increase in population from 1840 through 1845. *Census of the State of New-York, for 1835*, 12, http://purl .nysed.gov/nysl/11021918; *Census of the State of New-York, for 1845*, 11, https:// nysl.ptfs.com/data/Library1/06042012/88797.PDF; United States, Bureau of the Census, and Leslie T. C. (Leslie Tse-chiu) Kuo, *Census of New York State by Counties, Cities & Towns, 1840–1940* (Ithaca, NY, 1941), 55; "1840 Federal Census: African Americans of Cayuga County, New York," Judith Wellman, coordinator, in cooperation with the Cayuga County, NY, Historian's Office, accessed 26 June 2023, https://www.cayugagenealogy.org/census/1840/africana.html.

33. According to the US Census, by 1850 only 49 of Auburn's 263 African Americans lived in Ward 2, the quarter of the city that included New Guinea. In other words, by 1850, far *fewer* than 49 African Americans (that is, much less than 18 percent of the city's African American population) remained in the former Black stronghold. Judith Wellman, coordinator, in cooperation with the Cayuga County, NY, Historian's Office, "African Americans in the 1850 Federal Census for Cayuga County, New York, Auburn, NY, Surname Section 'A' thru 'H,'" accessed 26 June 2023, https://www.cayugagenealogy.org/census /afriamer/1850aub1.html#top; "African Americans in the 1850 Federal Census for Cayuga County, New York, Auburn, NY, Surname Section 'J' thru 'Y,'" accessed 26 June 2023, https://www.cayugagenealogy.org/census/afriamer /1850aub2.html; and "1840 Federal Census: African Americans of Cayuga County, New York," accessed 26 June 2023, https://www.cayugagenealogy.org /census/1840/africana.html.

34. "Uncovering," 10, 17, 35, 54, 57. On Deborah De Puy's death in 1879, she was remembered with admiration as a "zealous supporter of the African Methodist Episcopal Zion church, and at the annual donation parties for the benefit of the pastor, [she] was always a prominent character." "Local Necrology," *Collections of Cayuga County Historical Society, Number Nine* (Auburn, NY: Knapp, Peck & Thomson, 1891), 72.

35. "Abijah Fitch, Grantor Deeds, 1823–36" and "Sales to Blacks," Cayuga

County Historian's Office, Auburn, NY. Abijah Fitch sold land to Mary Ann Newark in December 1845. Fitch Family File, Book 72 201, Cayuga County Historian's Office.

36. Quincy T. Mills, *Cutting along the Color Line: Black Barbers and Barber Shops in America* (Philadelphia: University of Pennsylvania Press, 2013), 27.

37. Harry Freeman spent an unknown span of time in the Cayuga County poorhouse, leaving it on April 19, 1845. He died December 20, 1845, at the age of ninety-two. See "Uncovering," 81, citing Cayuga County poorhouse records. See also Michael S. Myers, "Recollections of Auburn: A Paper Read before the Cayuga County Historical Society, November 19, 1878," in *Collections of Cayuga County Historical Society Number Seven* (Auburn, NY: Knapp, Peck & Thompson, 1889), 117. Numerous deeds, in combination with census records, show that Henry Polhemus was among the white men who sold land in and beyond New Guinea to white buyers. See, for example, 16 September 1834, Book UU, 116, Cayuga County Historian's Office. See also vertical file "Polhamus" [*sic*], Cayuga County Historian's Office. I thank Jessica Armstrong for her impressive research on Auburn's historical deeds.

38. "Trial of Wm. Freeman," *Cayuga Patriot*, 15 July 1846, 2; "Trial of Wm. Freeman," *Cayuga Patriot*, 8 July 1846, 1. Newark, who was born in 1793, came to Auburn in 1820. 1840 Federal Census, Ancestry.com Library Edition. See also B. F. Hall, 324. Aaron Demun seems to have been a brother to Prentice (Prentiss) Brown, who married Freeman's aunt Jane Freeman. Demun was only one year older than Freeman. He later served in the Civil War as part of the Colored Troops. See 1830 Federal Census, 1900 Federal Census, Civil War Pension Index, and US Colored Troops Military Service Records, all on Ancestry.com.

39. B. F. Hall, 200. On the color of the coat, see B. F. Hall, 191.

40. B. F. Hall, 200. See also "Horrid Murder," *Auburn Journal and Advertiser*, 18 March 1846, 1.

41. "Cayuga County," *Auburn Journal and Advertiser*, 9 April 1844, 2. Van Nest's birth year of 1805 is recorded on his gravestone in the Sand Beach Cemetery in Fleming, NY. "Trial of Wm. Freeman," *Cayuga Patriot*, 15 July 1846, 2; B. F. Hall, 199–200.

42. B. F. Hall, 258, 75–76, 80, 324, 327.

43. Advertisement in *Auburn Journal and Advertiser*, 22 January 1845, 3; advertisement in *Auburn Journal and Advertiser*, Nov. 11, 1846, 3 (the advertisement ran in November, but it is dated 1 April 1846). Quincy served for burglary in the first degree. *Auburn Prison, Registers of Male Inmates Discharged (ca. 1816)-1894, 1908–1942*, 194 (*numbered 97*), New York State Archives, Albany, NY. Because prisoners were forbidden from looking at each other's faces, one might unknowingly serve alongside an acquaintance—as when Freeman was unaware

that he was imprisoned with Jack Furman. It is therefore unsurprising that neither man said he recognized the other from prison.

44. B. F. Hall, 191. Many Black-owned barbershops in New York served only
white men. A visiting Englishman, Henry Bradshaw Fearon, described this phenomenon in detail in 1848. However, Fearon witnessed a Black man asking a
white-serving Black barber for a shave and being turned away in humiliation—
which suggests that some Black men did expect to be shaved alongside white
men, and therefore some integrated barbershops existed. Freeman apparently
believed that Quincy's shop was open to Black as well as white men. Henry
Bradshaw Fearon, *Sketches of America, A Narrative of a Journey of Five Thousand Miles Through the Eastern and Western States of America*, 2nd ed. (London:
Longman, Hurst, Rees, Orme, and Brown, 1848), 58–60.

45. "Trial of Wm. Freeman," *Cayuga Patriot*, 8 July 1846, 1.

46. B. F. Hall, 44.

47. "Trial of Wm. Freeman," *Cayuga Patriot*, 8 July 1846, 1; B. F. Hall, 44,
257–58.

48. B. F. Hall, 258.

49. For an excellent overview of the history of wages for prison labor in the
early United States, see L. D. Weyand, "Study of Wage-Payment to Prisoners as
a Penal Method," *Journal of Criminal Law and Criminology* 10, no. 4 (1920): 558–
91 (hereafter Weyand). Europe, too, had systems of paying prisoners, including, in France, the *pécule*. When Gustave de Beaumont and Alexis de Tocqueville visited the Auburn State Prison in 1831, they commented on the absence
of a *pécule*, which they called "excessively severe" because all people, including
prisoners, have an "incontestable right" to benefit from their labor. Gustave de
Beaumont and Alexis de Tocqueville, *On the Penitentiary System in the United
States and Its Application in France*, trans. Francis Lieber (1833; reprint, Carbondale: Southern Illinois University Press, 1964), 70 (hereafter Beaumont and
Tocqueville).

50. *First Annual Report of the Board of Managers of the Prison Discipline Soci-
ety, Boston, June 2, 1826* (Boston: Perkins and Marvin, 1830), 30–32; *Fifth Annual
Report of the Board of Managers of the Prison Discipline Society, Boston, 1830* (Bos-
ton: Boston Type and Stereotype Foundry, n.d.), 360/30; *Third Report of the
Prison Association of New York* (New York: published by the Association, 1847),
68–70; Doc. Assembly, 75th sess., vol. 1, no. 20, 7 January 1852, 34–36; *Twenty-
Second Annual Report of the Executive Committee of the Prison Association of New
York, Transmitted to the Legislature January 29, 1867* (Albany, NY: C. Van Ben-
thuysen & Sons, Printers, 1867), 460. See also Orlando Faulkland Lewis, *The
Development of American Prisons and Prison Customs, 1776–1845: With Special
Reference to Early Institutions in the State of New York* (Albany, NY: published by

the Prison Association of New York, 1922), 53, 67, 92, 153, 167, 205, 220, 334; and Weyand, 562–63. On payment to prisoners in Pennsylvania, see Jen Manion, *Liberty's Prisoners: Carceral Culture in Early America* (Philadelphia: University of Pennsylvania Press, 2015), 36.

51. On the refusal to pay overstints in the Auburn State Prison, see *First Annual Report of the Board of Managers of the Prison Discipline Society, Boston, June 2, 1826* (Boston: Perkins and Marvin, 1830), 32.

52. Dorothea Dix, *Remarks on Prisons and Prison Discipline in the United States*, 2nd ed. (Philadelphia, PA: Joseph Kite & Co., 1845), 11–12. Dix critiqued aspects of the Auburn System, including its absence of overstints, while praising the Pennsylvania System of incarceration for providing them. Dix, 12. Dix did not wholly condemn or support either the Auburn or the Pennsylvania Systems. [Samuel Gridley Howe et al], *Report of a Minority of the Special Committee of the Boston Prison Discipline Society Appointed at the Annual Meeting, May 27, 1845* (Boston: William D. Ticknor and Company, 1846), 45.

53. "Trial of Wm. Freeman," *Cayuga Patriot*, 8 July 1846, 2; Dimon, 38; B. F. Hall, 94, 180, 247, 338, 445; *Daily Cayuga Tocsin*, 4 July 1846, 2; Anonymous, *A Peep into the State Prison, at Auburn, N.Y. with an Appendix, By One Who Knows* (pub. for the author, 1839; copyrighted 1838), 35.

54. Doc. Senate, 64th sess., vol. 2, no. 54, 25 March 1841, 14; William Henry Seward Jr., "Youthful Recollections," 16 March 1903, typewritten manuscript, William Henry Seward Papers, 1801–1872, Box 120, 3, River Campus Libraries, Special Collections, University of Rochester, Rochester, NY; Reed, 213; James Stuart, *Three Years in North America, In Two Volumes* (Edinburgh: printed for Robert Cadell, Edinburgh, 1833), 1:69.

55. Doc. Senate, 66th sess., vol. 3, no. 9, 16 January 1843, 20, 31, 52; Doc. Assembly, 63rd sess., vol. 1, no. 18, 15 January 1840, 9, 54; Doc. Assembly, 64th sess., vol. 2, no. 31, 12 January 1842, 48, 53; $250.91 in 1840 was worth more than $7,500 today.

56. B. F. Hall, 37, 47 (and also 21, 39); "The Murder of the Van Ness [*sic*] Family," *Albany* [New York] *Evening Journal*, 16 March 1846, 2.

57. Kellie Carter Jackson, *Force and Freedom: Black Abolitionists and the Politics of Violence* (Philadelphia: University of Pennsylvania Press, 2019), ebook, 3, 29; Henry Highland Garnet, "An Address to the Slaves of the United States of America," in *Walker's Appeal, with a Brief Sketch of His Life. And also Garnet's Address to the Slaves of the United States of America* (New York: J. H. Tobitt, 1848), 92, 94, 96, 95. Reprinted by DigitalCommons@University of Nebraska-Lincoln, https://digitalcommons.unl.edu/etas/8 and https://digitalcommons.unl.edu/cgi/viewcontent.cgi?filename=0&article=1007&context=etas&type=additional.

58. "Trial of Wm. Freeman," *Cayuga Patriot*, 15 July 1846, 2.

59. "Horrid Murder!," *Auburn Journal and Advertiser*, 18 March 1846, 1; "Trial of Wm. Freeman," *Cayuga Patriot*, 15 July 1846, 2. Andrew W. Arpey dates Freeman's visit to Hyatt as taking place on Monday March 9, 1846, but Hyatt stated that Freeman visited his shop a week prior to March 12, which dates the visit to about March 5. Arpey, *The William Freeman Murder Trial: Insanity, Politics, and Race* (Syracuse, NY: Syracuse University Press, 2003), 10 (hereafter Arpey).

60. "Trial of Wm. Freeman," *Cayuga Patriot*, 15 July 1846, 2. See Arpey, 10; B. F. Hall, 73, 186–88; and "More Disclosures of the Van Ness [*sic*] Massacre," *New York Daily Herald*, 21 March 1846, 1. It is possible that Gabriel assisted Freeman at Hyatt's shop rather than Simpson's. After the murders, Gabriel—but none of the white artisans—was accused of being Freeman's accomplice. James Bostwick interrogated Gabriel but released him when it became clear that Gabriel had no relationship with Freeman. "Appointment of Keeper," *Auburn Journal and Advertiser*, 18 March 1846, 2.

61. "Trial of Wm. Freeman," *Cayuga Patriot*, 15 July 1846, 2.

62. B. F. Hall, 250.

63. "Trial of Wm. Freeman," *Cayuga Patriot*, 1 July 1846, 3; B. F. Hall, 389, 405.

64. B. F. Hall, 40, 405. See also "Trial of Wm. Freeman," *Cayuga Patriot*, 1 July 1846, 3.

65. Slight paraphrase from B. F. Hall, 40.

66. "Trial of Wm. Freeman," *Cayuga Patriot*, 8 July 1846, 1; B. F. Hall, 46, 211, 324, 344, 359; slight paraphrase from "More Disclosures of the Van Ness [*sic*] Massacre," *New York Daily Herald*, 21 March 1846, 1.

Chapter Five

1. Time and Date moon calendar, https://www.timeanddate.com/moon/@5107505?month=3&year=1846; Benjamin F. Hall, *The Trial of William Freeman for the Murder of John G. Van Nest, Including the Evidence and the Arguments of Counsel, with the Decision of the Supreme Court Granting a New Trial, and an Account of the Death of the Prisoner, and of the Post-Mortem Examination of his Body by Amariah Brigham, M.D. and Others* (Auburn, NY: Derby, Miller & Co. Publishers, 1848), 323, 36, 51, 248–50, 261, 266, 407, 409 (hereafter B. F. Hall).

2. Anna Peterson Post, *Historical Sketch of the Town of Fleming* (Auburn, NY: Fenton Press, 1923), 16 (hereafter Post). On the rain, see B. F. Hall, 274.

3. Department of the Interior, "New York SP Sand Beach Church," National Register of Historic Places and National Historical Landmarks Program Records, 2013–2017, accession number TR-0079-2017-0097, National Archives at College Park, https://catalog.archives.gov/id/75316727; B. F. Hall, 293.

4. "William Freeman," *Cayuga Tocsin*, 9 April 1846, 4; B. F. Hall, 208–9.

5. B. F. Hall, 208–9.

6. B. F. Hall, 200, 345; "Horrid Murder," *Auburn Journal and Advertiser,* 18 March 1846, 1. The Van Nests' home was located at what is now 5923 West Lake Road, Fleming, NY. See Linda Ober, "Selling Point: Ghosts," *Auburn Pub,* 21 November 2005, https://auburnpub.com/news/local/selling-point-ghosts /article_658c6f50-1506-569c-812a-8633b08325d1.html. See also "William Freeman," *Cayuga Tocsin,* 9 April 1846, 4.

7. Sheila Saft Tucker, *The Township of Fleming Cayuga County New York, 1823– 1973* (Auburn, NY: Brunner the Printer, 1973), 44, 97–99; Post, 36; "Cayuga County," *Auburn Journal and Advertiser,* 9 August 1844, 2; A. B. Winfield, *Sermon at the Interment of the Bodies of John G. Van Nest, Mrs. Sarah Van Nest, G. W. Van Nest, Their Son, and Mrs. Phebe Wykoff [sic], Who Were Murdered March Twelfth Inst., By a Colored Man Named William Freeman, Preached in the R. D. Church, at Sand Beach, Owasco Lake, March Fifteenth* (Auburn, NY: Napier Press of J. C. Merrell & Co., 1846), 12. George Van Nest was born in 1844 and Peter in 1845; on these birth years, see the US Census for 1850 under "Peter Vanest" [sic] and Tucker, 48. Some sources suggest that Peter was older than George, but census data, combined with the fact that Peter never seems to have interacted with Freeman, suggests that Peter was barely one year old at the time of the murders.

8. "Trial of Wm. Freeman," *Cayuga Patriot,* 15 July 1846, 1; B. F. Hall, 77, 192.

9. David Dimon, *The Freeman Trial: Presenting the Testimony Given in this Remarkable Case, with Comments* (Auburn, NY: Dennis Bro's & Thorne, 1871), 22.

10. B. F. Hall, 200, 265–66; "William Freeman, the Murderer," *Albany Evening Journal,* 19 March 1846, 2. See also B. F. Hall, 51; *Auburn Journal and Advertiser,* 18 March 1846, 2.

11. B. F. Hall, 43, 51, 226, 248, 255, 266; "In the Matter of the Inquisition on the Death of John G. Van Nest Sarah Van Nest, and George W. Van Nest and Verdict of Jury, Ashbel Winigar, Coroner, Filed March 14, 1846," 15, Cayuga County Historian's Office, Auburn, New York, 7 (hereafter coroner's report); *Auburn Journal and Advertiser,* 18 March 1846, 2. A few primary accounts claim that Freeman stabbed Sarah before John. This seems unlikely, however, because John died instantly and did not cry out, whereas Sarah screamed. If Sarah had been stabbed first, John would have been alerted and would not have been caught unawares.

12. B. F. Hall, 266; coroner's report, 5.

13. Slight paraphrase from *Auburn Journal and Advertiser,* 18 March 1846, 2; coroner's report, 4, 11.

14. B. F. Hall, 18, 37, 81, 208, 213, 266, 331.

15. B. F. Hall, 214; slight paraphrase from B. F. Hall, 201.

16. "William Freeman, the Murderer," *Albany Evening Journal,* 19 March 1846, 2; coroner's report, 8, 17; B. F. Hall, 84, 171–72, 201, 208.

17. B. F. Hall, 345, 283; coroner's report, 11–14. Because the house was dark

and the moon was bright, Freeman was visible to Holmes and Van Arsdale, who were in the front sitting room, but not vice versa.

18. B. F. Hall, 323, 267.

19. B. F. Hall, 193, 202.

20. B. F. Hall, 84, 194, 212; "Murder of John G. Van Nest and Family," *Cayuga Patriot*, 18 March 1846, 2.

21. "William Freeman, the Murderer," *Albany* [New York] *Evening Journal*, 19 March 1846, 2; B. F. Hall, 204, 209, 213, 235, 284, 345.

22. B. F. Hall, 205, 208, 212; "Trial of Wm. Freeman," *Cayuga Patriot*, 15 July 1846, 1.

23. B. F. Hall, 212.

24. J. W. Loguen, *The Rev. J. W. Loguen as a Slave and as a Freeman: A Narrative of Real Life*, reprint, ed. and introduced by Jennifer A. Williamson (Syracuse, NY: Syracuse University Press, 2016), 200, 217, 220; original work published 1859. On nineteenth-century American taverns, see Christine Sismondo, *America Walks into a Bar: A Spirited History of Taverns and Saloons, Speakeasies and Grog Shops* (New York: Oxford University Press, 2011); and Steven Barleen, *The Tavern: A Social History of Drinking and Conviviality* (Westport, CT: Greenwood Press, 2019).

25. B. F. Hall, 203, 206.

26. On nineteenth-century Black men's work in the horse industry, see Katherine C. Mooney, *Race Horse Men: How Slavery and Freedom were Made at the Racetrack* (Cambridge, MA: Harvard University Press, 2014); Edward Hotaling, *The Great Black Jockeys: The Lives and Times of the Men Who Dominated America's First National Sport* (Rockland, CA: Forum, 1999); and Mim Eichler Rivas, *Beautiful Jim Key: The Lost History of a Horse and a Man Who Changed the World* (New York: William Morrow, 2005).

27. "Trial of Wm. Freeman," *Cayuga Patriot*, 15 July 1846, 1; B. F. Hall, 204, 206.

28. B. F. Hall, 204.

29. Slight paraphrase of "Trial of Wm. Freeman," *Cayuga Patriot*, 15 July 1846, 1.

30. "Trial of Wm. Freeman," *Cayuga Patriot*, 15 July 1846, 1; B. F. Hall, 206.

31. B. F. Hall, 204, 206; "Trial of Wm. Freeman," *Cayuga Patriot*, 15 July 1846, 1.

32. B. F. Hall, 204, 206.

33. B. F. Hall, 206.

34. "Trial of Wm. Freeman," *Cayuga Patriot*, 15 July 1846, 1; B. F. Hall, 205.

35. A. B. Chambers, ed., *Trials and Confessions of Madison Henderson, Alias Blanchard, Alfred Amos Warrick, James W. Seward, and Charles Brown, Murderers of Jesse Baker and Jacob Weaver, as Given by Themselves; and a Likeness of Each, Taken in Jail Shortly after Their Arrest* (Saint Louis: Chambers & Knapp, 1841), 9.

36. See, for example, John Brown, *Slave Life in Georgia: A Narrative of the Life, Sufferings, and Escape of John Brown, a Fugitive Slave, Now in England*, ed. L. A. Chamerovzow (London: privately printed, 1855), 13.

37. Keith Green notes that "multiple kinds of captivity, confinement, and bondage structured the lives and stories of people of African descent." Green, *Bound to Respect: Antebellum Narratives of Black Imprisonment, Servitude, and Bondage, 1816–1861* (Tuscaloosa: University of Alabama Press, 2015), 7.

38. B. F. Hall, 205, 206.

39. B. F. Hall, 205–6.

40. "More Disclosures of the Van Ness [*sic*] Massacre," *New York Daily Herald*, 21 March 1846, 1; C. F. P., "The Horrible Murders in Cayuga," *Albany* [New York] *Argus*, 18 March 1846, 102.

41. "More Disclosures of the Van Ness [*sic*] Massacre," *New York Daily Herald*, 21 March 1846, 1; B. F. Hall, 207.

42. B. F. Hall, 206.

43. Slight paraphrase of B. F. Hall, 205.

44. B. F. Hall, 206–7. On the normal cacophony of nineteenth-century taverns, see Sismondo, 100.

45. B. F. Hall, 207. The first quotation in this paragraph is a slight paraphrase.

46. "More Disclosures of the Van Ness [*sic*] Massacre," *New York Daily Herald*, 21 March 1846, 1; B. F. Hall, 205–7.

47. B. F. Hall, 210.

48. B. F. Hall, 81, 210–11.

49. B. F. Hall, 207–11.

50. "Trial of Wm. Freeman," *Cayuga Patriot*, 15 July 1846, 1.

51. "Trial of Wm. Freeman," *Cayuga Patriot*, 15 July 1846, 1; B. F. Hall, 62.

Chapter Six

1. "Horrid Murder!," *Auburn Journal and Advertiser*, 18 March 1846, 1; Benjamin F. Hall, *The Trial of William Freeman for the Murder of John G. Van Nest, Including the Evidence and the Arguments of Counsel, with the Decision of the Supreme Court Granting a New Trial, and an Account of the Death of the Prisoner, and of the Post-Mortem Examination of his Body by Amariah Brigham, M.D. and Others* (Auburn, NY: Derby, Miller & Co. Publishers, 1848), 197, 203, 208 (hereafter B. F. Hall); "In the Matter of the Inquisition on the Death of John G. Van Nest Sarah Van Nest, and George W. Van Nest and Verdict of Jury, Ashbel Winigar, Coroner, Filed March 14, 1846," 15, Cayuga County Historian's Office, Auburn, New York, 7 (hereafter coroner's report); A. B. Winfield, *Sermon at the Interment of the Bodies of John G. Van Nest, Mrs. Sarah Van Nest, G. W. Van Nest, Their Son, and Mrs. Phebe Wykoff [sic], Who Were Murdered March Twelfth Inst., By a Col-*

ored Man Named William Freeman, Preached in the R. D. Church, at Sand Beach, Owasco Lake, March Fifteenth (Auburn, NY: Napier Press of J. C. Merrell & Co., 1846), 13; D. H. "The Awful Tragedy in Cayuga," *Harbinger*, 4 April 1846, 272.

2. Coroner's report, 13.

3. Coroner's report, 4; B. F. Hall, 202.

4. *Daily Cayuga Tocsin—Extra*, 19 March 1846, n.p., William L. Clements Library, University of Michigan, Ann Arbor (hereafter *Tocsin Extra*); "Letter from Frances Miller Seward to Augustus Henry Seward," 18 March 1846, Seward Family Digital Archive, University of Rochester; William Henry Seward Jr., "Youthful Recollections," typewritten manuscript, 3½–4, William Henry Seward Papers, 1801–1872, Box 120, River Campus Libraries, Special Collections, University of Rochester, Rochester, NY; "Letter from Frances Seward to William Henry Seward," qtd. in Frederick W. Seward, *William H. Seward; An Autobiography from 1801 to 1834. With a Memoir of His Life, and Selections from His Letters* (1877; reprint, New York: Derby and Miller, 1891), 787 (hereafter Frederick W. Seward).

5. "The Horrid Murders at Auburn—Great Excitement!" *Albany* [New York] *Argus*, 20 March 1846, 2; B. F. Hall, 203.

6. One newspaper reported that the crowd numbered more than two thousand people and included at least two church deacons. "Shocking Atrocity," *Liberator*, 27 March 1846, 2.

7. "Horrid Murder!," *Auburn Journal and Advertiser*, 18 March 1846, 1; B. F. Hall, 200, 202; "The Murder of the Van Ness [*sic*] Family," *Albany* [New York] *Evening Journal*, 16 March 1846, 2.

8. *Tocsin Extra*; "Shocking Atrocity," *Liberator*, 27 March 1846, 2; Rev. J. M. Austin, "Reminiscences of the Freeman Trial," *Daily Advertiser*, [Auburn, NY], 4 March 1873, n. p., River Campus Libraries, Special Collections, University of Rochester, Rochester, NY (hereafter Austin 1873); "The Horrid Murders at Auburn—Great Excitement!" *Albany* [New York] *Argus*, 20 March 1846, 2.

9. "Shocking Atrocity," *Liberator*, 27 March 1846, 2. See also B. F. Hall, 64.

10. Austin 1873; *Tocsin Extra*.

11. "The Horrid Murders at Auburn—Great Excitement!," 2; John Austin, *Evangelical Magazine and Gospel Advocate* [Utica], 10 April 1846.

12. John Mather Austin, *Journal*, vol. 3, 4 March 1846, Andover-Harvard Theological Library, Harvard Divinity School (hereafter Austin, *Journal*); Austin 1873.

13. "Freeman Trial Recalled, Reminiscences Suggested by an Old Cell," *Auburn Morning Dispatch*, 27 May 1888, 2; *Auburn Journal and Advertiser*, 25 March 1846, 1; *Auburn Journal and Advertiser*, 25 March 1846, 1.

14. "Sentence of Freeman," *Auburn Journal and Advertiser*, 29 July 1846, 2.

15. "Examination of Wm. Freeman," *Auburn Journal and Advertiser*, 18 March

1846, 2. The newspapers reported on the debunking of the rumor of revenge. See, for example, *St. Lawrence Republican*, 24 March 1846, 3.

16. "Trial of Wm. Freeman, On the Preliminary Issue of Present Insanity," *Cayuga Patriot*, 1 July 1846, 2; "The Murder of the Van Ness [*sic*] Family," *Albany* [New York] *Evening Journal*, 16 March 1846, 2; B. F. Hall, 349 (see also 299 and 348); "Trial of Wm. Freeman, On the Preliminary Issue of Present Insanity," *Cayuga Patriot*, 8 July 1846, 1; "Account of Freeman Trial?," unsigned and undated holograph trial transcript, Box A20, Cayuga Museum of History and Art & Case Research Laboratory, Auburn, NY, n.p. (hereafter Account of Freeman Trial?); "The Horrible Murders in Cayuga," *Albany Argus*, 20 March 1846, 1; *Cayuga Patriot*, 18 March 1846, 3.

17. William Henry Seward Jr., "Youthful Recollections," 16 March 1903, type-written manuscript, William Henry Seward Papers, 1801–1872, Box 120, 4, William Henry Seward Papers, 1801–1872, River Campus Libraries, Special Collections, University of Rochester, Rochester, NY; *Auburn Journal and Advertiser*, 4 March 1846; "Letter from Frances Miller Seward to Augustus Henry Seward," 6 April 1846, Seward Family Digital Archive, University of Rochester.

18. Deborah Bronson, stepdaughter of Dr. Joseph Pitney, recalled that around the time of the War of 1812, Cayugas and other Native Americans routinely "walked into a house without knocking, and were liable to appear at any moment in any part of it, begging." She described a neighbor who "went upstairs to bed" and "was naturally quite terrified to find a drunken Indian behind her door. She was so frightened that she did not stay to descend the stairs in the ordinary manner, but jumped directly over the balustrade to the floor of the hall." Mrs. Deborah Bronson, "On Recollections of My Early Life in Auburn, By Mrs. Deborah Bronson, Read Before the Cayuga County Historical Society, March, 8, 1881," 4–5. In file, "Recollections of My Early Life in Auburn, Mrs. Deborah Bronson, March 8, 1881, Manuscript," at Cayuga Museum of History and Art & Case Research Laboratory, Auburn, NY.

19. "Letter from Frances Miller Seward to Augustus Henry Seward," 18 March 1846, Seward Family Digital Archive, University of Rochester; "Letter from Frances Seward to William Henry Seward," qtd. in Frederick W. Seward, 786.

20. *Auburn Journal and Advertiser*, 25 March 1846, 1; Warren [no first name], "Correspondence of the Atlas," *Boston Daily Atlas*, 9 June 1846, n.p.; B. F. Hall, 62, 232, 503.

21. "Rev. John M. Austin," *Trumpet and Universalist Magazine*, 7 July 1849, 14; Karen Dau, "John Mather Austin," Dictionary of Unitarian & Universalist Biography, Unitarian Universalist History & Heritage Society, https://uudb.org/articles/johnmatheraustin.html; Austin, *Journal*, vol. 3, 26 March 1846; B. F. Hall, 247–48.

22. B. F. Hall, 249.

23. "Trial of Wm. Freeman, On the Preliminary Issue of Present Insanity," *Cayuga Patriot*, 8 July 1846, 1, 2; "Account of Freeman Trial?," unsigned and undated holograph trial transcript, Box A20, Cayuga Museum of History and Art & Case Research Laboratory, Auburn, NY, n.p.

24. B. F. Hall, 36, 62, 81, 208, 213, 266, 267, 331; David Dimon, *The Freeman Trial: Presenting the Testimony Given in this Remarkable Case, with Comments* (Auburn, NY: Dennis Bro's & Thorne, 1871) 11, 18, 37, 42 (hereafter Dimon); "Account of Freeman Trial?"

25. *Auburn Journal and Advertiser*, 25 March 1846, 1.

26. B. F. Hall, 242.

27. B. F. Hall, 45, 286; see also Dimon, 23.

28. B. F. Hall, 78, 212.

29. "Trial of Wm. Freeman, On the Preliminary Issue of Present Insanity," *Cayuga Patriot*, 15 July 1846, 2; "Trial of Wm. Freeman the Negro on the Preliminary Issue of Present Insanity," *Daily Cayuga Tocsin*, 1 July 1846, 2.

30. "Horrible Murder," *Augusta* [Georgia] *Chronicle*, 24 March 1846, 2; "Horrible Butchery," *Maysville* [Kentucky] *Eagle*, 24 March 1846, 5; "The Murder in Auburn, N.Y.," *Alexandria* [Virginia] *Gazette*, 21 March 1846, 4; *Scioto Gazette* [Chillicothe, Ohio], 26 March 1846, 2; "The Horrible Murder in Cayuga," *Monoquet* [Indiana] *Kosciusko Republican*, 8 April 1846, 1; "The Auburn Murder," *Wisconsin Argus* [Madison, Wisconsin], 14 April 1846, 1; "Murderer Arrested," *North American* [Philadelphia, Pennsylvania], 19 March 1846, 1; *National Intelligencer* [Washington, DC], 20 March 1846, 3; "Freeman's Trial," *Sun* [Baltimore, Maryland], 6 July 1846, 4; "An Eloquent Plea for a Murderer," *Bridgeton* [New Jersey] *Chronicle*, 29 August 1846, 2.

31. *Cayuga Patriot*, 18 March 1846, 2.

32. *Auburn Journal and Advertiser*, 18 March 1846, 2; *Syracuse Journal* quoted in the *Morning Courier and New York Enquirer*, 20 March 1846, both quoted in Andrew W. Arpey, *The William Freeman Murder Trial: Insanity, Politics, and Race* (Syracuse, NY: Syracuse University Press, 2003), 32; "Trial of Wm. Freeman, On the Preliminary Issue of Present Insanity," *Cayuga Patriot*, 8 July 1846, 2; "The Horrible Murders in Cayuga," *Albany Argus*, 18 March 1846, 102; "Further Particularities of the Butchery at Auburn," *Brooklyn Daily Eagle and Kings County Democrat*, 17 March 1846, 2; "William Freeman," *Cayuga Tocsin*, 9 April 1846, 4.

33. *Tocsin Extra*.

34. "Freeman the Murderer," *Auburn Journal and Advertiser*, 25 March 1846, 2, emphasis in original. Two weeks later, the *Cayuga Tocsin* republished Clough's illustration on a magnified scale: three newspaper columns wide, occupying more than a quarter of the tabloid-sized page. "The Murderer, William Free-

man," *Cayuga Tocsin*, 9 April 1846, 4; *Auburn Journal and Advertiser*, 1 April 1846, 2.

Chapter Seven

1. Philip English Mackey, *Hanging in the Balance: The Anti-Capital Punishment Movement in New York State, 1776–1861* (New York: Garland Publishing, 1982).

2. See, for example, Michel Foucault, *Discipline & Punish: The Birth of the Prison*, trans. Alan Sheridan (1977; reprint, New York: Vintage Books, 1995); and David J. Rothman, "Perfecting the Prison: United States, 1789–1865," in *The Oxford History of the Prison: The Practice of Punishment in Western Society*, ed. Norval Morris and David J. Rothman (New York: Oxford University Press, 1995), 114.

3. "More Disclosures of the Van Ness [sic] Massacre," *New York Daily Herald*, 21 March 1846, 1.

4. A. B. Winfield, *Sermon at the Interment of the Bodies of John G. Van Nest, Mrs. Sarah Van Nest, G. W. Van Nest, Their Son, and Mrs. Phebe Wykoff [sic], Who Were Murdered March Twelfth Inst., By a Colored Man Named William Freeman, Preached in the R. D. Church, at Sand Beach, Owasco Lake, March Fifteenth* (Auburn, NY: Napier Press of J. C. Merrell & Co., 1846), 3–4, 12–14 (hereafter Winfield).

5. Andrew W. Arpey, *The William Freeman Murder Trial: Insanity, Politics, and Race* (Syracuse, NY: Syracuse University Press, 2003), 15, 43 (hereafter Arpey). On the history of the insanity defense, see Allen D. Spiegel and Marc B. Spiegel, "The Insanity Plea in Early Nineteenth Century America," *Journal of Community Health* 23, no. 3 (June 1998): 227–47. On Freeman's case within this history, see Kenneth J. Weiss and Neha Gupta, "America's First *M'Naghten* Defense and the Origin of the Black Rage Syndrome," *Journal of the American Academy of Psychiatry and the Law* 46, no. 4 (December 2018): 503–12.

6. Winfield, 14–15.

7. Frederick W. Seward, *William H. Seward; An Autobiography from 1801 to 1834. With a Memoir of His Life, and Selections from His Letters* (New York: Derby and Miller, 1891), 788; "The Horrible Murders in Cayuga," *Albany* [New York] *Argus*, 20 March 1846, 2.

8. John Mather Austin, *Journal*, Andover-Harvard Theological Library, Harvard Divinity School (hereafter Austin, *Journal*), vol. 3, 22 March 1846; "Shocking Atrocity," *Liberator*, 27 March 1846, 2; J. W., "Five Reasons Why Freeman should be Hung" [sic], *Prisoner's Friend*, 19 August 1846, 131. In 1846, Universalists in Cayuga County were organized in opposition to capital punishment. See Arpey, 25.

9. Walt Whitman, "Hurrah for Hanging!" *Brooklyn Eagle*, 23 March 1846 and "Our Answer to a Reasonable Question," *Brooklyn Eagle*, 24 March 1846, in *The Collected Writings of Walt Whitman, The Journalism, Vol. 1: 1834–1846*, ed. Herbert Bergman, Douglas Noverr, and Edward Recchia (New York: Peter Lang, 1998), 300, 302, emphasis in original. Whitman acknowledged the legitimacy of Freeman's resistance, but he also voiced pity in terms similar to Austin's (and indeed, Whitman read the Auburn newspaper in which "Justice" was published). Freeman, Whitman wrote, was a "neglected, ignorant and depraved negro," an "uneducated, friendless outcast" who "has never had the benefit of any kind of teaching or counsel; and never lived within any fixed moral or religious influences." Whitman, "Hurrah for Hanging!," 300. Paul Christian Jones comments on Whitman's use of sentimentalism in his antigallows arguments, especially in relation to the Freeman case. See Jones, "'That I could look … on my own crucifixion and bloody crowning': Walt Whitman's Anti-Gallows Writing and the Appeal to Christian Sympathy," *Walt Whitman Quarterly Review* 27, no. 1 (2009): 1–27.

10. These data and their interpretation were championed in the South as proof that slavery was necessary to control African Americans. See, for example, John C. Calhoun, *Errors in Sixth Census. Letter from the Secretary of State* (Washington, DC: US Department of States, 1845). The census was challenged, especially in the North. See, for example, Edward Jarvis, *Insanity among the Coloured Population of the Free States* (Philadelphia, PA: T. K. & P. G. Collins, printers, 1844). On the 1840 census and its reverberations in the Freeman case, see Jeannine Marie DeLombard, *In the Shadow of the Gallows: Race, Crime, and American Civic Identity* (Philadelphia: University of Pennsylvania Press), 226–31.

11. "Trial of Wm. Freeman the Negro," *Daily Cayuga Tocsin*, 4 July 1846, 2.

12. "Trial of Wm. Freeman, On the Preliminary Issue of Present Insanity," *Cayuga Patriot*, 15 July 1846, 2.

13. Scholar Neil Harris would later name this mode of spectatorship the "operational aesthetic." Harris, "The Operational Aesthetic," in *Humbug: The Art of P. T. Barnum* (Chicago: University of Chicago Press, 1973), 61–89.

14. "Siamese Twins," broadside, Waterloo, NY (Waterloo, NY: printed by Charles Sentell, Observer office, Waterloo, N.Y., 1832), New-York Historical Society, NYHS SY1832 no. 85; John Jerome Hrkach, "Theatrical Activity and Other Popular Entertainment along the Turnpikes of New York State from the End of the American Revolution to the Beginning of the Civil War" (PhD diss., City University of New York, 1990), 310; Documents of the Senate of the State of New-York, 63rd sess., vol. 2, no. 48, 17 February 1840, 63–64, 88; Austin, *Journal*, vol. 3, 23 September 1842; 27 September 1842; and 29 September 1842. Austin attended Stratton's performance and enthused about it. Austin, *Journal*, vol. 4, 6 August 1847; 7 August 1847.

15. *Auburn Journal and Advertiser*, 25 March 1846, 2.

16. "Letter from Frances Miller Seward to Augustus Henry Seward," 18 March 1846, Seward Family Digital Archive, University of Rochester; "Letter from Frances Seward to William H. Seward," qtd. in Frederick W. Seward, *William H. Seward; An Autobiography from 1801 to 1834. With a Memoir of His Life, and Selections from His Letters* (New York: Derby and Miller, 1891), 786–87 (hereafter Frederick W. Seward).

17. "Letter from Frances Miller Seward to Augustus Henry Seward," 18 March 1846, Seward Family Digital Archive, University of Rochester; "Letter from Frances Miller Seward to Augustus Henry Seward," April 6, 1846, Seward Family Digital Archive.

18. Peter Hughes, "Universalism, Universalists," in *Encyclopedia of Christianity Online*, doi:http://dx.doi.org/10.1163/2211-2685_eco_U.24. Austin attended antislavery conventions and meetings as well as lectures by Frederick Douglass, Gerritt Smith, Henry Highland Garnet, Lunsford Lane, George Latimer, Charles L. Remond, William Lloyd Garrison, and others. Austin, *Journal*, vol. 3, 24 May 1842; 24 November 1842; 31 May 1843; 11 April 1844; 28 May 1844; 16 October 1845; 12 August 1847. On December 3, 1845, he wrote in his journal, "From my *soul*, I *abominate* and *hate* slavery *in all its forms*—but especially American Slavery" (emphasis in original). It is important to note that pessimistic religious traditions such as Calvinism also led believers to reform movements. Different paths could lead to similar destinations.

19. John Mather Austin, *Arguments Drawn from the Attributes of God, in Support of the Doctrine of Universal Salvation* (Boston: A. Tompkins, 1844), 106, emphasis in original.

20. Justice [John Mather Austin], "The Late Murder," *Auburn Journal and Advertiser*, 18 March 1846, 2 (hereafter "The Late Murder"); Henry Hall, *The History of Auburn* (Auburn, NY: Dennis Bro's & Co., 1869), 150–51. The choice of pseudonym is theologically significant: Mather called "Justice" "One of the Main Pillars of Universal Salvation." Austin, *Arguments Drawn from the Attributes of God*, xii.

21. John Austin, *Evangelical Magazine and Gospel Advocate* [Utica, NY], 10 April 1846; Austin, *Journal*, vol. 3, 4 July 1846, emphasis in original; Justice [John Mather Austin], "The Late Murder," 2.

22. "William Freeman," *Liberator*, 24 April 1846, 68; "Ex-Governor Seward in Defence of Freeman," *Universalist Watchman, Repository and Chronicle*, 2 October 1846, 89; *Prisoner's Friend*, 8 April 1846, 55; "William Freeman," *National Anti-Slavery Standard*, 28 May 1846, 208; Donald B. Cole, *Martin Van Buren and the American Political System* (Princeton, NJ: Princeton University Press, 1984), 90. The possible connection between Tyler and "Fleming" appears in the *Cayuga Tocsin*, 20 May 1840, 2, which identifies Fleming as an assistant keeper at the Auburn State Prison who recently had to fight to retain his position. This de-

scription matches Tyler's experience. See also *Cayuga Tocsin*, 29 April 1840, 2; and *Cayuga Tocsin*, 24 March 1841, 2.

23. Austin, *Journal*, vol. 3, 29 June 1846.

24. Austin, *Journal*, vol. 3, 12 December 1844; 17 February 1846, emphasis in original.

25. Austin, *Journal*, vol. 3, 26 March 1846; Benjamin F. Hall, *The Trial of William Freeman for the Murder of John G. Van Nest, Including the Evidence and the Arguments of Counsel, with the Decision of the Supreme Court Granting a New Trial, and an Account of the Death of the Prisoner, and of the Post-Mortem Examination of his Body by Amariah Brigham, M.D. and Others* (Auburn, NY: Derby, Miller & Co. Publishers, 1848), 251 (hereafter B. F. Hall).

26. Austin, *Journal*, vol. 3, 26 March 1846; 31 May 1846; 1 June 1846.

27. Frances Seward described herself as "disapproving of capital punishment at all, under any circumstances." "Letter from Frances Miller Seward to Augustus Henry Seward," 25 June 1846, 2–3, Seward Family Digital Archive, University of Rochester.

28. Austin, *Journal*, vol. 3, 4 April 1846; 2 March 1846. In 1846, twenty-five hundred dollars was worth more than eighty thousand dollars today.

29. Scott W. Anderson, *Auburn, New York: The Entrepreneurs' Frontier* (Syracuse, NY: Syracuse University Press, 2015), 111, 115, 222, 235.

30. "Letter from Frances Miller Seward to Lazette Miller Worden," 1 July 1846, 3, Seward Family Digital Archive, University of Rochester. Among friends and family, William Henry Seward was known as "Henry." See also Arpey, 51–54.

31. Seward to Weed, 29 May 1846, Weed Papers, University of Rochester, quoted in Walter Stahr, *Seward: Lincoln's Indispensable Man* (New York: Simon & Schuster, 2012), 101 (hereafter Stahr); Frederick W. Seward, 810; William Henry Seward Jr., "Youthful Recollections," typewritten manuscript, 4, William Henry Seward Papers, 1801–1872, Box 120, River Campus Libraries, Special Collections, University of Rochester, Rochester, NY; "Letter from Frances Miller Seward to Lazette Miller Worden," 1 July 1846, 3, Seward Family Digital Archive; "Letter from Frances Miller Seward to Augustus Henry Seward," 15 June 1846, 1, Seward Family Digital Archive.

32. Stahr, 101.

33. Seward to Weed, 29 May 1846, qtd. in Frederick W. Seward, 810; "Murder Trials," *Auburn Journal and Advertiser*, 3 June 1846, 3.

Chapter Eight

1. The eyewitness who came closest to describing Freeman's assessment of his mental impairment was Deborah De Puy. She said she asked him "what made him appear so dull. He said he didn't know." Benjamin F. Hall, *The Trial*

of William Freeman for the Murder of John G. Van Nest, Including the Evidence and the Arguments of Counsel, with the Decision of the Supreme Court Granting a New Trial, and an Account of the Death of the Prisoner, and of the Post-Mortem Examination of his Body by Amariah Brigham, M.D. and Others (Auburn, NY: Derby, Miller & Co. Publishers, 1848), 46 (hereafter B. F. Hall).

2. "Letter from Frances Miller Seward to Lazette Miller Worden," 7 June 1846, Seward Family Digital Archive.

3. Dennis Tilden Lynch, *An Epoch and a Man: Martin Van Buren and His Times* (New York: Horace Liveright, 1929), 316, 377–78, 497–98; William L. Mackenzie, *The Lives and Opinions of Benj'n Franklin Butler and Jesse Hoyt* (Boston: Cook & Co., Publishers, 1845), 58–64; Edward M. Shepard, *Martin Van Buren* (Boston: Houghton, Mifflin and Company, 1888), 1; "John Van Buren," National Park Service, September 17, 2022, https://www.nps.gov/mava/learn/historyculture/john-van-buren.htm; John Niven, *Martin Van Buren: The Romantic Age of American Politics* (New York: Oxford University Press, 1983), 291–92, 480–81, 544.

4. B. F. Hall, 217; Frederick W. Seward, *William H. Seward; An Autobiography from 1801 to 1834. With a Memoir of His Life, and Selections from His Letters* (New York: Derby and Miller, 1891), 811 (hereafter Frederick W. Seward); Warren [pseud.], "Correspondence of the Atlas," *Boston Daily Atlas*, 9 June 1846; "Auburn and Albany United," *Auburn Journal and Advertiser*, 27 May 1846, 2; Earl Conrad, *Mr. Seward for the Defense* (New York: Rinehart & Company, Inc., 1956), vii.

5. B. F. Hall, 57, 180, 247, 338, 445, 120–39, emphasis added.

6. B. F. Hall, 94, 109.

7. B. F. Hall, 43–45, 48, 61, 81–82.

8. "Trial of Wm. Freeman the Negro, on the Preliminary Issue of Present Insanity," *Daily Cayuga Tocsin*, 3 July 1846, 2.

9. B. F. Hall, 52–54. See also John Mather Austin, *Journal*, Andover-Harvard Theological Library, Harvard Divinity School (hereafter Austin, *Journal*), vol. 3, 27 June 1846, 413.

10. David J. Rothman, *The Discovery of the Asylum: Social Order and Disorder in the New Republic* (rev. ed., Boston: Little, Brown, and Company, 1990), 62–78 (hereafter Rothman 1990).

11. Austin, *Journal*, vol. 3, 4 July 1846, 415–16, emphasis in original. This quotation is from Austin's journal, not Seward's closing. Only one paragraph of Seward's closing to the preliminary trial is extant.

12. B. F. Hall, 141.

13. B. F. Hall, 143; Leonard W. Levy, *The Law of the Commonwealth and Chief Justice Shaw* (Cambridge, MA: Harvard University Press, 1957), 211, qtd. in Andrew W. Arpey, *The William Freeman Murder Trial: Insanity, Politics, and Race*

(Syracuse, NY: Syracuse University Press, 2003), 43 (hereafter Arpey); Charles Patrick Ewing, *Insanity: Murder, Madness, and the Law* (Oxford University Press, 2008), xviii–xiv. Freeman's insanity defense was not New York's first, but the case was the first to be decided according to the McNaughton definition of insanity. New York's appellate court then made the McNaughton rules standard for state law, and for this reason *Freeman v. People* remains a touchstone in legal history. Kenneth J. Weiss and Neha Gupta, "America's First *M'Naghten* Defense and the Origin of the Black Rage Syndrome," *Journal of the American Academy of Psychiatry and the Law*, 46, no. 4 (December 2018): 503–12. According to LexisNexis, Freeman's case has been cited nearly 150 times.

14. Arpey, 43.

15. B. F. Hall, 143.

16. He preached from James 1:4: "let patience have its perfect work, that you may be perfect and complete, lacking nothing." Austin, *Journal*, vol. 3, 5 July 1846, 417.

17. Austin, *Journal*, vol. 3, 6 July 1846, 418, emphasis in original.

18. Austin, *Journal*, vol. 3, 5 July 1846, 417–18, emphasis in original.

19. Austin, *Journal*, vol. 3, 6 July 1846, 418.

20. Frederick W. Seward, 815.

21. Austin, *Journal*, vol. 3, 6 July 1846, 418; Frederick W. Seward, 815.

22. Austin, *Journal*, vol. 3, 10 July 1846, 419; "The Trial of William Freeman for the Murder of John G. Van Nest, Auburn, New York, 1846," in *American State Trials*, ed. John D. Lawson (St. Louis: Thomas Law Book Co., 1928), 16:359 (hereafter Lawson); B. F. Hall, 222; Paul Harris, *Black Rage Confronts the Law* (New York: New York University Press, 1997), 9.

23. Lawson, 332, 335; B. F. Hall, 398.

24. The juror was Henry Cooley. Documents of the Senate of the State of New-York (hereafter Doc. Senate), 67th sess., vol. 1, no. 18, 12 January 1844, 21. The witness was Ethan A. Worden. Documents of the Assembly of the State of New York (hereafter Doc. Assembly), 64th sess., vol. 2, no. 31, 12 January 1842, 47. See also Doc. Senate, 66th sess., vol. 1, no. 9, 16 January 1843, 26. "Annual Report of the Inspectors of the State Prison at Auburn," Doc. Senate, 69th sess., vol. 2, no. 46, 30 January 1846, 95; Robert T. Swaine, *The Cravath Firm and Its Predecessors 1819–1947* (New York: Ad Press, 1846), 1:94; Jeffrey A. Mullins, "Shifting Our Focus on New York's Rural History: Politics, Prisons, and Social Reform," *New York History*, Summer–Fall 2016, 447; DeAlva Stanwood Alexander, *Political History of the State of New York, Vol. II: 1833–1861* (New York: Henry Holt and Company, 1906), 35, https://www.gutenberg.org/files/22591 /22591-h/political2.html; Scott W. Anderson, *Auburn, New York: The Entrepreneurs' Frontier* (Syracuse, NY: Syracuse University Press, 2015), 226.

25. On the rivalry and "pamphlet war" between the Auburn and Pennsyl-

vania Systems, see Adam Jay Hirsch, *The Rise of the Penitentiary: Prisons and Punishment in Early America* (New Haven, CT: Yale University Press, 1992), 65–66; Rebecca M. McLennan, *The Crisis of Imprisonment: Protest, Politics, and the Making of the American Penal State, 1776–1941* (New York: Cambridge University Press, 2008), 62; and Rothman 1990, 81–88. On the spread of the Auburn System in the United States, see Ralph S. Herre, "The History of Auburn Prison from the Beginning to about 1867" (PhD diss., Pennsylvania State College, 1950), 210–22 (hereafter Herre).

26. [Samuel Gridley Howe et al], *An Essay on Separate and Congregate Systems of Prison Discipline* (Boston: 1846), 6, 11–12; Dorothea Dix, *Remarks on Prisons and Prison Discipline in the United States*, 2nd ed. (Philadelphia, PA: Joseph Kite & Co., 1845), 85–90; Doc. Assembly, 72nd sess., vol. 6, no. 243, 1849, 140. On the French preference for the Pennsylvania System, see also *London Lancet*, 1 July 1848, 58.

27. *Sixteenth Annual Report of the Board of Managers of the Prison Discipline Society, Boston, May, 1841* (Boston: Published at the Society's Rooms, 1841), 53; W. David Lewis, *From Newgate to Dannemora: The Rise of the Penitentiary in New York, 1796–1848* (1965; reprint, Ithaca, NY: Cornell University Press, 2009), 105–6; Herre, 71–73, 109–10. In pamphlets, public letters, and strategic alliances with reformers, Powers proclaimed his success in leading prisoners to spiritual redemption. Powers and a few other reformist leaders convinced many observers—in the nineteenth century and today—that redemption, not profit, defined the mission of the Auburn State Prison. See David J. Rothman, "Perfecting the Prison: United States, 1789–1865," in *The Oxford History of the Prison: The Practice of Punishment in Western Society*, ed. Norval Morris and David J. Rothman (New York: Oxford University Press, 1995), 117; Jennifer Graber, "Engaging the Trope of Redemptive Suffering: Inmate Voices in the Antebellum Prison Debates," *Pennsylvania History: A Journal of Mid-Atlantic Studies* 79, no. 2 (Spring 2012): 214–17; and Jennifer Graber, *The Furnace of Affliction: Prisons & Religion in Antebellum America* (Chapel Hill: University of North Carolina Press, 2011).

28. A. B. Winfield, *Sermon at the Interment of the Bodies of John G. Van Nest, Mrs. Sarah Van Nest, G. W. Van Nest, Their Son, and Mrs. Phebe Wykoff [sic], Who Were Murdered March Twelfth Inst., By a Colored Man Named William Freeman, Preached in the R. D. Church, at Sand Beach, Owasco Lake, March Fifteenth* (Auburn, NY: Napier Press of J. C. Merrell & Co., 1846), 14–15; *New York Daily Tribune*, 20 March 1846, quoted in Arpey, 24. See also Arpey, 31, 37, 75. For Winfield, Auburn's failure to reform Freeman did not tip the scales in favor of the Pennsylvania System but instead toward execution—an alternative to both systems of incarceration.

29. "Black Jacob, or Jack Hodges," *Boston Recorder*, 29 April 1842, 65; A[nsel] D. Eddy, *The Life of Jacob Hodges, an African Negro, Who Died in Canandaigua, N. Y., February, 1842* (Philadelphia: American Sunday-School Union, 1842), 41–42, 51–52 (hereafter Eddy); "Prison Discipline Society," *Boston Recorder*, 27 May 1842, 82.

30. Eddy, 93. See also *Seventeenth Annual Report of the Board of Managers of the Prison Disciplinary Society, Boston, May, 1842* (Boston: Published at the Society's Rooms, 1842), 5–26; New York State, Executive Pardons, New York State Archives, cited in Caleb Smith, "Jack Hodges' Conversions," unpublished paper, 2022. Smith provides the most thorough assessment of Jacob Hodges. Gershom Powers, like Lynds, was a Democratic appointee.

31. Eddy, 3.

32. White reformers' claim that Hodges isolated himself from the Black community was undermined by their own evidence. Eddy, for example, praised Hodges for avoiding other Black people. However, Eddy also wrote that when Hodges died, "coloured people of the village circulated reports that his body had been removed from the grave for the purpose of dissection." The community evidently responded with sufficient force to compel white officials to open Hodges's grave and display his body. Eddy sneers at these "credulous" African Americans, but he inadvertently shows that the Black community cared about Jacob Hodges enough to agitate on behalf of his bodily integrity. Eddy, 92.

33. B. F. Hall, 285–86.

34. B. F. Hall, 421–22.

35. B. F. Hall, 441, 443.

36. B. F. Hall, 287.

37. B. F. Hall, 287–88.

38. B. F. Hall, 441.

39. B. F. Hall, 443, 395. Seward had voiced a similar argument seven years earlier in his gubernatorial inaugural address: "The proportion of colored persons in the state to that of white persons is 1 to 48," Seward said, but the "proportion of colored persons in the state prisons is about 1 to 6. This class of our population is in a great measure deprived by its condition of the advantages of our schools." That is, white-run schools. "It is respectfully submitted whether a solicitous regard for the public welfare, justice to an injured race and the dictates of an enlightened humanity, do not require us to provide more effectually for their education." William Henry Seward, "Message of the Governor to the Legislature of the State of New-York," *Albany* [New York] *Argus*, 1 January 1839, 2.

40. *Liberator*, 27 March 1846, 2; B. F. Hall, 466. Most scholars agree that the libelous association between African Americans and criminality became widespread in the final quarter of the nineteenth century (the definitive source on

this point is Khalil Gibran Muhammad, *The Condemnation of Blackness: Race, Crime, and the Making of Modern Urban America* [Cambridge, MA: Harvard University Press, 2010]).

41. Lawson, 517–18; "Sentence of Freeman," *Auburn Journal and Advertiser*, 29 July 1836, 2; Austin, *Journal*, vol. 3, 24 July 1846, 425–26.

42. "Sentence of Freeman," *Auburn Journal and Advertiser*, 29 July 1836, 2, emphasis in original.

43. Austin, *Journal*, vol. 3, 24 July 1846. Nearly identical dialogue was reported in "Sentence of Freeman," *Auburn Journal and Advertiser*, 29 July 1836, 2, and other transcripts.

44. "Sentence of Freeman," *Cayuga Patriot*, 29 July 1846.

45. Austin, *Journal*, vol. 3, 24 July 1846, 425–26.

46. Austin, *Journal*, vol. 3, 24 July 1846, 425.

47. B. F. Hall, 474.

48. Lawson, 517–18.

49. Lawson, 517–18.

50. Lawson, 517–18; Austin, *Journal*, vol. 3, 24 July 1846, 425–26.

51. Austin, *Journal*, vol. 3, 24 July 1846.

Chapter Nine

1. "Exhibition of Oil Paintings!" *Auburn Daily Advertiser*, 22 October 1846, 3, Fulton History database, accessed 24 June 2023, https://fultonhistory.com /Fulton.html.

2. Elliot G. Storke, *History of Cayuga County, New York* (Syracuse, NY: D. Mason & Co., 1879), 498.

3. John Jerome Hrkach, "Theatrical Activity and Other Popular Entertainment along the Turnpikes of New York State from the End of the American Revolution to the Beginning of the Civil War" (PhD diss., City University of New York, 1990), 127 (hereafter Hrkach).

4. Henry Hall, *The History of Auburn* (Auburn, NY: Dennis Bro's & Co., 1869), 12–13, 36, 43, 177–78.

5. I refer to the paintings as "Mastin's" to mean that he owned them, not that he painted them.

The fourteen paintings are as follows: four paintings of William Freeman, one landscape (Niagara Falls), four history paintings (George Washington's headquarters, Milly Francis, the murder of Jane McCrea, and General George Putnam), and five scenes from the Bible.

Clearly, Mastin commissioned the four paintings of William Freeman between the murders in March 1846 and the show's debut in October 1846. The exact dates on which Mastin had his history, landscape, and Bible paintings made, however, are less certain. I believe that Mastin began accumulating his paintings in or shortly after 1835 because none of the history paintings has a source image earlier than 1835 and all four of the history narratives are taken verbatim or nearly verbatim from sources published in 1835 or 1836. If Mastin had begun collecting texts in 1835–1836 but had *not* commissioned any paintings at that time, it seems likely that he would have continued collecting texts *after* 1836. Most likely, Mastin collected his history and landscape sources in 1835–1836 and had the corresponding paintings executed shortly thereafter.

Of the five Bible images, three (Adam and Eve, Christ blessing the children, and Christ tempted by the devil) were advertised, and therefore completed, by 1846. Two more Bible scenes (of the crucifixion and the resurrection) were not initially advertised and had different dimensions: all the others were roughly eight feet high and ten feet wide, but these two were ten feet high and fourteen feet wide. All other paintings were unattributed, but Mastin identified the painters of the crucifixion and resurrection as "Elliot of N.Y. and Paulding of Utica" (Broadside, Mastin Collection [Collection 195], Folder 7, Fenimore Art Museum, Cooperstown, New York). James Paul Gold suggests that these artists are likely Charles Loring Elliot and Richard A. Paulding. Gold, "A Study of the Mastin Collection" (MA diss., State University of New York—Oneonta, Cooperstown Graduate Programs, 1967), 24–26 (hereafter Gold). These differences, along with the fact that the crucifixion and resurrection images were advertised only after 1846, suggests that Mastin added these Bible scenes later.

A puzzling outlier is Mastin's painting of General George Putnam riding his horse down stone steps. Mastin lifted his Putnam script from John Frost's *History of the United States: For the Use of Schools and Academies* (Philadelphia: Edward C. Biddle, 1836), 277. The source image, however, may have been published significantly later. Between 1845 and 1847, three companies—Sowle & Shaw, E. B. & E. C. Kellogg, and N. Currier—produced nearly identical lithographs of General Putnam riding his horse down stone steps. Any one of these could have been Mastin's source. Because Mastin's 1846 advertisement lists "The Escape of Gen. Putnam at Horse Neck" and the earliest known source image was disseminated in 1845, Mastin seems to have commissioned this painting between 1845 and 1846. It is unclear why he took his written source from a text of the mid-1830s, as he did the other three history paintings, but apparently waited to commission this fourth painting. Gold identifies a possible earlier source image in Colonel David Humphreys, *The Life and Heroic Exploits of Israel Putnam* (New York: E. Strong, 1834), 164. That image, however, has major compositional differences from Mastin's. If Mastin's painters did use this image as their reference, they revised the image far more than they did any of their other history works. Perhaps there is a yet-undiscovered visual source from 1836 and Mastin did indeed commission this painting alongside his other three history paintings.

The Niagara Falls painting is the only one of Mastin's collection that is not extant. In an undated note, an archivist at the Cayuga-Owasco Lakes Historical Society commented that a large painting of Niagara Falls had been observed at "the old Genoa firehouse, rolled up" and that it "may have been destroyed when the new house was built." "Family File: Mastin [esp. George] Marston," Cayuga-Owasco Lakes Historical Society, Moravia, NY. Mastin's script for this painting, too, is lost. However, Mastin cribbed two of his scripts from 1835 issues of the *Family Magazine*, and that same magazine included an article titled "Niagara Falls." It seems likely that Mastin cribbed this *Family Magazine* article for his Niagara script.

All Mastin's paintings except for the one of Niagara Falls are owned by the Fenimore Art Museum (formerly the New York State Historical Association) in Cooperstown, NY. The Fenimore Art Museum's George J. Mastin Collection (collection no. 195) contains Mastin's handwritten scripts, clippings, broadsides, images, and other documents pertaining to Mastin's life and show. The archives hold James Paul Gold's excellent MA dissertation, which includes an interview with Mastin's grandson (hereafter John Booker Mastin in Gold) and biographical and genealogical information.

In 1845, George Mastin got swindled in the notorious "Carver's Grant" land hoax. See "Indenture made between W. G. Mastin of the county of Cayuga and the state of New York... and George J. Mastin [of Genoa, New York], April 5, 1845," Jonathan Carver Land Grant-Related Deeds and Papers, Minnesota Historical Society, St. Paul, MN.

6. On the attempted revolts of 1846, see Herbert Aptheker, *American Negro Slave Revolts: Nat Turner, Denmark Vesey, Gabriel, and Others* (New York: Columbia University Press, 1943), 337–38.

7. Hrkach, 342, 344, 47–49; Heather Nathans, *Slavery and Sentiment on the American Stage, 1787–1861* (New York: Cambridge University Press, 2009), 183.

8. "Celebrates 95th Birthday," *Genoa* [New York] *Tribune*, 5 March 1909, 1.

9. Gold, 5–14.

10. John Booker Mastin in Gold, 142; Dick Norman, "Genoa and Vicinity," *Moravian Republican-Register*, 5 February 1932, Cayuga County Historian's Office; John Booker Mastin in Gold, 150; "Broadside," Mastin Collection, Collection 195, Folder 7, Fenimore Art Museum, Cooperstown, NY. Two similar broadsides are reproduced in Gold. The men in the Mastin family were notably tall. See John Booker Mastin in Gold, 149.

11. *The Family Magazine* was a short-lived but popular general-interest magazine known for its prophrenology stance. Frank Luther Mott, *A History of Amer-*

ican Magazines, 1741–1930 (Cambridge, MA: Belknap Press of Harvard University Press, 1958), 1:363–64, 448.

12. Samuel Y. Edgerton Jr., "The Murder of Jane McCrea: The Tragedy of an American Tableau d'Histoire," *Art Bulletin* 47, no. 4 (December 1965): 483 (hereafter Edgerton). See also Lloyd E. Divine Jr., *On the Back of a Turtle: A Narrative of the Huron-Wyandot People* (Columbus: Trillium, an Imprint of the Ohio State University Press, 2019), 122–24. Smirke titled his drawing *The Murder of Lucinda*, but the book Smirke illustrated included a footnote explaining that Lucinda was a pseudonym for Jane McCrea. Edgerton, 484.

13. This message traveled as far away as the British House of Commons, where Edmund Burke used the case of Jane McCrea to argue against a military alliance with Native Americans. Britannica Online Encyclopedia, s.v. "Jane Mc-Crea," accessed 25 June 2023, https://www.britannica.com/biography/Jane-McCrea. Some scholars argue that propagandistic uses of Jane McCrea helped recruit soldiers for the Revolutionary army—and particularly to build support for the 1779 Sullivan Expedition, which brought John Hardenbergh, as a soldier, to the land that would become Auburn. Vitoria Rushworth, *Battles of the American Revolution, Saratoga* (Pelham, NY: Benchmark Education Company, 2005), 16.

14. "Mastin's Spiel," handwritten manuscript, George J. Mastin Collection (collection no. 195), folder 2, Fenimore Art Museum, Cooperstown, NY (hereafter "Mastin's Spiel"). Mastin's script eliminated references to Francis's location in Florida and membership in the Creek nation. These facts were included in Mastin's source text, Henry Trumbull's *History of the Indian Wars: to which is prefixed a short account of the discovery of America by Columbus, and of the landing of our forefathers at Plymouth, with their most remarkable engagements with the Indians in New England, from their first landing in 1620, until the death of King Philip, in 1679* (1836; reprint, Boston: Phillips and Sampson, 1846), 225–26. (We know that the 1836 edition was Mastin's source because only in that edition does the image bear the caption that Mastin copied in his handwritten script.) By eliminating references to Florida and the Creeks, Mastin made Milly Francis speak within his suite of history paintings of Revolutionary New York. Mastin's painters went even further to relocate Francis: they stripped the Creeks of the robes they wore in Trumbull's source image and re-dressed them identically to the Huron-Wendats whom Jane McCrea encountered in New York. This visual testimony, along with the artful silences in Mastin's script, misdirected audiences to understand the attempted burning as a story of Revolutionary New York. Because Francis's story, unlike that of Pocahontas, was obscure, few members of Mastin's audiences would have recognized the act of importation. For more information about Milly Francis, see Dale Cox, *Milly Francis: The Life & Times of the Creek Pocahontas* (Bascom, FL: Old Kitchen Books, 2013).

15. George Mastin, letter to Mrs. S. G. Mastin, Dixon, Solano County, California, 24 June 1884. Transcribed in Gold, 137–38.

16. "Exhibition of Oil Paintings!" *Auburn Daily Advertiser*, 22 October 1846, 3.

17. Advertisement, *Cayuga Patriot*, 14 September 1836, qtd. in Hrkach, 111. See also "Auburn Museum," advertisement in the *Auburn Free Press*, 23 January 1833, clipping in Cayuga County Historian's Office. Chedell's, like many museums of its day, resembled Charles Willson Peale's Philadelphia Museum. Chedell's Museum was, as Peale described his own museum, "a world in miniature." David R. Brigham, *Public Culture in the Early Republic: Peale's Museum and Its Audience* (Washington, DC: Smithsonian Institution Press, 1995), 171n1.

18. "Mastin's Spiel."

19. "Mastin's Spiel." Mastin's script indicates that he began his narration with the painting of the exterior of the house, moved to the painting of George and John Van Nest, returned to the painting of the exterior with an emphasis on Phebe Wyckoff, and then continued to the third painting, the pietà.

20. J. M. A. [John Mather Austin], "The Murder near Auburn," *Evangelical Magazine and Gospel Advocate* (Utica, NY), 10 April 1846, 117; "Exhibition of Oil Paintings," *Auburn Daily Advertiser*, 22 October 1846, 3.

21. "Mastin's Spiel."

22. "Childhood," *Blackwood's Magazine* 12, no. 67 (1822): 139–45, cited in Robin Bernstein, *Racial Innocence: Performing American Childhood from Slavery to Civil Rights* (New York: New York University Press, 2011), 6. For a full analysis of childhood innocence, ignorance, and whiteness, see Bernstein, especially 6–8, 41, 90, and 247n26.

23. "Mastin's Spiel."

24. "Mastin's Spiel."

25. "Mastin's Spiel." Hersey's claim was unlikely and unsubstantiated. Hersey had his own complex relationship to the case because Jack Furman, whose accusation put Freeman in prison for horse theft, was his stepfather. Benjamin F. Hall, *The Trial of William Freeman for the Murder of John G. Van Nest, Including the Evidence and the Arguments of Counsel, with the Decision of the Supreme Court Granting a New Trial, and an Account of the Death of the Prisoner, and of the Post-Mortem Examination of his Body by Amariah Brigham, M.D. and Others* (Auburn, NY: Derby, Miller & Co. Publishers, 1848), 195–96 (hereafter B. F. Hall).

26. See Christine Stansell, *City of Women: Sex and Class in New York, 1789–1860* (New York: Knopf, 1986), 194; and Timothy J. Gilfoyle, "Street-Rats and Gutter-Snipes: Child Pickpockets and Street Culture in New York City, 1850–1900," *Journal of Social History* 37, no. 4 (Summer 2004): 183.

27. "Mastin's Spiel."

28. J. M. A. [John Mather Austin], "The Murder near Auburn," *Evangelical Magazine and Gospel Advocate* (Utica, NY), 10 April 1846, 117; B. F. Hall, 64.

New York State had outlawed public hangings in 1835, but Mastin was either ignorant of or indifferent to this fact. Michelle Henry, "New York's Last Hanging," *New York Archives*, Summer 2005, 6.

Chapter Ten

1. "The Trial of William Freeman for the Murder of John G. Van Nest, Auburn, New York, 1846," in *American State Trials*, ed. John D. Lawson (St. Louis: Thomas Law Book Co., 1928), 16:517–18.

2. Keven Barrett, "Thompson, Joseph Pascal," *Oxford African American Studies Center*, 31 May 2013, https://doi.org/10.1093/acref/9780195301731.013 .38032. Joseph Pascal Thompson, a minister and later bishop, is sometimes confused with Joseph Parrish Thompson, another abolitionist and minister with the AME Zion Church who preached in New York State in the second half of the nineteenth century.

3. John Mather Austin, *Journal*, Andover-Harvard Theological Library, Harvard Divinity School (hereafter Austin, *Journal*), vol. 3, 5 August 1846, 431.

4. Henry Hall, *The History of Auburn* (Auburn, NY: Dennis Bro's & Co., 1869), 280 (hereafter H. Hall); "Uncovering the Freedom Trail in Auburn and Cayuga County, New York," Judith Wellman, project coordinator, sponsored by the City of Auburn Historic Resources Review Board and the Cayuga County Historian's Office, 2005, 81, citing Cayuga County poorhouse records (hereafter "Uncovering"), 55, 154; C. Griffin, *A Sketch of the Origin of the Colored Man: His Great Renown; His Downfall and Oppression; Also, The Prejudice Which Did Exist, and Still Exists to a Certain Extent, Against Him* (Auburn, NY: Auburnian Steam Printing House, 1882), 43. *Griffin* was sometimes spelled *Griffen* or *Griffiths*. See "Uncovering," 55, 201–6. Griffin's little-known pamphlet, which is available as a full text on Readex, deserves further study. J. W. Hood, *One Hundred Years of the African Methodist Episcopal Zion Church, or, The Centennial of African Methodism* (New York: AME Zion Book Concern, 1895), 191, 216.

5. The list of founders and trustees appears in H. Hall, 280. On Hopkins's abolitionism, see "A Bypath in Bygone Cayuga. Memories of Auburn c 1901. Author Unknown. Read before CCHS. Manuscript," 18, Cayuga Museum of History and Art & Case Research Laboratory, Auburn, NY. On Hewson, see William Mawbey Brown and Francis Bazley Lee, *Biographical, Genealogical, and Descriptive History of the State of New Jersey* ([Newark, NJ ?]: New Jersey Historical Publishing Company, 1900), 286. On Terrill and Wright, see Elliot G. Storke, *History of Cayuga County, New York* (Syracuse, NY: D. Mason & Co., 1879), 181.

6. By Kate Clifford Larson's count, approximately five hundred self-liberators passed through Auburn between 1831 and 1861. Kate Clifford Larson, *Bound for*

the Promised Land: Harriet Tubman, Portrait of an American Hero (New York: Ballantine Books, 2003), 156 (hereafter Larson).

7. See, for example, Austin, *Journal*, vol. 3, 2 August 1846; 8 September 1846; 9 September 1846; 11 September 1846; 21 September 1846; 9 October 1846; 15 June 1847; 25 August 1847; 18 February 1848; and 5 December 1848.

8. Austin, *Journal*, vol. 4, 21 January 1848, 155; vol. 4, 15–18 April 1848, 181–82; Josiah Henson, *The Life of Josiah Henson, Formerly a Slave, Now an Inhabitant of Canada, as Narrated by Himself* (Boston: Arthur D. Phelps, 1849), 75–75.

9. See Austin, *Journal*, vol. 4, 29 December 1846; 12 August 1847; 23 September 1847; 16 April 1848; 18 August 1848; 30 March 1849; 5 August 1849; "Frederick Douglass," *Cayuga Chief*, 5 April 1849, 2; *Cayuga Chief*, 20 August 1850, 2.

10. "Anti-Slavery Meeting," *Auburn Journal and Advertise*, 27 September 1843, 2; *Auburn Journal and Advertiser*, 17 February 1841, 3; *Auburn Journal and Advertiser*, 29 December 1841, 3; *Auburn Journal and Advertiser*, 20 April 1842, 3; *Auburn Journal and Advertiser*, 1 February 1843, 3; Austin, *Journal*, vol. 3, 16 October 1845, 332; "Anti-Slavery Conventions in Cayuga County," *National Anti-Slavery Standard*, 14 April 1842, 3; *National Anti-Slavery Standard*, 12 February 1846, 147; *National Anti-Slavery Standard*, 19 February 1846, 151; *National Anti-Slavery Standard*, 8 October 1846, 75; *National Anti-Slavery Standard*, 12 November 1846, 94; *National Anti-Slavery Standard*, 21 January 1847, 135.

11. In 1850, Luke Freeman owned sixteen hundred dollars in property, which made him the second wealthiest Black man in Auburn. Platt Freeman, who may have been related to Luke, also was qualified to vote because he owned eight hundred dollars in property. See 1850 Federal Census; and "African Americans in Cayuga County, New York in 1850," database developed as part of the "Survey of Sites Relating to the Underground Railroad, Abolitionism, and African American Life in Auburn and Cayuga County, 1820–1870," Judith Wellman, coordinator, https://www.cayugagenealogy.org/census/afriamer/index50.html.

12. Leslie Harris, *In the Shadow of Slavery: African Americans in New York City, 1626–1863* (Chicago: University of Chicago Press, 2003), 222, 267 (hereafter Harris); Phyllis F. Field, *The Politics of Race in New York: The Struggle for Black Suffrage in the Civil War Era* (Ithaca, NY: Cornell University Press, 2009), 45–48 (hereafter Field).

13. For more on the Constitutional Convention in relation to the Freeman case, see Andrew W. Arpey, *The William Freeman Murder Trial: Insanity, Politics, and Race* (Syracuse, NY: Syracuse University Press, 2003), 50–51 (hereafter Arpey).

14. "Negro Suffrage," *Cayuga Patriot*, 11 March 1846, 2.

15. For examples of side-by-side reportage, see *Auburn Journal and Advertiser*, 25 March 1846, 1, and *Cayuga Patriot*, 18 March 1846, 3.

16. Seward to Alvah Worden, 22 March 1846, Weed Papers, University of Rochester, quoted in Walter Stahr, *Seward: Lincoln's Indispensable Man* (New York: Simon & Schuster, 2012), 100. See also Arpey, 51–53. On Seward's views on Black suffrage and the New York State Constitution, see Field, 48, and William Henry Seward, Letter to the Editor, 31 March 1846, *National Anti-Slavery Standard*, 23 April 1846, 2.

17. Jeffrey A. Mullins makes this argument in "Race, Place and African-American Disenfranchisement in the Early Nineteenth-Century American North," *Citizenship Studies* 10, no. 1 (February 2006): 77–91. Seward fretted that Freeman had damaged suffrage efforts—and the Whig Party—but in fact, Seward himself flip-flopped on the issue of Black male voting. See William Henry Seward to William Jay and Gerrit Smith, 22 October 1838, in William H. Seward, *Works*, ed. George E. Baker (New York: Redfield, 1853), 3:428, cited in Jane H. Pease, "The Road to the Higher Law," *New York History* 40, no. 2 (April 1859): 120; "Letter from William H. Seward," *National Anti-Slavery Standard*, 23 April 1846, 186; Sarah L. H. Gronningsater, "Practicing Formal Politics without the Vote: Black New Yorkers in the Aftermath of 1821," in *Revolutions and Reconstructions: Black Politics in the Long Nineteenth Century*, ed. Van Gosse and David Waldstreicher (Philadelphia: University of Pennsylvania Press, 2020): 116–38; and Paul Finkelman, "The Protection of Black Rights in Seward's New York," *Civil War History* 34, no. 3 (1988): 211–34.

18. Harris, 268, citing William G. Bishop and William H. Attree, *Report of the Debates and Proceedings of the Convention for the Revision of the Constitution of the State of New York* (Albany, NY: printed at the office of the *Evening Atlas*, 1846), 1018; S. Croswell and R. Sutton, *Debates and Proceedings in the New-York State Convention, for the Revision of the Constitution* (Albany, NY: printed at the office of the *Albany Argus*, 1846), 783–84, 785–86, emphasis added.

19. Harris, 267; Field, 61; "Cayuga County Official Canvass, 1846," *Auburn Journal and Advertiser*, 18 November 1846, 3; James McCune Smith to Gerrit Smith, 31 March 1855, in *The Works of James McCune Smith, Black Intellectual and Abolitionist*, ed. John Stauffer (New York: Oxford University Press, 2006), 305 (hereafter McCune Smith); J. C., "Away with the $250 Suffrage!—Equal Rights, and Nothing Less!" *North Star*, 2 November 1849.

20. P. Gabrielle Foreman, "Black Organizing, Print Advocacy, and Collective Authorship: The Long History of the Colored Conventions Movement," in *The Colored Conventions Movement: Black Organizing in the Nineteenth Century*, ed. P. Gabrielle Foreman, Jim Casey, and Sarah Lynn Patterson (Chapel Hill: University of North Carolina Press, 2021), 24 (hereafter *Colored Conventions Movement*); Josiah Henson, *An Autobiography of the Rev. Josiah Henson ("Uncle Tom") from 1789 to 1881* (London: Schuyler, Smith & Co., 1881), 123–24. On the vitality of women in the colored conventions, see Foreman, 33–44.

21. Henry Highland Garnet, "An Address to the Slaves of the United States of America," in Henry Highland Garnet and David Walker, *Walker's Appeal, with a Brief Sketch of His Life. And also Garnet's Address to the Slaves of the United States of America*, (New-York: J. H. Tobitt, 1848), 94–96. Reprinted by Digital Commons@University of Nebraska-Lincoln, https://digitalcommons.unl.edu /etas/8 and https://digitalcommons.unl.edu/cgi/viewcontent.cgi?filename=0 &article=1007&context=etas&type=additional; *Minutes of the National Convention of Colored Citizens: Held at Buffalo on the 15th, 16th, 17th, 18th, and 19th of August, 1843 for the Purpose of Considering their Moral and Political Condition as American Citizens* (New York: Piercy & Reed, 1843), 13; Colored Conventions Project Digital Records, accessed 26 June 2023, https://omeka .coloredconventions.org/items/show/278. On Garnet's "Address" and its impact on Black radical thought, see Kellie Carter Jackson, *Force and Freedom: Black Abolitionists and the Politics of Violence* (Philadelphia: University of Pennsylvania Press, 2019); Derrick R. Spires, "Flights of Fancy: Black Print, Collaboration, and Performance in 'An Address to the Slaves of the United States of America' (Rejected by the National Convention, 1843)," in *Colored Conventions Movement*, 125–53; and Anna Mae Duane, *Educated for Freedom: The Incredible Story of Two Fugitive Schoolboys Who Grew Up to Change a Nation* (New York: New York University Press, 2020), 96–105.

22. *Proceedings of the National Convention of Colored People, and Their Friends, Held in Troy, N.Y., on the 6th, 7th, 8th, and 9th October, 1847* (Troy, NY: Steam Press of J. C. Kneeland and Co., 1847), 10; Colored Conventions Project Digital Records, accessed 26 June 2023, https://omeka.coloredconventions.org/items /show/279 (hereafter Troy convention).

23. Troy convention, 13–14, 31.

24. Auburn was generally not well-represented at the colored conventions. One of the few participants from the city was Nicholas Bogart. Likely participating along with his wife, Harriet Bogart, he attended the convention of 1840 in Albany, 1841 in Troy, 1844 in Schenectady, and 1845 in Geneva. Another participant from Auburn was the Reverend William Cromwell, who was associated with the AME Zion Church. See Convention of the Colored Inhabitants of the State of New York, "Minutes of the State Convention of Colored Citizens, Held at Albany, on the 18th, 19th, and 20th of August, 1840, for the purpose of considering their political condition," Albany, NY, 1840, Colored Conventions Project Digital Records, accessed 26 June 2023, https://omeka.coloredconventions.org /items/show/620; and "Uncovering," 37–38, 44–45.

25. James McCune Smith to Gerrit Smith, 31 March 1855, in McCune Smith, 316. McCune Smith wrote these words in 1855, so it is not possible to prove that he had read Seward's defense by 1847. Seward's closing speech was most energetically distributed in the months immediately following the trial, however, so

it seems likely that McCune Smith read Seward's argument prior to the Troy convention.

26. Austin, *Journal*, vol. 4, 23 September 1847, 119; 12 August 1847, 104; *National Anti-Slavery Standard*, 12 February 1846, 147; 19 February 1846, 151; 8 October 1846, 75; 12 November 1846, 94; 21 January 1847, 135.

27. Troy convention, 19–20.

28. Troy convention, 6.

29. Troy convention, 8–9.

30. Frederick Douglass to Amy Post, 28 October 1847. River Campus Libraries, Special Collections, University of Rochester, Rochester, NY.

31. Troy convention, 31; "A Lesson in Life and Death," *North Star*, 30 June 1848. I take the phrase "contempt and pity" from Daryl Michael Scott's important book by that title. Daryl Michael Scott, *Contempt and Pity: Social Policy and the Image of the Damaged Black Psyche 1880–1996* (Chapel Hill: University of North Carolina Press, 1997). The respective narratives of Freeman as villain and victim can also be described, in the terms of historian Ibram X. Kendi, as "segregationist" and "assimilationist." Ibram X. Kendi, *Stamped from the Beginning: The Definitive History of Racist Ideas in America* (New York: Bold Type Books 2016), 5, 2.

32. Larson, xvii, 302; Dorothy Wickenden, *The Agitators: Three Friends who Fought for Abolition and Women's Rights* (New York: Scribner, 2021), 96 (hereafter Wickenden). According to most scholars, Tubman likely met the Wrights in Philadelphia through Martha Coffin Wright's sister Lucretia Coffin Mott. Larson, 155–56; see also Wickenden, 17, 64.

33. Wickenden, 21–22, 137, 92; Milton C. Sernett, *Harriet Tubman: Myth, Memory, and History* (Durham, NC: Duke University Press, 2007), 110–11 (hereafter Sernett); Scott W. Anderson, *Auburn, New York The Entrepreneurs' Frontier* (Syracuse, NY: Syracuse University Press, 2015), 111, 115, 118, 221, 235.

34. Wickenden, 95, 138. Prior to Wickenden's research, scholars commonly credited William Henry Seward with the sale of land to Tubman. See, for example, Sernett, 257. For more on the sale of the land, see Larson 163–66. On the Auburn Bank and its ties to the Auburn State Prison, see Anderson, 125–26. The relationship between Tubman and Nicholas and Harriet Bogart, Black abolitionists and activists, deserves future attention. The Bogarts worked for the Seward family for fifty years. In 1862, Tubman entrusted the Seward household with the care of her niece Margaret Stewart—who may have been Tubman's birth daughter. Stewart's daughter Alice H. Brickler wrote in 1939 that Frances Seward took primary responsibility for Stewart. Jean M. Humez, *Harriet Tubman: The Life and the Life Stories* (Madison: University of Wisconsin Press, 2003), 270. Most scholars have taken Brickler's words at face value and have not considered the role of the Bogarts in Stewart's care. However, when Tubman

transferred her niece to the Seward household in 1862, she surely considered all aspects of that arrangement—including the presence of employees Harriet and Nicholas Bogart. On the Bogarts or Margaret Stewart, see "Uncovering," 37, 39; Larson, 199–200; and Wickenden, 195–96.

35. Ralph S. Herre, "The History of Auburn Prison from the Beginning to about 1867" (PhD diss., Pennsylvania State College, 1950), 90, 216. On the publication history of Tubman's multiple narratives, see Sernett, 107.

36. Gershom Powers, *A Brief Account of the Construction, Management, & Discipline &c, &c, of the New-York State Prison at Auburn, Together with a Compendium of Criminal Law* (Auburn, NY: U. F. Doubleday, 1826), 68; "Uncovering," 54, 57, 99, 114–15, 179; "African Methodist Zion's Church," *Northern Christian Advocate*, 10 November 1847, 127.

37. Sarah H. Bradford, *Scenes in the Life of Harriet Tubman* (Auburn, NY: W. J. Moses, printer, stereotyped by Auburn, NY: Dennis Bro's & Co.,1869), 19–20.

38. I take the term "carceral capitalism" from Jackie Wang's excellent *Carceral Capitalism* (Cambridge, MA: MIT Press, 2018). I take the term "prison land" from Brett Story, *Prison Land: Mapping Carceral Power across Neoliberal America* (Minneapolis: University of Minnesota Press, 2019). "Prison land" refers to the fact that carcerality is not limited to institutions like prisons or jails, but instead saturates physical, cultural, and economic landscapes.

Afterlives

1. The defense argued that several jurors should not have been seated because they had preformed opinions as to Freeman's sanity; the defense also pointed to errors in some jurors' swearing-in process. Seward also objected to Whiting's charge to the jury in the preliminary trial, which he said incorrectly limited the definition of sanity. David Wright, "Points for the Defense—Errors of the Court in Jury Selection," holograph, file in Box A20, "Files of relevance to William Freeman Trial," Cayuga Museum of History and Art & Case Research Laboratory, Auburn, NY; "Freeman vs. The People," "Cases Argued and Determined in the Supreme Court of the State of New-York, in January 1847," in Hiram Denio, *Reports of Cases Argued and Determined in the Supreme Court and in the Court for the Correction of Errors of the State of New-York* (Albany, NY: Gould, Banks & Gould, 1849), 4:2–41; Andrew W. Arpey, *The William Freeman Murder Trial: Insanity, Politics, and Race* (Syracuse, NY: Syracuse University Press, 2003), 125–29. One of the jurors to whom Seward objected was named Benjamin Beach; I have been unable to ascertain whether this juror was related to John Beach, the cofounder of the Auburn State Prison.

2. Blanchard Fosgate, "Case of William Freeman, the Murderer of the Van

Nest Family," *American Journal of the Medical Sciences* (October 1847), 30; David Dimon, *The Freeman Trial: Presenting the Testimony Given in this Remarkable Case, with Comments* (Auburn, NY: Dennis Bro's & Thorne, 1871), 6, 75 (hereafter Dimon); John Mather Austin, *Journal*, Andover-Harvard Theological Library, Harvard Divinity School, vol. 3, 26 July 1847; William H. Seward, Letter to Amariah Brigham, 15 August 1847, Lucy Scribner Library, Skidmore College, https://digitalcoll.skidmore.edu/record/4462; Benjamin F. Hall, *The Trial of William Freeman for the Murder of John G. Van Nest, Including the Evidence and the Arguments of Counsel, with the Decision of the Supreme Court Granting a New Trial, and an Account of the Death of the Prisoner, and of the Post-Mortem Examination of his Body by Amariah Brigham, M.D. and Others* (Auburn, NY: Derby, Miller & Co. Publishers, 1848), 504 (hereafter B. F. Hall); "Letter from Frances Miller Seward to William Henry Seward, August 21, 1847," Seward Family Digital Archive, University of Rochester, https://sewardproject.org /18470821FMS_WHS1; C. S., "Death of William Freeman," *Prisoner's Friend*, 1 September 1847, 139.

3. Dimon, 75; B. F. Hall, 505; "Freeman Trial Recalled, Reminiscences Suggested by an Old Cell," *Auburn Morning Dispatch*, 27 May 1888, 2. The doctors who performed the autopsy included Lansingh Briggs, Amariah Brigham, and Blanchard Fosgate, all of whom had testified at Freeman's trial. B. F. Hall, 497–98. Austin later claimed that Seward initiated and paid for Freeman's autopsy. Rev. J. M. Austin, "Reminiscences of the Freeman Trial," *Daily Advertiser*, [Auburn, NY], 4 March 1873, n. p., River Campus Libraries, Special Collections, University of Rochester, Rochester, NY.

4. "The Case of Luke Freeman," *Auburn Daily Union*, 27 July 1859; "Uncovering the Freedom Trail in Auburn and Cayuga County, New York," Judith Wellman, project coordinator, sponsored by the City of Auburn Historic Resources Review Board and the Cayuga County Historian's Office, 2005, citing Cayuga County poorhouse records," 114–15; "Funeral of Luke Freeman," *Auburn Daily Advertiser & Union* 18, no. 35 (11 April 1863); "In Re Estate of Catherine M. Freeman, Deceased," Box 173, file 0013, Cayuga County Records Retention, Auburn, New York. This is the 1867 probate record for Luke Freeman's wife, Catherine, who should not be confused with his mother Kate.

5. "Riot at Auburn," *Albany* [New York] *Journal*, 6 July 1846; *Daily Cayuga Tocsin*, 4 July 1846, 4. County records list John De Puy as having died on June 6, 1847 of unstated causes. If this record is accurate, John De Puy died two months before William Freeman. "Cayuga County Deaths 1847–1850," accessed 26 June 2023, https://www.cayugagenealogy.org/vital_records/1847/47d.htm#1. In Cayuga County in 1861 and 1862, a man named John De Puy was indicted for assault and battery with the intent to kill. This was likely John De Puy Jr.—that is, the son of Freeman's brother-in-law. "State of New York, Cayuga Oyer and

Terminer, The People Against John DePuy, Indictment for Assault & Battery With Intent to Kill, 10 October 1861," Cayuga County Historian's Office, Auburn, NY; "State of New York, Cayuga Oyer and Terminer, The People Against John DePuy, Indictment for Assault & Battery with Intent to Kill," 23 August 1862, Cayuga County Historian's Office, Auburn, NY.

6. "Uncovering," 54, 57–58, 99.

7. The slave narrative took its familiar shape in the second half of the 1840s. During this same half-decade, the number of slave narratives increased dramatically. In the 104 years between 1740 and 1844, thirty-six known slave narratives were published. From 1845 to 1849, however, twenty-one slave narratives were published, with an additional thirty-three appearing in the 1850s. William L. Andrews, *To Tell a Free Story: The First Century of Afro-American Autobiography, 1760–1865* (Urbana: University of Illinois Press, 1986), 333–42; see also "North American Slave Narratives," Documenting the American South, University of North Carolina–Chapel Hill, 2021, http://docsouth.unc.edu/neh/chronauto bio.html.

8. William Henry Seward, *Autobiography of William H. Seward from 1801 to 1834: With a Memoir of his Life and Selections from his Letters from 1831 to 1846* (New York: D. Appleton, 1877), 822.

9. Frederick W. Seward, *William H. Seward; An Autobiography from 1801 to 1834. With a Memoir of His Life, and Selections from His Letters* (New York: Derby and Miller, 1891), 822.

10. Karen Dau, "John Mather Austin," *Dictionary of Unitarian and Universalist Biography*, Unitarian Universalist History & Heritage Society, accessed 26 June 2023, https://uudb.org/articles/johnmatheraustin.html.

11. Ralph S. Herre, "The History of Auburn Prison from the Beginning to about 1867" (PhD diss., Pennsylvania State College, 1950), 63; Blanchard Fosgate, *Spain: Antagonism of Races the Cause of its Social Disorder* (Auburn, NY: Wm. J. Moses' Publishing House, 1869); "Dr. E. Humphrey's Vegetable Ointment," *Cayuga Patriot*, 6 July 1842, 4; "In Chancery— Seventh Circuit—Nelson Beardsley vs Henry Polhemus and John London," *Auburn Journal and Advertiser*, 15 February 1843; "Supreme Court," *Albany* [New York] *Argus*, 28 October 1845; "Sheriff's Sale, *Cayuga Chief*, 6 August 1850. Polhemus died in 1858. Card catalog s.v. "Polhemus, Hon. Henry," Cayuga County Historian's Office, Auburn, NY, cards 1–3, citing Auburn Daily Advertiser, 18 September 1858 and 4 October 1858; *Report of the Select Committee of the Assembly of 1851, Appointed to Examine into the Affairs and Conditions of the State Prisons of this State, Transmitted to the Legislature*, January 7, 1852 (Albany, NY: Charles Van Benthuysen, Printer to the Legislature, 1852), 171; Elliot G. Storke, History of Cayuga County, New York (Syracuse, NY: D. Mason & Co., 1879), 224.

12. Over the next forty years, Mastin performed in three distinct waves.

From 1846 to 1851, he performed in Auburn, Ovid, and other sites in New York State. George Mastin, letter to Mrs. S. G. Mastin, Dixon, Solano County, California, 24 June 1884; transcribed in Gold, "A Study of the Mastin Collection" (MA diss., State University of New York—Oneonta, Cooperstown Graduate Programs, 1967), 137–38. In 1852, when Mastin married and began having children, he seems to have taken a break from touring. Sometime before 1870, he commissioned two additional Bible paintings. Between 1871 and 1875, Mastin printed several advertising broadsides and went back on the road with a revamped show: he now had fourteen paintings and was accompanied by the Erin Twin Brothers, who performed a double clog dance. Mastin's reentry into show business coincided with the death of William Henry Seward in 1872, which spurred a new wave of interest in the William Freeman trial—which in turn guaranteed fresh audiences for Mastin's show. In the 1880s, when Mastin was in his seventies, he printed a new set of broadsides and again restaged his show—but this time he seems to have stayed close to home, performing in Genoa in 1886 and 1887 (other locations are also likely). See "Exhibition," *Ovid Bee* (New York), 18 November 1846, 2; Dick Norman, "Genoa and Vicinity," Moravian Republican-Register, 5 February 1932, Cayuga County Historian's Office; "The County: Genoa," *Auburn Daily Bulletin*, 1 February 1887; *Weekly Auburnian*, 28 February 1887; and John Booker Mastin interview in Gold. On the dating of Mastin's broadsides, see Gold, 29. When not touring, Mastin stored his paintings in an attic. On a clear day each spring, he unfurled the immense paintings in a field. Neighbors—old ones who remembered, young ones who remembered the old ones remembering—gathered. As his audience watched, Mastin gently brushed each canvas, removing dust. He repeated this ritual annually until his death in 1910. Gold, 35–36, 145; "Oldest Resident Dead," *Genoa Tribune*, 23 September 1910, clipping in Cayuga County Historian's Office, Auburn, NY; "Funeral of Mr. Mastin," *Genoa Tribune*, 30 September 1910. In 1954, the New York State Historical Association bought the paintings from Mastin's niece and had them restored. The paintings now occupy a storage facility in Cooperstown, New York.

13. The Sachem [likely Thurlow Weed Brown], "A Night of Blood: A Legend of the Lake," *Cayuga Chief*, 26 April 1849, 2. The serialization continued through 3 May 1849, 2; 10 May 1849, 2; 17 May 1849, 2; 24 May 1849, 2; 31 May 1849, 2; 7 June 1849, 2; 14 June 1849, 2; 21 June 1849, 2; 19 July 1849, 2; 26 July 1849, 2; and 9 August 1849, 2. After twelve installations, the novel abruptly stopped with Freeman evading lynching and being jailed for the murder of the Van Nests (the author probably intended to write more). Thurlow Weed Brown (who should not be confused with Seward's friend and adviser Thurlow Weed) was a white temperance activist and the editor of the *Cayuga Chief* in Auburn and later in Wisconsin.

14. During Freeman's trial, stories of Black villainy and victimhood were rivals, but by the century's end the stories had integrated. These apparently opposing stories became entangled, for example, in an 1895 article in the *New York Times*. The article, published apropos of nothing, described Freeman as a "brutal, insensate murderer" who killed because of an "inherent diabolism in him and his race"—but also as a "groveling, insensible object" of "pity" who killed because of a "noisome atmosphere of cruelty and injustice" and "neglect shown to the moral, intellectual, and religious instruction of the colored people." "The Case of William Freeman," *New York Times* 17 November 1895, 32.

15. Daryl Michael Scott, *Contempt and Pity: Social Policy and the Image of the Damaged Black Psyche 1880–1996* (Chapel Hill: University of North Carolina Press, 1997) (hereafter Scott); Ibram X. Kendi, *Stamped from the Beginning: The Definitive History of Racist Ideas in America* (New York: Bold Type Books 2016), 5, 2, emphasis in original.

16. Khalil Gibran Muhammad, *The Condemnation of Blackness: Race, Crime, and the Making of Modern Urban America* (Cambridge, MA: Harvard University Press, 2010) 3, 35–87 (hereafter Muhammad). See also George M. Fredrickson, *The Black Image in the White Mind: The Debate on Afro-American Character and Destiny, 1817–1914* (New York: Harper and Row, 1971), 256–82; and Michelle Alexander, *The New Jim Crow: Mass Incarceration in the Age of Colorblindness* (New York: New Press, 2010). On the relationship between the mass criminalization of Black people and American carcerality, see Elizabeth Hinton and DeAnza Cook, "The Mass Criminalization of Black Americans: A Historical Overview," *Annual Review of Criminology* 4 (January 2021): 261–86, https://www.annual reviews.org/doi/abs/10.1146/annurev-criminol-060520-033306.

17. W. David Lewis argues that after 1848, New York's prison reformers dramatically increased their concern that environmental factors, especially inadequate education, caused crime. He shows, too, that Auburn's *Northern Christian Advocate* was a primary amplifier of these ideas. Freeman was thus at the epicenter of changes in penology that galvanized in Auburn and spread across New York and then nationally. See W. David Lewis, *From Newgate to Dinsmore: The Rise of the Penitentiary in New York, 1796–1848* (1965; reprint, Ithaca, NY: Cornell University Press, 2009), 277–80. For different periodizations of the "environmental" argument, see David J. Rothman, *The Discovery of the Asylum: Social Order and Disorder in the New Republic*, rev. ed. (Boston: Little, Brown, and Company, 1990), 62–78; and Muhammad, 7. The Moynihan Report, in yet another echo of the Freeman trial, particularly blamed women-led Black families, and therefore Black women, for social woes. See Office of Policy Planning and Research, *The Negro Family: The Case for National Action* (Washington, DC: US Department of Labor, 1965), 29–45 (this document is popularly called the

Moynihan Report). On the impact of the Moynihan Report on criminalization and incarceration, see Scott, 150–56; and Elizabeth Hinton, *From the War on Poverty to the War on Crime: The Making of Mass Incarceration in America* (Cambridge, MA: Harvard University Press, 2016), 20, 59–60, 74–76.

18. Douglas A. Blackmon, *Slavery by Another Name: The Re-Enslavement of Black People in America from the Civil War to World War II* (New York: Doubleday, 2008); Heather Ann Thompson, "Blinded by a 'Barbaric' South: Prison Horrors, Inmate Abuse, and the Ironic History of American Penal Reform," in *The Myth of Southern Exceptionalism*, ed. Matthew D. Lassiter and Joseph Crespino (New York: Oxford University Press, 2010), 79.

19. Auburn's license plate factory is a legacy of white mechanics' agitation against competition from incarcerated workers. The mechanics' campaign resulted in an 1894 amendment to New York's constitution that abolished prison contracts with for-profit entities. This amendment did not end New York's prison labor, but instead reserved it for the manufacture of products exclusively for state use. Since then, various governmental organizations have arisen to oversee this process. The current version is called Corcraft. As the New York State Preferred Source for governmental supplies, Corcraft employs between 1,850 and 2,100 prisoners per year. In Corcraft-run factories, prisoners make license plates as well as office furniture, eyeglasses, uniforms, soap, bedding, recycling bins, and more. The commodities sell to public schools, government offices, and other state markets. Corcraft pays workers between $.16 and $.65 per hour and sells prison-made goods for approximately $50 million per year. On Northern white mechanics' opposition to competitive prison labor, see Blake McKelvey, *American Prisons: A History of Good Intentions* (Montclair, NJ: Patterson Smith, 1977), 117–22; and Glen A. Gildemeister, *Prison Labor and Convict Competition with Free Workers in Industrializing America, 1840–1890* (1977; reprint, New York: Garland Publishing, 1987), 196–255. Opposition from labor activists in the South made prison contracts decline similarly in that region. See Heather Ann Thompson, "Blinded by a 'Barbaric' South: Prison Horrors, Inmate Abuse, and the Ironic History of American Penal Reform," in *The Myth of Southern Exceptionalism*, ed. Matthew D. Lassiter and Joseph Crespino (New York: Oxford University Press, 2010), 79. On prison labor and the amendment to the New York State Constitution, see Constitution of the State of New York, 11–12, accessed 26 June 2023, https://www.nysenate.gov /sites/default/files/ckeditor/Sep-22/586_ny_state_constitution_-_generic _version.pdf; and Kathleen Maguire, "Industry," in *Encyclopedia of American Prisons*, ed. Marilyn D. McShane and Frank P. Williams III (New York: Garland Publishing, 1996), 253. On labor in the Auburn Correctional Facility, see New York Department of Correction and Community Supervision, "Prison

Rape Elimination Act (PREA) Audit Report, Adult Prisons & Jails," Auburn Correctional Facility, 6 May 2020, 2–3, 9-10, https://doccs.ny.gov/system/files /documents/2020/05/auburn-correctional-facility-final-prea-audit-report -5.6.2020.pdf; Zellnor Myrie, "About Those License Plates: New York Needs to Pay Prisoners More for Producing them, and for Their Other Labor," *New York Daily News*, 23 August 2019, https://www.nydailynews.com/opinion/ny -oped-about-those-license-plates-20190823-fo4an7lzwvfazn3f63q5eetj6m -story.html; and Christopher Robbins, "NY's New License Plates Will Still Be Made by Prisoners Earning 65 Cents an Hour," *Gothamist*, 23 August 2019, https://gothamist.com/news/nys-new-license-plates-will-still-be-made-by -prisoners-earning-65-cents-an-hour. On Corcraft, see Corcraft, "Who We Are," https://corcraft.ny.gov/; American Civil Liberties Union and the University of Chicago Law School Global Human Rights Clinic, "Captive Labor: Exploitation of Incarcerated Workers," 2022, 58, 95, https://www.aclu.org/sites /default/files/field_document/2022-06-15-captivelaborresearchreport.pdf; Legal Aid Society, "2022 Joint Legislative Budget Hearing, Committee on Workforce Development: Ending Forced Prison Labor in New York State," 31 January 2022, 10, https://nyassembly.gov/write/upload/publichearing/001269 /003581.pdf, 10; and New York State of Opportunity, Office of General Services, "List of Preferred Source Offerings," December 2022, https://ogs.ny.gov /system/files/documents/2022/12/the-list-of-preferred-source-offerings .pdf. In 1890, the Auburn State Prison garnered additional fame as the site of the first execution by electricity—in the electric chair, an eerie recapitulation of the chair-based "shower-bath" implemented during Freeman's incarceration.

20. Ruth Wilson Gilmore, quoted in "If You're New to Abolition: Study Group Guide," *Abolition Journal*, 25 June 2020, https://abolitionjournal.org /studyguide/. For more information about prison abolition, see Angela Y. Davis, Gina Dent, Erica Meiners, and Beth Richie, *Abolition, Feminism, Now* (Chicago: Haymarket, 2021); Liz Samuels, "Improvising on Reality: The Roots of Prison Abolition," in *The Hidden 1970s: Histories of Radicalism*, ed. Dan Berger (New Brunswick, NJ: Rutgers University Press, 2010), 131–204. Two exceptionally important abolitionist organizations are Incite! (https://incite-national .org/, accessed July 2023) and Critical Resistance (https://criticalresistance .org/, accessed July 2023). For the history of Critical Resistance, see "Critical Resistance to the Prison-Industrial Complex," *Social Justice* 27, no. 3 (2000) and CR10 Publications Collective, ed., *Abolition Now! Ten Years of Strategy and Struggle against the Prison Industrial Complex* (Oakland, CA: AK Press, 2008). Fundamentally and crucially, the prison abolition movement opposes prison reform. William Freeman's experiences support this perspective by showing how cycles of prison reform work to perpetuate carceral systems (see chapter 3 of this book).

Author's Note

1. While I occasionally sketch possibilities, these moments of speculation are clearly identified. Some facts are disputed, emerging from contradictory witness testimony. For disparities that have no consequence for the book's overall claims, I narrate events in the way I consider most likely and then note alternatives in the endnotes. In the case of disputes that are consequential, I flag them in the body of the text. A few minor paraphrases are noted in the citations; all other quotations come directly from primary sources.

2. Saidiya Hartman, "Venus in Two Acts," *small axe* 26 (June 2008): 1–14 (hereafter Hartman, "Venus").

3. See, for example, Benjamin F. Hall, *The Trial of William Freeman for the Murder of John G. Van Nest, Including the Evidence and the Arguments of Counsel, with the Decision of the Supreme Court Granting a New Trial, and an Account of the Death of the Prisoner, and of the Post-Mortem Examination of his Body by Amariah Brigham, M.D. and Others* (Auburn, NY: Derby, Miller & Co. Publishers, 1848), 259.

4. "Deed—John H. Hardenbergh and his wife to Allen Warden and Asaph Leonard, July 23, 1829," Hardenbergh Archives, File "Hardenbergh, Deeds and Land Grants," item 141, Cayuga Museum of History and Art & Case Research Laboratory, Auburn, NY.

5. See Hartman, "Venus"; Saidiya Hartman, *Wayward Lives, Beautiful Experiments: Intimate Histories of Riotous Black Girls, Troublesome Women, and Queer Radicals* (New York: W. W. Norton & Company, 2019); Tavia Nyong'o, *Afro-Fabulations: The Queer Drama of Black Life* (New York: New York University Press, 2019), especially 6–7, 20; Tiya Miles, *All That She Carried: The Journey of Ashley's Sack, a Black Family's Keepsake* (New York: Random House, 2022). Jane Clark, a woman who freed herself from slavery in Maryland and escaped to Auburn in 1859, is important but less well known. For a transcription of Jane Clark's twelve-page handwritten narrative along with a contextualizing introduction and historical corroboration, see Robin Bernstein, "Jane Clark: A Newly-Available Slave Narrative," *Commonplace: The Journal of Early American Life*, accessed 26 June 2023, http://commonplace.online/article/jane-clark/.

6. W. David Lewis, *From Newgate to Dannemora: The Rise of the Penitentiary in New York, 1796–1848* (1965; reprint, Ithaca, NY: Cornell University Press, 2009), 123.

7. Koritha Mitchell, *Living with Lynching: African American Lynching Plays, Performance, and Citizenship, 1890–1930* (Urbana: University of Illinois Press, 2011); Koritha Mitchell, *From Slave Cabins to the White House: Homemade Citizenship in African American Culture* (Urbana: University of Illinois Press, 2021); Koritha Mitchell, "Identifying White Mediocrity and Know-Your-Place Aggres-

sion: A Form of Self Care," *African American Review* 51, no. 4 (Winter 2018): 253–62.

8. Angela Y. Davis, "From the Prison of Slavery to the Slavery of Prison: Frederick Douglass and the Convict Lease System," in *The Angela Y. Davis Reader*, ed. Joy James (Malden, MA: Blackwell Publishers, 1998), 91; Kevin Quashie, *The Sovereignty of Quiet: Beyond Resistance in Black Culture* (New Brunswick, NJ: Rutgers University Press, 2012); Derrick Spires, *The Practice of Citizenship: Black Politics and Print Culture in the Early United States* (Philadelphia: University of Pennsylvania Press, 2019), 13.

Index

Page numbers in italics refer to images.